95

£3

STEAMSHIP TRAVEL IN THE INTERWAR YEARS

Tourist Third Cabin

Lorraine Coons and Alexander Varias

AMBERLEY

First published 2016

Amberley Publishing
The Hill, Stroud
Gloucestershire, GL5 4EP

www.amberleybooks.com

British Library Cataloguing in Publication Data.
A catalogue record for this book is available from the British Library.

ISBN: 978 1 4456 4986 3 (print)
ISBN: 978 1 4456 4987 0 (ebook)

Typesetting and Origination by Amberley Publishing.
Printed in Great Britain.

Contents

Acknowledgements

This revised and updated book owes much to many people who are too numerous to name. In addition to those we acknowledged for their invaluable assitance in our previous edition, *Tourist Third Cabin: Steamship Travel in the Interwar Years,* we thank the following for their help recently and without whom the continued progress of our work would not have been possible.

To begin, we thank Georgina Coleby, our editor at Amberley Publishing, who enthusiastically embraced our revised and expanded work and who has been so helpful these last months.

We appreciate the contributions of the following people who made available various archival sources and illustrations: Sian Wilks of the Cunard Archives at the University of Liverpool; Nancy Chauvet of Association French Lines in Le Havre; and Astrid Drew of the Steamship Historical Society of America Archives.

We thank our teaching institutions, Chestnut Hill College and Villanova University, for their support and encouragement in our teaching and research endeavors. Special thanks to Sandra Suprenuk and Elisa Wiley of Villanova University for their time and assistance.

Finally, and most importantly, we thank our families and friends who have always been there and without whom our work would never have come to fruition.

Preface

Two world wars and the emergence of global terrorism have reminded us of the dependence of travel and tourism upon peace and tranquility. For people to venture abroad, war has to be absent from the world scene and people's sense of safety and security assured. Exceptions abound in the form of adventurers pursuing travel experiences in circumstances of danger and risk. Furthermore, peace is rarely found universally without some form of conflict in a pocket or two of the earth. In some cases, 'peace' hardly describes an era's character accurately, so prescient are the conflicts or their potential for eruption. General suggestions of peace during an era are assumed only when stark contrasts are drawn to the very recent past. These perceptions, nonetheless, are crucial for large numbers of travelers and tourists to make the decision to leave home for a while.

Such an era was the interlude between the First and Second World Wars, unique in having the epithet 'the interwar years'. The era could be called a time of peace, though with a sense of caution regarding its fragility and vulnerability to conflict. After all, ethnic violence in Turkey, the Caucuses, the Middle East, and other regions and revolutionary, cataclysmic fallout from movements like Bolshevism in Russia and Fascism in Italy provided a variety of volatile accents. With Western economies still sluggish and explosive conditions prevailing in Weimar Germany, the European scene was anything but tranquil during that transitional time.

Nevertheless, the exuberant release of post-war energy was felt especially in the United States, which was able to savor both victory in war and a financial boom. Though 'tempered' by the restrictions of Prohibition, the roaring twenties ensued, and their mood was conveyed across the Atlantic Ocean to war-weary societies desiring some form of festivity, even in their ongoing tension and despair. The party mood was as a result felt on Parisian streets like Boulevard Montparnasse, in London's Bloomsbury section, and in Berlin cabarets. Jazz musicians, singers and dancers gave an added dimension to the modernistic experiments of the artistic revolution that had begun before the First World War. A new urge to travel was also part of this scenario, and connected to it was a resumption of transatlantic steamship travel that had been so interrupted by the conflict. Releasing pent-up travel urges that had been restrained for those four years, Americans and Europeans took to the sea and displayed the excitement of the new era. Steamship lines, accordingly, went on a buying spree and cast new plans for building more modern liners that themselves were connected to the times – as evident in contemporary accounts in writing, theater and cinema. Passengers' aims here were primarily to use the liners as means to reach distant destinations. Shipboard culture was evident during that time of transatlantic crossing (measuring between four and seven days), but the goal of reaching a port of disembarkation surpassed the desire simply to 'cruise' for no other reason.[1] If one avoided sea-sickness and other travails, the voyage offered its delights and passengers could wrap themselves up in the sailing, dining, wining and other experiences available to them. Yet wrapped around that consciousness was the very real other journey experienced once the ship began to sail.

Not much remains from that era. There had, until recently, been four relics of the twentieth century's array of liners. Four hulls; four ships. Decaying, floating, transformed, still sailing, planned to sail. The *Queen Mary*, the SS *United States*, the *France* (later called *Norway*), the *Queen Elizabeth 2*. These were the remnants of twentieth-century ocean liners, representing the age when travel across the Atlantic was conceivable only or primarily by ship and the airplane was only a distant future dream or threat. In the case of one, the *Queen Elizabeth 2*, construction began and the maiden voyage was taken after air travel had already assumed its superior status and ocean liners began to be envisioned as dinosaurs – impressive, mammoth structures supreme at one time, but now extinct and without purpose. Sadly the *QE2* has been put out of service and its possible fate as a floating hotel yet to be determined by developers driven primarily by profit, not by historic preservation.

Cunard Line's *Queen Mary* project resulted in a replacement for the *QE2* – the *Queen Mary 2*, which has been sailing for over a decade. Can we be assured that the ocean liner has returned? In truth, the *QM2*, like the *QE2*, serves both as a transatlantic liner and as a cruise ship. Following the success of James Cameron's film, *Titanic*, nostalgia prevailed within the maritime audience, which yearned for new luxurious ships to satisfy the needs of the opulent and the upwardly mobile classes. Few of the resulting ships can even faintly be called 'liners'. Unlike its predecessors, the *QM2* has verandahs for its passengers – a feature associated with cruise ships built after the 1980s. Owned by Carnival Cruise Line, Cunard has designed a transatlantic liner with even more cruise ship features than the *QE2*. A walk around the public spaces of the ship, and into certain rooms, brings to the surface an undeniable echo of the past. That past comes to life when taking the Cunard Heritage Trail, which nobly serves the purpose of assuring that passengers do not lose sight of the history of transatlantic sailing. Yet a stroll into other prominent areas brings one to the world of the cruise ship of today. History endures, but nostalgia has gained the upper hand over the type of functional purpose that characterized the age of the ocean liners.[2]

During the period from 1900 to 1939, ocean liners provided the only practical means for mass travel either way between Europe and North America and were characterized by luxury and increased size and speed. At the same time, questions of function and design were subjects of debate and reflected key cultural transformations of the time. As in the case of train systems, metro stations and other areas of vitally practical transportation systems, the construction and design of ocean liners drew the attention of masses of people at the national and local level – even of those who had no hope to travel on them. The liners were a matter of national pride and concern, not just a focus of private companies. At 150,000 tons and with the greatest length of any passenger ship, *Queen Mary 2* would ordinarily have swelled British pride with its British name and maritime heritage. However, it is under the ownership of Carnival Cruise Line and was constructed in a French shipyard. These realities contradict its national qualities as it is an international product. If it had been built during the 1930s such would not have been the case, as national identity mattered most.

In the world of cruise ships today we find vessels coming in at over 200,000 tons in some cases, awkwardly affixed to specific cruise itineraries only designed to satisfy leisure needs and certainly not necessary to life except if one wishes to suggest that travel and enjoyment are necessary to life. You do not have masses emigrating, business people hurrying to reach a meeting on the other side of the ocean, or movie stars going to a shooting site on board today's cruise ships. Instead, paraphrasing the words of a Marlon Brando character in the early 1950s or those of Jack Kerouac, 'you just go'. And so, cruise ships today are filled with people who simply travel in a circle of enjoyment and escape and experience no hurry at all.

Not so in the age when the Blue Riband was the much coveted prize sought by all shipping companies as it honored the ship crossing the North Atlantic in the shortest time. It goes without saying that the particular ship's speed was the maximum then possible. While 'pleasure cruising' was already evident by the 1880s and 1890s, for the masses of people traveling on ship, necessity was the main impulse.

The four ships mentioned above, as relics, really are testimonies to that past in ways that no cruise ships today can be because they are virtually all we have left from that era, although now there are only three. They are seen, however, in different capacities. The *Queen Mary*, of Cunard-White Star, built during the early 1930s, now serves as a hotel, convention center, and museum in Long Beach, California. Along the docks of Philadelphia, the *United States*, (the last liner to earn the Blue Riband) rusts away, its interior furnishings all removed and sold at auctions to nostalgia lovers, its owners valiantly hoping to convert her into an East Coast version of the *Mary*. French Line's last great ship, the *France*, renamed the *Norway*, was operated by Norwegian Cruise Lines, serving mostly as a Miami-based Caribbean cruise ship, although on some occasions making transatlantic voyages intended to rekindle thoughts and echoes of her glorious record of the 1960s. She was received with great enthusiasm by adoring crowds in Le Havre, who savored memories of her brief career as a French Line ship. Even greatly reduced speed and the reality of alterations to her structure could not erase the *France/Norway*'s essential character as a transatlantic liner, rendered all the more poignant by a stroll within the inner promenade and a view of her lines and smoke stacks from portside or, better yet, a tender. In the main dining room, one could see the cascading staircase, which served to provide passengers with a *grande descente* along the way to their table. Her career came to a tragic and undignified end after an explosion in the engine room in 2003, which led to her scrapping after being renamed for a final time the *Blue Lady*. Despite dreams among many fans of conversion into a hotel/ museum somewhere, nothing could save the *France* from that end. While nothing has happened yet, the *Queen Elizabeth 2* also evokes much concern as no real plans have been made to preserve her, regardless of her distinguished history and chapter in the long history of Cunard. History is amazingly neglected in the current world of turmoil and instability.

Other shattered echoes of the age are found. In one of the Metropolitan Museum's former cafés, one could see a mural from the *Normandie* in homage to the great works of Art Deco found on French Line's great liner. It is now stored elsewhere as that area of the museum has been redesigned to make way for the Roman galleries. *Normandie* relics are also paradoxically found in a church or in collectors' homes. Large fragments of paneling from Cunard's *Mauretania* dominate the atmosphere of the Bristol pub named in its honor, and the original letters MAURETANIA that once graced one side of the ship's hull are now placed atop the door. It is a virtual return to the pre-First World War era when you pass through the door, prepare to order a pint at the bar, and then marvel at the original paneling once lining the ship's staterooms or public spaces. The Le Havre Maritime Museum similarly holds large numbers of wood paneling from the old *France*, once described as the 'floating Versailles' – fragments which were, in fact, rescued from a trash heap. Other artistic works from ocean liners have made their way into special dining rooms of contemporary cruise ships as background for passengers. Objects and fragments from the *Titanic*, once nestled within the famous hull, abound in ever-growing numbers rescued from their former sea-bottom abode. Steamship buffs purchase other bits of liners at auction, from catalogs, and, now, from online websites.

The feelings generated by walking through the old liners were quite alien to those felt on contemporary ships. Transatlantic ships also differed from each other. Each had a different character. Passengers experiencing the *Olympic*, *Paris*, *Berengaria* and the *Leviathan* during the 1920s found sharply contrasting features among them even though all were products more or less of the previous fifteen years of shipbuilding. On the other hand, these ships seemed similar when compared to Italian Line's *Rex* and French Line's *Ile de France* arriving on the scene at the end of the twenties and to the massive liners emerging from the shipyards during the 1930s – most notably French Line's *Normandie* and Cunard-White Star Line's *Queen Mary* and *Queen Elizabeth*. Even the lettering of company names on publicity brochures and posters indicated a transformation of liner character. The cursive writing on earlier posters reflecting an antique flavor gave way to the linearity of lettering of the 1930s most embodied in Art Deco.

Passengers walking through the *Mauretania* (if they succeeded in transgressing the class barriers) were immersed in a unique maritime world. First Class space, like the smoking and dining rooms and adjoining corridors, enveloped them in upper-class Edwardian opulence suggesting an aristocratic castle or manor. Wood paneling provided a sense of warmth and tradition. Oaks used for the paneling were well varnished and inlaid. In the case of the *Mauretania*, dark colors conveyed heaviness. On the other hand, Cunard's *Aquitania* had wood painted in shades of off-white to different effect. Both liners conveyed aristocratic splendor in various shades, at least in their First Class quarters. Visits to Second Class revealed rooms stripped of such ornamentation and showing a bit more of the functional underpinnings of the ship. The mechanical and strictly functional reality of the ship was especially revealed in Steerage. Pipes showed themselves. Images of popular dining rooms show people sitting in rows at long tables rather than in the separate round- or square-cut tables demanded by First Class. If elites perceived dining as an artful, leisurely activity, the popular classes had no choice but to see it as a strictly necessary activity, not a way of passing the time in enjoyment. What one witnessed in visiting the various sections of these liners was a reflection of the old restrictive feudal order albeit in a mechanical world driven forward by the turbine engines of the ship.

A similar visit during the 1930s on the *Normandie* revealed something quite different. The strictness of feudalism had given way to a more relaxed mood. First Class space was still exclusively reserved for the wealthy, but the castle/manor look had been replaced by an airier and more modern ambience. Lightness and modernism conveyed a mood of splendor and opulence but in more leisurely forms. Formality and elitism were tempered by feelings of ease and confidence. Heavy woods were replaced by other materials, and glass was used widely to refract the illuminated public spaces. Even when woods were used, they were lighter than on the older liners. Passengers privileged to inhabit this world felt a connection to the vivid changes in style, art and music, even if they did not say so directly. Being modern and contemporary was itself an elitist stand. It was the relaxed formality found in Astaire/Rogers films through which dancers flowed across the stage effortlessly.

The *Normandie*'s First Class dining room, smoking room and other spaces were elite in this sense, and not in the manner of its predecessors. First Class passengers desiring that old environment had to opt for the liners that were growing more and more antique by the moment. Entry into Second and Third Class quarters revealed, however, just as real a detachment from the elite. Decor was more modest and less flashy, with utilitarian features pronouncing their accents to remind the more modest passengers of the world they were 'stuck in'. Class divisions were still present, even during the time of democratization.

This book appears at a rather unique moment regarding the history of travel by ship. On the one hand, the release in 1997 of the film, *Titanic*, created a mass wave of excitement that not only saw more numbers of people deciding to travel by ship, but also frenzied interest in the purchase of ship memorabilia and the hopes that new 'authentic' liners would be built. Even cruise ships began placing in their dining rooms and lounges old murals and panels from earlier liners long sent to the scrappers. The wave of enthusiasm provoked countless television documentaries about ocean liners, a multitude of lectures at sea on the same subject, and one book after another that served to satisfy what was becoming a true mass audience for ship buffs. At the center of it all was the *Titanic*, which continued to be visited by marine archaeologists and adventurers of all kinds. For those not wanting to pay the fare or daring to venture into the Atlantic's depths and observe the decaying hull up close, the option was there to see live footage of the vessel on cable television.

Yet the image of that famous ship also evokes a new shudder. The events of 11 September 2001 have, in addition to shattering human lives, shaken the foundations of travel, which has faced great difficulties as travel firms, cruise companies and airlines continue to face financial problems. Fear of travel has been tangible since those terrible days and the current situation in the Middle East has added to that emotional climate. Safety does not seem ensured by technological advances, and the *Titanic*'s fate serves to reinforce that sentiment. Even so, one also senses an ongoing enthusiasm for travel and for a new age of ship voyages that had been shaped in previous years.

Our book focuses on the social and cultural history of twentieth-century steamship travel as seen in Cunard Line and French Line – two large companies representing different nations that tapped into the transatlantic market during the period from 1919 to 1939. As defeat and post-war sanctions had caused German decline in passenger ship travel, Britain and

France were most poised to tap into the new market of the immediate post-war years, and their efforts over the next two decades set the pace for much of the steamship scene, although other countries had great roles to play as well.[3]

Before the First World War, most passengers coming to America traveled in Steerage Class as immigrants to the 'promised land', seeking a more materially prosperous life. This situation changed after the Russian Revolution as the United States reversed its 'open arms' policy and the American Congress passed the Dillingham Immigration Restriction Act in May 1921.

Such a political move had the effect of an earthquake upon European steamship companies that had thrived on transporting the masses of immigrants to Ellis Island – especially from eastern and southern Europe. The lines were now faced with the realisation that the steerage trade was about to collapse and that the bulk of travelers would have America as their point of departure rather than Europe. As there was such a strong middle class in the United States and so much prosperity abounded there, it was safe for them to conclude that Americans would make up the bulk of travelers making the transatlantic crossing to visit a European continent that was not nearly so affluent. In addition, steamship travel would involve a return passage home. Steerage was replaced by a new class of passage, Tourist Third Cabin, as an entirely new breed of mass tourist was in the making. The concept of pleasure cruising likewise began to catch on, enticing a largely American audience.

One of the classes connected to the Industrial Revolution that began asserting its right to leisure and seeking to demonstrate its worth to the aristocracy was the bourgeoisie. By the twentieth century, seashore resorts began catering to a largely middle-class audience, and by the 1920s such egalitarianism was evident in all varieties of tourism, including steamship travel.

Yet a rigid social hierarchy remained evident aboard these 'floating palaces' of luxury. Classes continued to be kept separate, and ship personnel knew their place. Money was the strictest criterion for segregation. As with all taboos and regulations, crew and passengers tried to overstep them as curiosity got the better of their caution. Interaction between passengers of different classes and between passengers and shipboard personnel was evident and texturized the overall experience of life both on the promenade and lido as well as 'below the decks'.

Many facets of the new emerging culture were reflected in the increased visibility of women on board – both as workers and travelers. In an age when women had just obtained the right to vote in many Western societies, their greater presence on ocean liners is noteworthy. Women were venturing out without male escorts and traveling across the ocean for both business and pleasure. Young women, in particular, sought employment on board the floating palaces far away from the protection of their families. What made them wish to work at sea? Could it offer possible upward social mobility and a chance to experience high adventure? Were they indeed 'new women'?

The interwar years saw advertising assume a more prominent and intrusive force than was previously known. As with automobile companies like Ford and cooking specialists like Betty Crocker, the steamship lines saw advertising as key in their luring of the new mass audience. Marketing of the new floating palaces was critical. With competition between lines before and after the Second World War becoming stronger, companies employed various marketing strategies. Posters played a central role in such strategies. Displayed on building walls, kiosks and other areas of cities, posters were highlighted both by traditional aesthetics and modernistic styles – whether to advertise cabarets, theater, cinema, or the ever-changing world of transportation dramatized by faster trains, spacious steamships and revolutionary airplanes.

Questions arise as to the place of poster art in luring prospective travelers. What types of messages were poster artists trying to convey? Many posters enticed people with images of exotic, newly discovered areas of the world at a time when interest in archaeological excavations grew and captured people's imaginations. Some ships elaborately decorated public lounges in imitation of Minoan palaces or Egyptian pyramids. In other cases, the lavish public areas on board as well as the spectacular embellishments of furniture and murals provided other types of material suitable for poster display.

At the same time, the question of interior design and the decorative arts also created contrasting alternatives of tradition and modernism. Furniture, vases and other floating objects could reflect either the heritage of traditional period style or more modern forms associated with currents like the Bauhaus. Ocean liner management commissioned artists like Vanessa Bell (sister to Virginia Woolf) to create canvases for ship interiors like that of the *Queen Mary* to make them moving exhibitions of modernism. This process extended to the design of ship interiors. If the *Titanic-Mauretania* generation preferred the heavy wood and elaborate decor of the *France*, other travelers opted for the more streamlined, modernistic interiors of the *Paris* or the *Normandie*, which represented a direct acceptance of industrial production and the style of Art Deco found in train stations, hotels and New York City skyscrapers. Coming at a time when architect-designers like Le Corbusier cast a prophetic aura around the modernism of ocean liners as splendid reflections of industrial production, this debate was likely to create controversy – and it did.

The outbreak of the Second World War put an end to this new era of transatlantic steamship travel as the end of the First World War began it. One direct form of borrowing from the First World War's heritage was for nations to 'embrace' ocean liners and to convert them into troop carriers, as had been true of the *Mauretania* and *Paris* to name but two. The use of White Star's *Britannic* as a hospital ship was most dramatic as it sank in Greek waters in 1915 after hitting a mine.

With the Second World War, liners of over 80,000 tons like the *Normandie*, the *Queen Mary* and *Queen Elizabeth* were converted into troop carriers and dramatically symbolized the nationalism attached to the steamships even in times of peace. While the latter two ships carried out their mission, the *Normandie* ended its spectacular, but brief, history in a tragic fire in 1942 at New York's piers that damaged its hull but spared many of its decorative works that were slated for exhibit as art. Meanwhile, the two *Queens* continued their wartime work even after the war ended as they transported countless European war brides to the United States to create domestic lives with husbands they had met and married during the war. Ships also acquired the purpose during this troubled time of moving refugees from their unstable troubled homelands to areas that seemed more accommodating to their needs.

Yet even as the Second World War was being fought, plans for a new postwar recovery were set in place. With the Second World War's enormous toll on French Line and Cunard-White Star Line ships and with the concept of regular transatlantic air travel for passengers wishing to travel faster now in sight, the two, by necessity, continued their earlier efforts at enticing masses of non-wealthy people to recommence traveling. But it was apparent that the threat from the air – so vital in concluding the war – was now taking a new turn. Faster and larger airplanes would convey passengers across the Atlantic in hours rather than the four days that ocean liners required. The beginning of one era and the end of another were apparent. It is ironic that the element of speed that doomed mass transatlantic steamship travel was promoted by the shipping companies themselves, not only in faster and bigger vessels but in enterprises and publicity gimmicks also – such as the famed and prized Blue Riband, last claimed by the SS *United States*. An unintentional by-product of this fact was, however, the massive success of cruise ship travel from the 1970s to the present. That desire to go on a sea

journey without thought of a functional purpose had already
been discovered by the steamship companies themselves during
the 1920s as a means by which they could generate revenue.
The demise of regular transatlantic service after the 1950s and
the emergence of mass cruising has brought the final irony:
that whatever crossings do occur now will be as a result of
the ventures of cruise lines and the movies. A more complete
reversal of causes could not be envisioned.

Lorraine Coons and Alexander Varias

Chapter One

Ocean Liners and the New Vistas of Interwar Society

In his cinematic masterpiece *And the Ship Sails On* (*E la nave va*), Federico Fellini characterized the unique life aboard a ship navigating the waters of the Mediterranean during the summer months of 1914 before the onslaught of 'the guns of August'. On board are a group of opera singers, critics, artists and members of the upper class escorting the ashes of a famed deceased soprano who had requested that her remains be scattered off the coast of one particular island. Even on their solemn mission, they march to the cadence of leisure and eccentricity. Dinners are very formal, refined affairs, although the waiters and cooks in the kitchen display a more frenzied, Chaplinesque attitude, colliding and fighting among themselves. The singers delight in showing off their talents, at one point attempting to outdo each other's vocal cords and impressing the stokers in the depths of the engine room, their operatic blasts accompanied by the churns of the engine. As the ship approaches its final destination, a group of Serbian refugees fleeing the chaotic conditions of the Balkans is brought on board and the humane captain offers them asylum from the Austrian warships chasing them. At one point, the refugees release their pent up spirits in exuberant energetic dances that capture the fancies of the First Class elite passengers who, in turn, attempt to join in. The frenzy leads to a final apocalyptic event of terror and destruction, ending the story, but followed by views of the staged sets of the Cinecittà studio used by Fellini and his film 'crew' to manipulate the audience.

Fellini's vision of the liner of 1914 brings to mind even on this solemn mission the vast political, social, cultural and military changes occurring in the world during the early twentieth century. Such transformations also inevitably embraced the maritime scene found in ocean liners and smaller ships. There was no escaping the dynamic and destructive change sweeping through human civilisation. Capitalist economies based on the new methods and products of the Second Industrial Revolution had shaped the movement of social classes both in upward and downward directions. Politics reflected these changes, and as nationalism overtook the traditional restraint of European diplomacy, the Western world was swept into the First World War with its massive bloodletting battles that followed on such a devastating level as to shape human life in its many manifestations over the next several decades.

The aftermath was both a consequence of the war and a rechanneling of historical currents now forced into accelerating speeds. Ocean liners themselves were to reflect that 'Janus-like' reality. With international change and volatility marked by a speeding up of the rhythm and pace of life, transatlantic traffic between Europe and America itself witnessed an ever growing and diverse number of passengers traveling across the ocean on liners that were faster and more massive than those known before. They also displayed strikingly novel designs in line with new debates shaking the artistic world.

All would be abruptly halted once again by another, even deadlier world war. Yet this short-lived era had its own unique character. The years between 1919 and 1939, known as the interwar years, were characterized as a return to 'normalcy'. They were at least years of greater peace when contrasted to the time of the two world wars, which serve as emotional 'bookends' to our perception of this fascinating era of intense cultural activity and exploration.

Travelers could take advantage of the relative peace in ways not possible during the terrible preceding or succeeding years. Numbers of newly designed ocean liners consequently left the slipways from the shipyards of St Nazaire in France, John Brown on Clydebank in Scotland, Newcastle-on-Tyne, and Liverpool in England, their steel plates assembled and riveted by large numbers of unionized workers who viewed them both as sources of employment and emblems of national pride. (See Figure 1.) Huge turbine-driven steam engines in the depths of the liners no longer required stokers feeding them coal because petroleum was the new fuel of the age. Increasingly, such steamships were identified with places and people sacred to the nation and became showcases of the industrial age, exhibiting unparalleled speed and monumental scale. In uncertain, tumultuous times, national pride seemed encased within the gigantic frames set to travel across the Atlantic at dizzying speeds.

The steamship lines at the center of this book prepared for the new century's demands, but they had been founded much earlier. Cunard Line was founded in 1840 under the guiding influence of Samuel Cunard. French Line was begun in 1855 as Compagnie Générale Maritime (later becoming Compagnie Générale Transatlantique) under the inspiration and influence of two brothers important to Napoleon III's national economy – Emile and Isaac Péreire. Although both companies, as evident, were indebted to the direction of key individuals, the enormity of their operations connected them to the larger national concerns of the age and made government support critical to their success.

Even before the First World War, it was evident that life aboard ocean liners like the *Mauretania*, *France*, and the *Olympic* constituted a true culture, partially reflecting the social setting back home. Since the time of the first transatlantic steamships like the *Britannia* and the *Great Britain* of the 1830s and 1840s, the liners had developed into vast floating cities. Travelers like Charles Dickens, Alexis de Tocqueville, Henry Adams and Mark Twain had noted the harsh conditions found aboard the pioneering vessels. In between bouts of sea sickness and the boredom connected to idleness, they hardly exuded words of praise for the ships' decor, which only served particular utilitarian needs with a few cushions of comfort evident now and then. Adams was amazed to see the changes evident in his 1890 voyage on the *Teutonic* that contrasted to his earlier voyages twenty years before. Technological progress in the maritime world was astonishing to behold. As he noted, 'To a man who had been stationary ... the *Teutonic* was a marvel. That he should be able to eat his dinner through a week of howling winter gales was a miracle. That he should have a deck stateroom, with fresh air, and read all night, if he chose by electric light, was a matter for more wonder than life had yet supplied, in its old forms.'[4]

As the nineteenth century went on, ocean liners displayed all the signs of progress and accompanying problems that characterized the age. The three decades preceding the First World War saw Cunard Line, White Star Line, French Line, Hamburg-America, and other steamship companies cater both to the increasingly luxurious tastes of elites and the masses of immigrants leaving Europe for New York's Ellis Island and a home in the United States. This situation was part of a larger context involving both undeniable technological progress and the social volatility felt by those with a precarious hold on life. Yet large numbers of prospective travelers, crowded around the piers of ports like Le Havre, Liverpool, or Hamburg, needed a large country with mythically endless potential to entice them to emigrate.

Since the 1870s tremendous changes had swept over Europe, beginning with the completion of German and Italian unification and new national rivalries that contributed to heightened states of military tension within the continent. Concurrently, the Second Industrial Revolution witnessed increased populations in ever-larger cities, the growing prominence of the middle classes, more prominent working classes that tended toward union activity and general strikes, and the growing participation of the masses in democratic politics. Though many of the new participants worked in liberal and socialist circles, conservatives sought increasingly to co-opt them as seen in the Roman Catholic Church's issuance of *Rerum Novarum* in 1891.

Revolutionary ideas still stirred orthodox Marxism, but anarchism also provided its own edge, with terrorism and assassinations of prominent leaders in several countries. The latter movement attracted peasants and craftsmen in backward areas like southern Italy in which, as with other parts of the non-industrialized continent, mass unemployment and impoverishment were part of a general condition of human misery. At the same time, Russia and other parts of Eastern Europe saw religious persecution chiefly of Jews. Racism and religious persecution flourished at an alarming level during this age which, after all, was colored by the Dreyfus Affair in France and the election of an anti-Semitic mayor in Vienna, capital of Austria-Hungary. The Dreyfus Affair involved the scapegoating of a Jewish captain in the French army on trumped-up charges of treason, while the Viennese election reflected the new political realities of mass extreme right wing politics, eventually exploited by Benito Mussolini and Adolf Hitler.

If this period thus saw corporate capitalists forge a new society of dynamic change and progress, the presence of masses of poor and persecuted people formed another social layer – in some cases applying pressure on the system, in others finding avenues of escape. With Britain, France, Germany and other countries, including the United States, increasingly imposing imperialist control over the undeveloped world, maritime transportation was already important in the making of global networks. The new steamships and the building of the Suez and Panama Canals were natural accompaniments to the wave of imperialism that saw Western societies parcel up much of the world. If the steamships enabled adventurers, entrepreneurs, business agents, government agents and others to reach the colonies, they also helped Europeans immigrate to the United States where it was believed work opportunities, religious toleration and freedom flourished in unprecedented degrees. The Age of Immigration forms a unique period in human history, linking complementary situations in Europe and America as those on the margins of their societies in one continent sought the employment and full range of preferred lifestyles that seemed available in the other. All was halted by the onslaught of the 'Great War'.

Europeans in 1919 saw the previous four years dominated by the war from a perspective of exhaustion and despair. In this, they differed from Americans who came into the war only during its final year and a half and emerged less weary and rather upbeat over their country's new place as the world's industrial leader and financial center. If social and political problems abounded, the epithet 'Jazz Age' still seemed to capture the rather fast-paced, energized world Americans experienced. As citizens of an international empire, larger numbers of Americans expressed more interest in travel abroad as they sought to discover foreign cultures. Prohibition may have restricted the avenues for self-expression and entertainment available domestically, but many Americans hoped to make up the difference by traveling overseas. Steamship lines took note of such a yearning as they promoted advertising campaigns intended to 'whet the appetite'. While the reality of Prohibition dampened the exuberance – except for bootleggers and runners of speakeasies – it also enhanced the yearning among travelers to visit areas with weaker currencies, abundant alcoholic beverages and other vestiges of 'exotic' life. An international culture of pleasure and leisure had emerged to which the steamship companies were strongly connected.

After 1918, Europe was witness, among other things, to downcast veterans returning home (often maimed, shell-shocked and disabled or disfigured by chemical gases), to ruined economies and new political situations, which included revolutionary socialist movements as had prevailed in the recent past in Russia (and nearly did so in Germany) and others that would emerge full-blown in the coming years as Fascism and Nazism, to carry out murderous policies of ethnic extermination and propel the West into a new world war. Despite this crisis-ridden atmosphere, the interlude also saw the American fixation on leisure conveyed across the Atlantic, with Europeans witnessing an explosion in new mores found in drinking, feasting, dance and promiscuity. It was this scene that Ernest Hemingway depicted as 'a movable feast' – a very apt term for the complex culture of Paris' Montparnasse area and the Berlin cabarets.

Because of the later rise to power of Adolf Hitler and the outbreak of the Second World War, the interwar years' frenzied cultural exuberance seems set against a growing abyss – like the 'dance macabre' of the fourteenth century when the Bubonic Plague raged throughout Europe.[5] Such a dance was a contrast to the swinging atmosphere found in Hollywood films. Not coincidentally did Jean Renoir cast a similar dance in the new setting in his important film, *Rules of the Game*, which depicts French elites' thoughtlessness on the eve of the new war. A microcosm of the plunge from frolicking festivity into the despair of the Second World War is found on the ocean liners, which for some time seemed nothing but floating pleasure enclaves, but which, with time, have come to represent the ominous world situation at the period's end. Much of the dynamic energy of the transatlantic experience was provided by new types of passengers, who more and more shaped the ships' character to align with the altered mores and values of the age.

Prior to the First World War, the bulk of passengers coming to America traveled in Steerage as immigrants to the 'promised land', searching for a better life. They left behind religious persecution, famine, pogroms and autocratic regimes to settle in the United States where the Statue of Liberty welcomed them to its shores. People from all parts of Europe boarded the great liners which would transport them to freedom. Between 1820 and 1920, 72 million Europeans left their countries, 34 million of whom sought asylum in the United States.[6]

Such 'huddled masses' could only travel Steerage Class on ocean liners like the *Deutschland* or the *Mauretania* (to name but a few). The numbers of people crammed together in such a way, however, provided great revenue for the shipping lines. Accordingly, large amounts of space on ever larger liners were opened up to accommodate such masses, though only in conditions that were spartan and utilitarian with the barest of furniture and implements necessary for satisfying basic human needs at a modicum. Steerage Class formed the bulk of the traffic of passenger-bearing liners traveling to and fro across the Atlantic Ocean.

Returning to England in 1842 on the *Britannia*, Dickens commented on the squalid living conditions 'below the decks' for emigrants who were treated as human cargo, with little care given to their comfort or health. By mid-century, William Inman, founder of Inman Line, changed the complexion of modern steamer travel with his introduction of a multi-class system, an 'opening up' or democratisation of ship travel that spurred substantial financial success and was copied by other steamship companies seeking their own share of this very lucrative market. Compared to conditions on some sailing ships, Steerage accommodations on board the newer transatlantic steamers were described as 'paradise', and the trip itself was cut from two months to two weeks.[7] By the late nineteenth century, companies had discovered the wisdom and good sense of catering to the needs of their Steerage passengers, who, as satisfied customers, might perhaps encourage friends by letter to travel with the same line. Although they supplied their own bedding and eating utensils, as had been true earlier, emigrant passengers now found markedly improved conditions on board. Dormitories were constructed in the hold space which carried sixteen bunk units. A table was placed in the center of the room where passengers took their modest meals, now included in the price of passage. Still, it was customary for emigrants to bring their own food to supplement the rations provided on board.

At the same time, wealthy First Class travelers demanded luxurious accommodation in the liners. By the end of the nineteenth century, Albert Ballin, Charles Mewès and Arthur Davis also saw vast possibilities in luring prosperous clients with luxury and splendor at sea. Ballin was the head of Hamburg America Line and keenly interested in the emerging taste of elites. As Mewès and Davis relied on upper class preferences for particular furnishings, decor and artistic fashions in designing the César Ritz hotels in Madrid, Paris and London, certain ideas and formulas came to mind almost instinctively as they now set about designing ocean liner interiors. Ballin convinced the two designers that the palatial look found in elite homes and hotels could also be transposed on a 'floating hotel'. The contrast between First Class luxurious quarters and Steerage Class recreated the divisions of the highest and lowest echelons of the European social structure. First Class passengers were naturally inclined as individuals to spend prodigious amounts in their quest to sustain a luxurious lifestyle and collectively represented a large sum of money for the lines. Yet the revenue which most mattered to the steamship companies came from the desperate, persecuted, impoverished 'passengers' in Steerage. In this case, the question of money assumed a mass, collective character of enormous consequence to the well-being of the lines. Indeed, it was only when accountants added that sum to the companies' assets that a rosy financial picture emerged, keeping them 'out of the red'.

The massive travel in Steerage nonetheless allowed for a great change in the level of luxury now afforded First Class passengers. If transatlantic travel had previously entailed austerity and sacrifice of luxury, such need not be the case any longer. Ballin, Mewès and Davis incorporated styles of interior design that could be described as Beaux-Arts, period, or historicist. Whether floating or aground, the style was instantaneously recognized and today would, in a different setting, be attached also to the whims of the jet set. At the time, the primary architectural aesthetic predilection of elites was for a palace setting as shaped by Medieval, Renaissance, Baroque and neo-classical styles, all of which could also be combined in unique arrangements – often in questionable combinations. If the ships' engines, funnels and streamlined hulls all clearly reflected the industrial age, the interiors preferred by First Class passengers suggested a throwback to a past age when aristocracy thrived. That they were themselves 'robber barons' and industrialists or financiers seemed mute. Elites desired an ambience filled with such details and flourishes – even though industrial machines were propelling them forward on the high seas.

Steamship lines devoted much time and effort to helping prospective immigrants move from the different parts of Europe to the ports of departure. French Line, for instance, opened sales offices in Paris, in the provinces, and in major cities throughout Europe to attract an ethnically diverse clientele since the French passenger trade was limited. Along these lines, it offered promotional packages which included rail transportation to Le Havre and accommodations in a hotel constructed specifically for passengers awaiting embarkation. Hamburg America Line under Ballin also addressed emigrants' needs with the construction in 1906 of the pleasant Emigrant Village located on 15 acres along the Elbe River and divided into two sections, an 'unclean side' and a 'clean side' that faced the water. When prospective passengers arrived, they proceeded to the showers where they were deloused.

After passing a physical examination, they were permitted to enter the 'clean side' where they could find inexpensive food and lodgings while awaiting embarkation. These situations would later be repeated upon arrival in Ellis Island. Italian emigration highlighted a large part of the passenger trade, and seeking to capture this large market, French Line experienced much competition from Cunard Line, which had established a direct line from Fiume to New York. After 1900, French Line sought to tap in to the lucrative Central European market and established offices in Austria, Bulgaria and Greece. Offices of steamship agents lured prospective clients with posters promising them a new and better life in America and describing the ship as their passport to liberation. In a move demonstrating the seeming equivalence of corporations and nations, Cunard Line itself paid Austria-Hungary a stipend requiring its government to deliver 20,000 emigrants annually for transport to America on its ships. Desperate to meet the annual quota, government agents often rooted out thousands of 'undesirable' subjects whom they happily exported to America, a practice which would end when the United States restricted the number of immigrants entering its ports.

The influx of emigrant travelers aboard the modern luxury steamships caused concern and dismay on the part of their 'social superiors' (First and Saloon Class passengers). R. A. Fletcher sought to reassure his readers in 1913:

> Most British lines will not carry emigrants from central Europe because of their dirty habits. This may seem unkind, but if you were to see the disgusting condition of some of the men and women who come from that part of the continent, you would not wonder at restrictions but would be surprised that they were ever allowed to enter a railway train – even a fourth-class continental – for a seaport or were allowed to embark.[8]

He advised his largely British audience to stay away from the 'cheap continental steamers' if they valued comfort and cleanliness as 'they cater to anyone who can pay low fares, and it is by these steamers that the mid and eastern European emigrant mostly travels.'[9] Even Robert Louis Stevenson, who in the late 1880s recorded his positive impression of life at sea in steerage in his book, *The Amateur Emigrant*, did not find much to admire in Steerage passengers. Although he preferred to spend his days at sea with Steerage companions whose energy and vitality in singing, dancing and storytelling was contagious, he described them (including himself) as a 'company of the rejected; the drunken, the weak, the prodigal ...We were a shipful of failures, the broken men of England.'[10]

One must keep in mind, when reading such accounts, that the attitudes and ideas connected to the pseudo-science of eugenics were in unfortunately wide usage.[11] Racism was evident when different races were judged to have corresponding emotional or spiritual qualities. With the notion of Orientalism also current, areas of Europe more removed from the 'heartland' of the western and central parts of the continent were deemed uncivilized and chaotic. Immigrants from areas such as southern Italy, Greece, the Balkans and Eastern Europe were accordingly viewed through the types of emotional 'lenses' witnessed above and whenever possible held at 'arm's length'. When contemplating the prospect of traveling alongside these immigrants, elite passengers contemplated the imprint left upon them by Russia's 'Asiatic' culture or the Islamic Ottoman Turkey, or their proximity of North African and Arab lands. Such geographical-cultural insinuations were intended to reinforce racist attitudes. If upper-class passengers could be intrigued and fascinated by the ways of such 'exotic' people (as seen in Fellini's film), an undeniable and strongly drawn prejudice was also apparent.

Racial attitudes and a changing political climate would affect the steerage trade. America's 'open door' policy changed after the Russian Revolution in 1917 and the subsequent attempts to spread Bolshevism abroad. Fearing the influx of communists, anarchists and other political subversives who might gain entry disguised as oppressed immigrants, the American Congress passed the Quota Law in May 1921 (also referred to as The Three Percent Act), which restricted annual immigration to 3 per cent of the foreign born population of the United States according to the 1903 census. Liberty's welcoming beacon was submerged in the translation of this suspicion into political law. By 1921, therefore, the American Congress passed the Dillingham immigration restriction acts, which greatly curbed the number of those able to get off in Ellis Island and gain legal entry to the United States. In 1922, 230,000 fewer Europeans made the crossing to New York than in the previous year.[12] The Johnson-Reed Act of 1924 cut that quota to 2 per cent and based it on the census of 1890. Notwithstanding the new quota, British immigrants were to constitute 50 per cent of the new arrivals, while Asian immigrants were virtually eliminated. No starker fact could testify to the types of racist policies being practiced. Fines were imposed on transportation companies that landed aliens in violation of United States Immigration Laws. Before the war, between 750,000 and 1 million Steerage passengers crossed over to America each year. After the implementation of the new immigration law of 1924, only 150,000 per year did so.[13]

These laws came in the wake of the 'Red Scare' in America, the principal architect of which was Attorney General A. Mitchell Palmer, who began a witch hunt in 1919 and paved the way for the McCarthy era in the 1950s. One of the notorious events characterizing the paranoia of the period was the trial of Nicola Sacco and Bartolomeo Vanzetti, two Italian immigrants charged with the murder of a paymaster and his guard during a robbery of a shoe factory in South Braintree, Massachusetts, on 15 April 1920. Both admitted to being devoted anarchists and communist sympathizers – a certain sign of their guilt in the eyes of the prosecution and judge. (The confusion of anarchism and Bolshevism being itself a symptom of the prevailing ultra-paranoia.) The two were convicted and electrocuted on 23 August 1927, despite international protests and appeals. America was determined to deal harshly with such perceived subversive elements before they brought Bolshevism to its shores, and restricting the entry of immigrants into American ports was seen as the most effective means of fulfilling this goal.

Soon after disembarking at Ellis Island, immigrants had previously undergone intensive scrutiny for various diseases, being associated in the process with illness and physical degeneration. Now they were also being linked with cultural decay, viewed as parasites seeking to invade a 'host' nation and create dangerous political movements. This predisposition to judge minorities and foreigners would not be the monopoly of America. Eugenics was an invention of Americans but traveled across the Atlantic and obviously influenced political movements there. It would become part of Adolf Hitler's broad plan to segregate Jews, gypsies and other minorities on the broader path aiming at their destruction.

The middle classes – that increasingly pervasive sector on the rise since the French Revolution (and well before that time) – did not find a corresponding area on board the liners attuned to their economic and cultural expectations. Yet the fact was that since the mid-nineteenth century, members of the middle classes had developed a desire to travel, and did so in greater numbers. As steamships became larger, more powerful and faster than earlier vessels like Isambard Brunel's *Great Britain* or Samuel Cunard's *Britannia*, the middle classes emerged as a potential source of great revenue for the companies. Still, the amount of space on board reserved for luxury First Class passengers and immigrants precluded much development of cabins and dining facilities reserved for the middle-class traveler. After the

First World War, as steamship companies confronted the reality that they could not rely upon Steerage Class for the bulk of their revenues, they naturally searched for a new source. They found it in the middle class and other less traditional travelers wishing to visit Europe as individual visitors and seeking only a modicum of comfort on board the ship. In the process, the category of Tourist Third Cabin as a novel class of passage on board the ocean liners was created. Whether this group would help fill the gap in profits was a question left open to the future. In any case, a number of strategies were unleashed to lure would-be travelers, and perhaps some adventurers, in the desperate hope that a solution to the crisis was at hand.

At the center of such strategy was the massive reliance on advertising, which in America during the 1920s was experiencing its first phase of widespread use. Cunard, White Star and French Lines, all of which had their principal offices in Europe, authorized their New York offices to launch advertising campaigns aimed at the First, Second and Tourist Class traveler. As a result, posters, brochures and other items were disseminated to attract prospective travelers by appealing either to their taste for comfort, their pocketbooks, or both.

The situation was enhanced even further when one took into consideration the make-up of the crew at this time. Indeed, transformations in the nature of shipboard personnel were themselves indications of the shifting maritime climate that reflected larger international developments. On-board crew were made up not only of traditional maritime workers but of other types of people who desired and/or found a career at sea. More and younger women were joining the ranks of seafarers on the mighty superliners of the Atlantic just as women back home were once again claiming their right to find gainful employment. The experience of a world war, which put them literally in the 'driver's seat' for the first time, convinced them that the notion of a woman's 'proper place' could be extended beyond the home into the workforce or the realm of travel. This diverse scene entailed that the ships pulsated with the varied rhythms and tones of the new age.

Steamship aesthetics gave further witness to the dynamic changes of the time. From the beginning of the twentieth century, ocean liners represented a twofold character in appearance and design. Their exteriors were undeniably products of the industrial age that nonetheless displayed a graceful beauty, seemingly uniting traditionalists and modernists if only because of their maritime reality. Ships were functional and beautiful at the same time – at least in most cases. The new liners were no different. Launched from massive shipyards like St Nazaire, Newcastle-on-Tyne, Liverpool, or Clydebank, they were machines in the making, having been put together by engineers, construction workers and riveters. As the funnels were put in place, the reality of their coal-driven propulsion loomed in massive three-dimensional form.

There were some hostile views of the new industrial ships. The romantic painter, Turner, portrayed a beautiful sailing vessel, the *Temeraire*, being pulled to its demise at the scrapyards by an ugly tug representing the new age. A nostalgic tribute to the stunning, breathtaking beauty of sailing vessels and scorn for the contemporary iron-clad tugs was undeniably present in this work.

Modern ships were machines in motion, like automobiles and trains, and it took time to admire their external aspect. Yet their interiors represented a throwback to aristocratic palaces and even seemed to cast an angry eye on the vivid realities of the modern world. Ballin's aristocratic mélange of assorted styles found in columns, balustraded staircases, high ceilings and other features made the concept of a floating hotel a reality. First Class passengers were prepared in proper dress to display themselves by the central staircase and other prominent public areas. They could pretend that they were part of an important historical moment, posing for the camera (ironically, another product of the industrial world). Historical paintings emphasizing traditional themes and subjects and aristocratic in character hung on the walls. Heavy wood paneling and other traditional materials like marble completed the look. The *Deutschland*, *Mauretania*, *Titanic*, and *France* were all designed according to this predilection for the traditional – or what came to be known as 'period revival'. From the last quarter of the nineteenth century, however, artistic styles in other areas of cultural life were multiplying in number and giving evidence of a world on the move in a revolutionary manner. In the process, new artists presented subjects and forms and colorist experiments that challenged both the entire notion of 'proper' works of art and the dependence upon traditional formulas and styles derived from history. Most obviously, avant-garde artists were revolutionizing painting and the other visual arts. Impressionism and post-impressionism offered artists like Monet, Pissarro, Cézanne, Van Gogh and Gauguin, among others, opportunities to experiment in color, light, form and composition and to challenge public expectations as to the proper nature of art. The avant-garde's works took them into an increasingly abstract direction that provoked both hostility and undeniable enthusiasm for a transformation in the artistic environment in which people lived, worked and traveled.

Architecture had been similarly affected by stylistic change and increasing redefinition of the nature of a building. In America, Henry Richardson, Louis Sullivan and Frank Lloyd Wright used modern materials to create more streamlined buildings with reduced amounts of applied ornament. Vienna's traditional streets also found modern buildings making their appearance as Secession School architects furthered the new architectural style. Gradually disappearing from view in American cities especially were columns, pediments, pilasters, entablatures and other devices used since the ancient world in varying ways to enhance the appearance of a structure. In the process, modern architecture increasingly displayed novel building techniques and materials as most evident and publically in two impressive engineering feats, which yet redefined aesthetic ideals. With the building of the Brooklyn Bridge and Eiffel Tower, modern engineering, as we shall see, imposed permanent effects on architecture, and ocean liners would inevitably reflect this development.

Launched into service during the twenties and thirties, liners like the *Ile de France*, the *Rex*, the *Bremen*, the *Normandie* and the *Queen Mary* gave maritime expression to the changing forms and values of a world transformed after the First World War. Indeed, they were an indelible public part of the world, and their presence provided people with a sense of the rapidly changing surface of the post-war world. This perception was true both in regard to their majestic, massive shapes and size and to the life promised on board. As their frames and hulls emerged in open-air settings, not enclosed within factory buildings like most industrial products, a growing excitement of their possibilities swept through audiences gathered to observe the modern production process at work – a process which was so monumental as to assume mythic and nationalistic status. Throughout the whole procedure, the national consciousness seemed suspended in awaiting the benefits and euphoric emotions that the final product would yield. An ocean liner was as mythic a phenomenon as one could witness in those disjointed days.

The *Ile de France* began setting the tone of the new liners. Its style and features echoed the works shown at the 1925 Exposition Internationale des Arts Décoratifs et Industriels Modernes in Paris, where Art Deco first received great publicity as an advanced and daring movement. While not as radical as the innovative works of the German Bauhaus, Art Deco still created a great splash in the design of ceramics, furniture, lighting fixtures and interior architectural space and the *Ile de France* absorbed the spirit of its influence.

Meanwhile, across the English Channel, the shipyards were creating ships commissioned by Cunard Line and White Star Line that kept much more to the period look, although slowly incorporating the modern in a more restrained manner. These companies were more concerned with keeping to the maritime traditions embraced by many passengers. For such travelers, navigational expertise was the most important ingredient and supreme goal of that long heritage. Modernistic artistic expression was to be kept to the peripheries. The British liners were certainly considered majestic and caused onlookers to catch their breath, but their interiors seemed archaic as though their designers seemed to stop short of embracing the spirit of twentieth-century style.

The liners of these two nations thus seemed to be resuming a rivalry and competition that went back to the invasion of William the Conqueror, the Plantagenets, the Hundred Years' War, and Napoléon, to mention but a few of the more salient moments of strife. Now the rivalry was relatively mild; France and Britain were not at war with each other. They had been allies in the most recent war and would be so in the next. Nevertheless, as the *Aquitania* and the *Ile de France* on the one hand, and the *Normandie* and *Queen Mary* and *Queen Elizabeth* on the other sailed into the open seas, the heads of the respective companies kept an eye on one another in assuming national responsibility for achieving either the most beautiful ship or the fastest and most massive. The race for the prized 'Blue Riband' was but one part of the rivalry between the British and French steamship companies. Other considerations included aesthetic design, hull length, the ship's height from water line to top of smoke stacks, the comfort of cabins, and quality of cuisine. Despite the hatred of traditional militarism emanating from the horrors of the First World War, nationalism itself was still alive and well during the interwar years not only in Italy and Germany, where it swelled into the evil forms of Fascism and Nazism, but also in

France and Britain. Even in a traditional form, French and British nationalism flourished as both powers sought to re-solidify their status as empires, having now obtained mandates in the Near East, and wanting to ensure that their international presence was duly recognised by the upstart United States and other nations. If their economic situations were a bit shaky and uncertain, they could still point to their ocean liners as obvious manifestations of their national importance.

Much had transpired to shake the sense of permanence and stability that the more conservatively minded preferred. Political volatility was evident throughout the West with the revolutionary novelties in Russia and Italy serving as warnings of things to come. Germans, still bitter over the harsh provisions of punishment in the Versailles Treaty, lived within the Weimar Republic where shifting coalitions prevented any government from being in place for very long. They worried about collapsing economic conditions. France, also war-weary and weakened, pressured Germany through such measures as the 1923 invasion of the Ruhr Valley to pay for its post-war reparations. The result for Germany after a chain of events unfolded was soaring inflation and the radical drop in middle-class property values. Economic sluggishness was rampant throughout Europe – a sharp contrast with the unprecedented bull market and high level of consumerism in the United States until the onslaught of the Depression after the October 1929 Wall Street crash.

Metamorphoses in a variety of cultural arenas were visible. Ezra Pound's and T. S. Eliot's modernist poems were examples of the streamlined language expressing complex symbolic metaphor. Stravinsky's, Schoenberg's and Bartok's musical innovations were matched by jazz to surround listeners with novel harmonies and dissonances. Cabarets displayed new forms of popular dance even as ballet had seen Diaghilev, Nijinksy and Isadora Duncan lead the way earlier on in novel choreographic arrangements. By the 1920s, earlier Cubists and Fauvists seemed less provocative in their experiments in painting, but Expressionism, Surrealism and other styles continued to tantalize gallery audiences with new forms of visual bafflement and bewilderment.

The sensation of drifting between continents fit the general public mood of flux among political and social systems, economic experiments, transformed cultural venues, and novel mores and behavior traits. Whether referred to as 'the waste land' of 'the hollow men' or 'the second coming', the European landscape was inhabited by men and women whose faith in the old order of things had been shattered by the world war and the seismic quivering emanating from the various fissures indicated above. The experience of ocean liner travel moved with the times as passengers' expectations of accommodations, forms of dress, end destinations and other matters had changed in so many ways. Speed, size and the scale of comfort and luxury had by now become measured in a different light, with the character of pre-war liners now regarded as antiquated and the novelty of contemporary forms more highly appreciated. With the airplane becoming ever more prominent, the steamship companies had to move to keep up with the public imagination and provide some obvious contrasts. It was also the case that class barriers now became subject to debate and resentment – especially with the arrival of the new class of passengers who perhaps aspired to the delights of the top classes.

Transatlantic liners served other causes besides those found in national rivalries. This era was marked not only by ongoing tension connected to the First World War, but by pacifism and diplomatic efforts to reduce world tensions, especially during the 1920s. If the League of Nations was not the force once envisioned by Woodrow Wilson, various pacts and accords were signed to lessen the possibilities for conflict and to humanize conflict when it did occur. During that decade we see such agreements as the Locarno Treaty and the Geneva Protocol (intended to make the treatment of prisoners of war more humane). The Rapallo Treaty signed by Germany and the Soviet Union also brought the latter country into the domain of nations once again – one with which the West could possibly conduct relations. While this view changed with the development of Stalinism, the renewal of dialog helped spur the resumption of travel to the estranged country. Out of self-interest and the search for new profits, steamship lines naturally were to lead the way in renewed contacts. They also exploited the audience for international dialog found in students, professors and other intellectuals to tailor voyages of reconciliation, educational discovery, and even the continual healing of wounds and sad memories connected to the First World War.

White Star Line announced its re-entry into the Russian trade in 1930 after agreements with the Soviet Union had been signed. It thus became the first shipping company to introduce service between New York and Leningrad. Brochures for trips on the *Olympic*, *Homeric* and *Majestic* invited tourists to view for themselves 'these vast new experiments in government'. Affordable round-trip fares of $280 in Tourist Third Cabin accommodations were offered. White Star Line worked with Sovtorgflot (the Soviet State Shipping Company) and Intourist Company, a separate Soviet state organization which arranged escorted land tours ranging from five to thirty days at a cost varying from $80 to $360. White Star Line also sought a new audience in the small remaining immigrant trade, transporting Soviet citizens who had been able to secure exit visas to America. 'Preferred category passengers' included wives and children (under age twenty-one) of American citizens, parents of American citizens, and wives and children of alien residents in the United States.[14]

Other exotic destinations meant to lure passengers included a thirty-day cruise organized by Cunard Line on the *Aquitania* to Egypt and the Mediterranean in 1932 with round-trip fares from New York ranging from as low as $250 for Tourist Class cabins to $540 for First Class accommodations.[15] Special trips billed as 'Scholars' Summer Cruises' were planned by White Star Line, whose *Doric* set sail from Oslo to Hamburg with 140 adults and 210 scholars. French Line's *Ile de France* and *Lafayette* both transported youths under twenty-five to Canada in August and September 1934 for a Voyage d'Amitié de la Jeunesse Française, which was arranged in coordination with the 400th anniversary of the discovery of Canada by Jacques Cartier and the Exposition of Toronto. As part of the concord of the age, large organized parties of students, educators and young professionals crossed the Atlantic on White Star ships with World Acquaintance Tours, the stated object of which was to promote 'international understanding among people of all lands through discussion and conferences with economic and social leaders in each country'.[16] Setting sail on 21 July 1933, the *Paris* carried French First World War veterans who were embarking on a 'goodwill visit' to the United States with the purpose of the voyage 'to pay a visit of courtesy to fellow war veterans of the American Legion, to thank them for the pilgrimage that they made to the battlefields in 1927, and to accept an invitation made by our delegates last year to revisit France in 1937.' The French government helped to fund the trip while the US Senate, adamantly clinging to isolationism, declined a request for funds.[17]

Such hopes for keeping to the spirit of reconciliation were later confirmed by the signing of the Kellogg–Briand Pact on 27 August 1928 in which the major European states, the United States, and Japan renounced war 'as an instrument of national policy'. The *De Grasse* and the *Colombie* offered land tours to the United States and Canada to its passengers who had sailed to New York to see the World's Fair during the summer of 1939. The International Exposition held in Paris in 1937 drew many American visitors who booked tour packages through French Line.

People experiencing the Second World War's unprecedented horrors could later assess the interwar years as a new version of the good old days, since the distance in time imbued them with hues of nostalgia and so many forms of progress revealed a world still on the move. It hadn't been clear then that times could become far more sinister. Change could be experienced as threatening or as an invitation to swing with the times in frolicking dance vibrating to the new music. Transatlantic steamship travel only evidenced this new reality in obvious and dramatic ways that took center stage among those who knew. As travel is transient in nature, its lessons are hard to pin. On the one hand, it could consist of a simple pursuit of leisure or escape, not reflecting the deeper problems of an age. At the same time, the presence of large masses of refugees fleeing terrible conditions revealed another side to the story. How the different classes of passenger occupied time on board, however, tells us something about expectations, since leisure does reveal values and desired forms attached to an age.

If ever an era was more divided between a continual sense of *angst* and the devotion to culture and pleasure it was the time of the interwar years. Few ages, in fact, have emitted both the desperate yearning for euphoria and the despair that seemed woven into history.

Following an unprecedentedly brutal war unleashing the new technological weapons, people everywhere dreaded the possible resumption of hostilities. All the more did the revolutionary realities of Bolshevism and Fascism make that threat ever more foreseeable and palpable. For that reason, as noted, the search for a permanent peace become ever more fervent.

On the other hand, as Paul Fussell has noted, the end of the war reawakened those pursuits suppressed during the four years of massive violence – pursuits connected to self-development, culture, leisure, and pleasure, among which was included travel. In the modern context, however, and due to that same technological change which contributed benefits as well as destruction, travel was able to attract more people (especially in the United States) who now found the means to board a liner and experience modern life in its many shades and varieties while sailing to a foreign port. The foreign and the exotic beckoned, and as a result, the Atlantic Ocean teemed with ships carrying people from America and Europe eager to witness lands of which they had only previously dreamt. Pushed to the background for Americans during the crossing was the war weariness and tension that would inevitably be felt in Europe upon disembarkation. As immigration faded in significance, those of the humbler classes who pursued that dream found themselves in the new category of Tourist Third Cabin.

Chapter Two

From Immigrants to Tourists: The Changing Complexion of Transatlantic Passengers

The strict immigration laws of the early 1920s forced steamship companies, which had benefitted from the booming steerage trade, to rethink their strategy for luring passengers. While companies traditionally focused their attention on First Class public space and accommodations, quality of food and service, the steerage trade, which captured little consideration from anyone, was what kept their account books well in the black. The 'floating palaces' would have turned into 'floating wrecks' had it not been for the revenue generated by the steerage trade. The end of steerage would most certainly have sounded the death knell for many steamship companies. Receipts of French Line fell from 235 million francs in 1920 to 87 million in 1923.[18]

An irrevocable shift in the Atlantic traffic followed. In search of a new audience, steamship companies focused on the middle classes who were eager candidates for affordable travel. 'Steerage' was replaced by a new class of passage, 'Tourist Third Cabin' (later simply referred to as 'Tourist'), and an entirely new breed of mass tourist was created. Dreary quarters were upgraded to accommodate teachers, students and tourists on a tight budget who were lured by company advertisements inviting Americans to explore Europe and other exotic parts of the globe. There was something very bohemian about the whole experience and 'Tourist Third Cabin' soon came to be christened the 'Left-Bank' class. United States Line sought to capitalize on America's reputation as one of the representative democratic nations and took the lead in promoting the new style of travel, offering free trips to reporters in exchange for favorable press.[19] It also sought to keep Americans on American liners, attempting to convince this predominant group of tourists that they would feel more at home on ships sailing their national flag. French Line publicity brochures advertising the new flagship of the fleet, *Normandie*, likewise invited Americans to travel in Tourist Class with no trepidations:

> To tired professors, to weary students, to all routine-bound jaded toilers, French Line travel makes an irresistible appeal. The appeal of suave, effortless living the age-old atmosphere of charming France.
>
> The gangplank serves as a barrier - a barrier between that life where ambition, work, nerve-twisting problems, fight for your peace-of-mind, and this ocean life of France which lulls you into unbelievable tranquility and quiet of spirit directly as you set foot on the shiny, polished deck.[20]

A new and improved Third Class section with more spacious public areas was maintained to accommodate the limited number of immigrants crossing the Atlantic.

Transatlantic travel itineraries were expanded. A new concept of 'pleasure cruising' was introduced to entice a clientele (80 per cent of whom were Americans) eager to embark on high adventure while taking minimal safety risks. One Tourist Third Cabin Class passenger described his fellow travelers as the 'solid middle class of the United States ... who feel more at home in Britain these days than we do in Europe. The European is apt to assume we are all very rich folk that have come over to squander our dollars ... Most of us are just hard-working people ... You British understand that.'[21] Europeans were also being lured by publicity brochures inviting them to visit American and Canadian world-class cities like New York, Chicago, Montreal and Québec, as well as spectacular natural sites like Niagara Falls or Yosemite.

Part of this new interest in tourism (on both sides of the Atlantic) came as a byproduct of economic modernization connected to the Industrial Revolution. A new class (the bourgeoisie/middle class) was created – one that claimed its equal right to leisure with the *grands notables*. No longer were summer vacations by the sea possible only for the wealthy. Seashore resorts began catering to a largely middle-class audience by the early twentieth century. Thomas Cook pioneered a new idea in travel in the mid-nineteenth century, taking groups on conducted tours, developing a business 'whose purpose it was to make travel easier and cheaper for people of modest means'.[22] Travel guides became popular companions to the would-be 'do-it-yourself' explorers. In addition to the well-respected Baedeker guides (first published in 1829), Jonathan Cape began publishing a series of Travelers' Library guides in 1926 – 5-by-7-inch books, bound in fine light blue, gold-stamped cloth, designed as pocket books for travelers.[23] By then, this egalitarianism had spread to all varieties of tourism including steamship travel.

The Second World War also contributed to the 'opening up' of travel to the masses. The 'Defense of the Realm' acts of 1914/15 restricted British private travel abroad. For four years, three months and seven days, British private citizens were held captive by their government and were not permitted foreign luxuries such as oranges, which, like other exotic items, had become rare commodities in England by 1916. Paul Fussell speaks of the 'tropical motif', which during the war had become 'a widespread imaginative possession of all in the trenches who were cold, tired, and terrified'. A favorite greeting card that soldiers sent home had a frieze of green and brown embroidered palm trees and a bright sun in the background with the inscription 'Greeting from the Trenches'.[24]

All aspects of British life had been rationed, and the Food Ministry adopted as its slogan 'Eat Slowly: You Will Need Less Food'. Domestic travel was limited as trains were frequently canceled and train passengers were discouraged by placards which reminded them that 'Unnecessary Traveling Uses Coal Required to Heat Your Homes'.[25] The same was true on the Continent. The passport, instituted in England in 1915 to restrict British travel abroad, became a permanent fixture for all countries after the war. Once hostilities ceased, there was a mass exodus of people leaving their familiar surroundings to explore distant shores about which they had dreamt during the war. To travelers of the 1920s, Fussell explains, 'the idea of travel is practically equivalent to the idea of ships, and the familiar spectacle of ships nearby ... induced curious, subtle, psychological ripples incident only to that time and place.'[26] The new Tourist Third Cabin accommodations made travel affordable for the middle classes. So it seemed to Evelyn Waugh's brother, Alec, himself a writer, who regarded his cabin as home: 'When people used to ask me how I could afford to do much traveling, I replied that I spent far less abroad than in a London flat. Travel, by ocean liner, was indeed in those days one of the cheapest ways of living, certainly for a freelance writer who carried his office with him and could work in his cabin or in a saloon.'[27] The laptop, with its promise of facilitating transportable work in a portable environment, was but a step away. Early in the twentieth century, Alec Waugh seems to be aspiring both to the compressed office and to the synthesis of work and leisure, in which neither realm is allowed to thrive by itself.

Aspiring writers could find inspiration and freedom on a liner in pursuing a novel, poem, or play. The image of a writer happy just to find creative freedom at sea became one of the age's stereotypes. A lifestyle was being born as Waugh tried to carry his writing with him – a desire that seems quite natural for artists who, after all, search for inspiration everywhere. Such intellectual, cultured, and often insecure, travelers stigmatized the masses of tourists who lacked any previous tradition or deep-founded need to travel (wanderlust), but who were now given the means to do so without the 'aura' associated with upper-class travel as once found in the 'Grand Tour'.

A transatlantic round-trip fare could cost the eager novice traveler as little as £20 or $110. Fussell attributes such bargains to the abundance of leftover troopships converted back to passenger vessels and to the large number of enemy ships seized as part of reparations, which put half of the world's ships under British control in the 1920s. Travel on the Continent was especially cheap since the pound and dollar were stronger than other foreign currencies. Hemingway found that in the 1920s, 'two people could live comfortably well in Europe on $5 a day and could travel'.[28] Cunard *Business News* told its American readers that the dollar's value to the British pound was 25 per cent greater than it formerly was. The gain on French francs would be 100 per cent, and even more in Italy, 'and if they should venture to Germany they can have marks almost for the asking'.[29] Such conditions indeed made European nations in the 1920s and 1930s vulnerable to fascist movements. The carefree American tourist who profited from Europe's post-war economic slump would later learn the dear price to be paid for such 'bargains'.

From the ranks of Tourist Third Cabin Class passengers in the interwar years, one could discern students, teachers and aspiring writers wishing to see great historical sites, exotic vistas, or a contrasting culture found across the Atlantic Ocean. From the social margins, one could also find card sharks, bootleggers, stowaways and others who made for a lively and complicated cast of characters aboard ships. With so many writers, outcasts, fun-lovers, go-getters, dance craze enthusiasts, and hard drinkers, the new category of passenger had few features in common other than the desire to travel cheaply, not requiring the luxury of First Class, which they could not afford in any case. That segregated First Class area of the liner was left to traditional, snobbish, pedigree families; prosperous, ambitious businessmen needing to arrive for work well rested and satiated; celebrities requiring an exclusive aura; politicians, and well-established writers and artists.

Shipping companies eagerly awaited the American 'invasion' in the summer of 1920 and more than 100,000 visitors who, according to *The Daily Mail*, considered London their 'mecca'. All eastbound crossings were heavily booked by both wealthy Americans and central Europeans and Scandinavians who were 'marooned in the New World owing to the hostilities on this side of the Atlantic' and were finally making their way home. Cunard Line assured prospective passengers a trouble-free experience. Once the ticket was purchased, Cunard would do the rest, company ads promised, even guaranteeing hotel accommodations if delays occurred.[30]

On the other side of the Atlantic, many Europeans saw the ship as their conduit to a better life in the Americas. At the end of 1919, *London's Daily News* predicted 'a big exodus from this country to America in the beginning of the New Year', which would include 'a large number of men and women who are dissatisfied with the unsettled state of affairs at home and mean to try hazards with fortunes in the west.' There was a sense that the disturbing effects of the war had been felt more by women than by men, and the paper predicted the departure of a large number of WAAC (Women's Army Auxiliary Corps) and WRNS (Women's Royal Naval Service) members.[31]

One important new source of revenue for Cunard, White Star, and other British shipping companies was the increasing number of single women emigrating from Europe to Canada.

The Canadian government had launched an active campaign to recruit needed workers in all trades and promised them employment, a great incentive for Europeans whose lives had been turned upside down by the war. Cunard Line publicity magazine promised rosy futures for women of all classes: 'Canada can absorb all the women Great Britain can send her.' Domestics, cooks, nurses, waitresses were in demand, and even the educated woman 'who is willing to undertake work of any kind ... will find that it will not be long before she will obtain employment in her own sphere.' Canada particularly welcomed middle-class women possessing a little capital, 'who bring with them something of the culture of the old country'.[32]

Cunard Line chairman, Thomas Royden, received an inquiry from Maurice Caillard, Esq. about the most economical and proper means of travel for a woman, twenty-eight years of age who had 'fallen on very tough times' and who had an offer of employment in Canada. Royden enthusiastically endorsed the company's newest class: 'Without a doubt a lady can travel with perfect decency and comfort if she goes Tourist Third. I would not hesitate to go that way myself, or send my own people, so I am not recommending something I don't believe in.'[33] Furthermore, Cunard assured parents that they need not be concerned about the safety of their daughters during their journey as the shipping lines had introduced a new position on board – 'conductress' – and the woman filling the job was to look after the well-being of the younger women and to see that they were in proper hands once in Canada. To meet this new demand, Cunard introduced a regular service between Liverpool–Belfast and Québec on board the *Caronia* and *Carmania*, both of which had been transferred from the New York service in 1924.[34] Amended immigration laws in July 1929 increased the number of emigrants from Great Britain and Ireland to the United States from 34,000 to 65,731. British shipping companies profited from this change. Among them was White Star, which noted in its publicity magazine in February 1930 that 'in spite of emigration difficulties Third Class still represents the largest proportion of the traffic moving, comprising 41 per cent of the carryings last year.'[35]

One new market for which shipping companies actively competed was the 'lady traveler' whose numbers were steadily increasing after the war. While wealthy widows and marriage-hopeful debutante types continued to make transatlantic voyages, more and more independent-minded 'new women' ventured out unescorted on travel adventures that took them across the high seas on the luxury liners in the interwar years. Cunard Line's *Aquitania* was billed as 'A Ladies' Ship' and publicity brochures sought to make women traveling alone feel especially welcome on board. On many sailings, women outnumbered men two to one in all classes.[36] Many teachers embarked on educational holidays, and businesswomen crossed the Atlantic to attend conferences, conventions, and the like.

In his travel essay, 'When the Going Was Good', Evelyn Waugh comments on the many vulnerable middle-aged widows who 'find themselves in control of more money than they have been used to; their eyes stray to the advertisements of shipping companies and find there just that assembly of phrases – half poetic, just perceptible aphrodisiac – which can produce at will in the unsophisticated a state of mild unreality and glamour.'[37] Cunard-White Star stewardess Edith Sowerbutts commented that such women were 'all dressed up to the nines, out on a big safari to ensnare unsuspecting males', but also acknowledged that certain men did not need much coaxing as 'it was a gigolo's paradise'. Sowerbutts was more critical of older female passengers, who 'complete with face lift, tummy-lift and breast lift', are married to younger men, all 'purchased with wealth'. She saw such women as pathetic 'travesties of womanhood' who 'hung onto their young husbands', keeping them on a tight leash.[38]

French Line's onboard newspaper, *L'Atlantique*, which carried news from around the world and articles advertising other ships of the fleet, began to include features on high fashion and other topics which were thought to attract a female readership.[39] One announcement informed lady readers 'that they are cordially invited by Mme Dresser, an American woman, to pay a visit to her salons, where they will find a most remarkable and unique collection of the latest creations by the leading Parisian designers.' Articles included tips on 'How to be Beautiful, Well and Happy! – Dancing as a Cure for Many Ailments', as well as advice on courtship and marriage: 'Maids Who Marry Millions – Cinderellas in Real Life'; 'Secrets of a Woman's Heart'; 'The Man I Loved – But Could Not Marry'; as well as a piece by Mrs Thomas Hardy, 'No Marriage Tiffs After 40. Wife of Celebrated English Novelist Says Quarrels Between Elderly Couples Are Positively Heartbreaking'. Other articles extolled the virtues of the traditional woman: 'Hero Worship and the Modern Girl – Woman Still Romantic in Spite of Modernism', and 'The French Woman' warned the reader that if a woman's goal in life is not marriage and motherhood, the 'nation faces jeopardy'.[40]

White Star Line stirred the imaginations of young female passengers in search of 'Mr Right' with an on-board publication, *Eve's Day*, a diary of a woman's ideal day at sea. After a luxurious breakfast served in bed, Eve dons silk stockings and 'a bewitching *crepe de chine* frock' and telephones home to inform Daddy that she has her eye on one special man. After lunch at the pool, she meets her new acquaintance, who, after seeing Eve in her new swim suit, calls her 'Aphrodite'. Now Eve's curiosity is sparked as she notes in her diary: 'Must look up Aphrodite and see who she is.' After a perfect evening of dancing and strolling on deck in the moonlight with her beau, she retires to her cabin, alone of course, to conclude her day's entry in her diary: 'Wouldn't it make a perfect honeymoon trip?'[41] On all transatlantic steamers, an elaborate shopping center could be found, which always included a jewelry store carrying an adequate supply of engagement rings, just in case![42]

Roydon Freeman warns the unattached male passenger that 'on board ship there is no peace for the bachelors. Girls who travel on mail-boats soon learn how to sort the males.'[43]

At the same time, shipping lines had become increasingly aware that a new age was upon them, with women becoming more and more the makers of their own destiny. The single woman traveler who ventured abroad unchaperoned was an example of this 'new woman'. Many of them traveled Tourist Third Cabin on ships, and companies competed for their business.

Cunard Line, for one, actively sought out these women by featuring articles in its publicity magazine considering questions thought to be of interest to them, such as 'Should Ladies Smoke in Public?', in which the author defended women's right to 'equal privileges' with men 'and to decide for themselves as to where they shall smoke'.[44] Another article on professions for women assured its readers that 'when intelligent women take up any occupation they make a success of it'. 'A Plea for the Bachelor Girl', found in one of the magazine's 'Ladies Corner' section, praised women:

> The most independent creature on the earth's surface is the true 'bachelor girl' ... [who] is her own mistress, and can order her leisure just as she chooses. Her hard earned money is her own, and there is no husband to whom she is responsible for the expenditure, thereof, ... If there is no one to praise her thriftiness, there certainly is no one to accuse her of extravagance ... The personality of the true bachelor girl is fresh and spontaneous. It is not crushed under the thing she imagines a husband would like her to be ... For company, if the bachelor girl is short of friends, there are always animals or parrots to love.[45]

L'Atlantique featured stories of Frenchwomen who were accomplished professionals, 'Women Doing Things' and

'Men the Modern Woman Likes', which stated that a woman 'only wants fair treatment and honest recognition of ability, irrespective of sex'. In such a way, the ongoing debate about woman's 'proper place' in the modern age was carried over to the high seas.

Shipping companies increasingly found themselves courting middle-class audiences. Once the economic barrier was lifted, students, teachers and other intellectually curious middle-class types could now contemplate travel abroad in comfort and safety. The introduction of 'pleasure cruising' further assured wary first-time travelers that they would not be abandoned in an alien environment abroad and left to fend for themselves. Now companies had to convince would-be passengers that they were welcome on board and that an ocean voyage was no longer to be viewed as an option available only to the wealthy. In an age in which rayon could easily substitute for silk, class lines increasingly were becoming blurred.

Ship brochures guaranteed a cabin to suit everyone's budget on the grand luxury liners in this democratic age, ranging from Third and Tourist Third Cabin to First Class. Separate brochures were published for each class of travel, with companies insisting on the respectability of travel in Tourist Third Cabin and Third Class to allay the fears of parents sending their daughters abroad to work, study, or travel. They sought to distance these new and improved classes of travel from the old steerage class and the negative connotations associated with it.

French Line introduced the '*classe unique*', the one class or 'one-cabin ship' with the *Chicago*, built in 1908 – the epitome of democracy at sea, which became a popular concept after the First World War.[46] Passenger accommodations varied on such ships, but public space was open to all. In this new style of travel, First Class was eliminated, while Second Class advanced in status to First and Third Class became second. While the names changed to reflect a greater democratization, class divisions remained securely in place with the middle class now getting its chance to play the role of the grands notables. This class of travel appealed to those people who preferred comfort to speed as these cabin ships were not contenders for the Blue Riband, and their tariffs, as a result, were more affordable to the middle classes. Passengers traveling on board these cabin ships were less concerned with luxury service than with getting the most for their money. Billed as 'family ships' by White Star Line, their brochures guaranteed passengers 'unrestricted use of broad decks and spacious, handsome public apartments.'[47]

Even on the standard luxury liners that maintained the three-class system, shipping companies sought to assure all prospective clients that they would be welcome on board. Cunard, White Star and French Line brochures promised their clients of more modest means that, regardless of the class of travel, they would be well cared for on their vessels. One French Line brochure guaranteed that 'a voyager may travel Tourist or Third Class on the *Normandie* and still be able to enjoy luxurious comfort and the keen delights of deck sports and other exceptional advantages – all within his ability to pay!' French Line advertised the *Normandie*'s maiden voyage in 1935 as offering round-trip prices beginning as low as \$245 for Third Class, \$315 for Tourist Class, and \$588 First Class for a fifteen-day journey.[48]

White Star Line publicity brochures allayed the fears of some of its white-collar clients by guaranteeing that anyone 'contemplating passage in Second Class, Tourist Third Cabin or Third Class … will find in these classes respectively the same careful thought for your comfort. The fittings, of course, will be somewhat less luxurious, but no less pleasing.' According to one passenger, however, the food was 'plain, substantial, utterly uninteresting but eatable', hardly a comment that any shipping company would want to include in its publicity brochures, which all boasted of elaborate, sumptuous, gourmet fare aboard their ships. Tourist Third Cabin clients were generally a satisfied lot and made no demands on the company as did its First Class passengers.

Special attention was paid to Third Class passengers, as Cunard recognized that the 'Third Class passenger of today may be the Saloon [First Class] passenger of tomorrow, and the treatment they receive now will determine their choice of Line then.' To that end, the 1927 *Cunard Rule Book for Crew* instructed the chief steward's staff to treat Third Class passengers with 'every civility and consideration', and that every effort should be made to serve the diverse nationalities ethnic food.

As a means of attracting prospective clients of all classes, steamship companies decided to allow public viewings of their 'traveling palaces'. White Star Line billed its flagship *Majestic* (formerly the *Bismarck*) as the 'largest steamship in the world' and opened it up for inspection to the curious public. On 13 August 1928, more than 10,000 visitors accepted the invitation to tour the ship. Railway companies, in cooperation with the steamship company, arranged excursions to Southampton for this purpose. The demand was so great that four special trains were run to the docks.[49] Calling itself the 'pioneer' of Tourist Third Cabin, White Star Line boasted that its ships carried 41,158 passengers in this class in 1928, 'the highest total also for one line since this class of travel was instituted'. To meet the increasing demand for this new class of travel, White Star announced in 1930 that it had converted the Second Class accommodations on the *Homeric* (formerly the *Columbus*) into Tourist Third cabin space. Other lines were quick to follow White Star's lead.

A Cunard publicity brochure described Tourist Third Class as a great innovation in luxury travel: '... so great has been the demand for this popular class in recent years that the whole of the palatial "Second Class" accommodation in the three mammoth express liners *Aquitania*, *Berengaria*, formerly the

Imperator, and *Mauretania* has now been placed unreservedly at the disposal of "Tourist Class" passengers.'[50] Cunard publicized passengers' comments about its ships, quoting from one passenger's very positive review: 'One's first thought on mounting the decks was that one had got into the First Class, so delightful were the spacious saloons, so comfortable and tastefully furnished they were ... I have traveled First on many liners, but I have no recollection of having been so comfortable as I was in the *Aquitania*'s tourist section.'[51]

Captain E. G. Diggle, Commander of Cunard Line's *Aquitania*, compared the ship to a floating city. As with any other city ashore, on board the floating city one finds 'people who are very rich, and who stay in the most select and exclusive districts of the city. There are also other visitors who cannot afford quite such luxurious apartments. These people can stay in any of three districts: the second class district, the tourist third cabin district or the third class district.' Realizing the luxurious First Class accommodations did not require a hard sell, Diggle focused on the lesser classes, assuring his readers that even Third Class is a respectable means of travel on board the new 'floating palaces' of his day: 'It must not be imagined that because of its name it is very terrible and dreary. People would be surprised to see the "type" of people in this class, and no one is ashamed of living there.' As in all other 'districts' on board, there was an inn (smoking room), a library and writing room, a concert lounge, and 'lots of deck space for the visitors to play games'.[52] As we will see later, this image of a ship as a city was a common metaphor used by shipping companies to entice potential passengers.

While company ads sought to reassure passengers that Tourist or Third were perfectly respectable classes of travel, writer Ludwig Bemelmans found it impossible to book a Third Class cabin on the *Normandie* on his return voyage to the United States. Having been upgraded to one of the suites de grand luxe, which resembled a veritable palace complete with private terrace, a servants' dining-room, and Lalique ashtrays on the Eastbound crossing, he chose to return in simpler accommodations: 'I wish to go downstairs, you understand, and find out how it is down there,' he told his booking agent. 'I now want to experience how a man feels who has no money, or very little and who has to eat and live in Third Class.' Horrified at the very thought, the man replied: '*Non, non, mais non, non, Monsieur Bemelmans - ça-ne-va-pas*! ...Victor Hugo did not become a hunchback in order to write Notre Dame de Paris.' The same suite was set aside for his family but Bemelmans was resolute. He was to travel in Third. The bewildered booking agent shrugged his shoulders and said, 'Enfin, I have nothing to say.' Bemelmans' status as a writer meant different things to both men. As one who belonged 'to the ultra-realist school of writers', Bemelmans felt compelled 'to go downstairs' to experience life 'below the decks'. To the French Line representative, however, the fact that Bemelmans was a writer made it imperative that he be extended every possible courtesy in exchange for good press, which 'is just why we wish you to write something very nice – ah, *la publicité, la publicité* – is very important ...'[53] French Line sought to put its best foot forward in showcasing the *Normandie* before the press and thus had no intention of having writers experience either Tourist or Third Class life aboard, regardless of how heartily they endorsed this democratic style of travel in their publicity brochures.

Once on board, the Tourist and Third Class passenger might not feel as welcome as brochures promised. Roydon Freeman correctly observed that class lines were much more tightly drawn at sea than on shore: 'In a three-class ship the money-barrier sharply divides the human race. On land a man may make friends with one much poorer than himself if he finds him attractive, but at sea the different-colored tickets come between them and divide up these human animals into separate cages, so that they can only observe one another through or over railings. And, owing to the ups-and-downs of life, these barriers are fixed not by intellect or refinement, but solely by money.[54]

In his account of ship travel before the First World War, *Travelling Palaces*, R. A. Fletcher describes the great fanfare with which First Class passengers were sent off. They were accompanied by a company representative who escorted them on a special train from London to the docks, where the captain and his officers were waiting at the top of the gangway to welcome them on board. No such ceremony was organized for the other classes. In fact, when a ship sailed at noon, there were normally three boat trains scheduled to depart from Waterloo station for Southampton between 7:30 and 9:00 a.m. – the first for Third Class passengers, the second for the Tourist Third Cabin and the last train reserved for the First Class. The ship's doctors presided over the embarkation. At the arrival of Third Class, the doctors carried out a medical examination of all passengers to ensure that no one would be turned back by health authorities at the port of disembarkation.[55] On the mixing of classes, Fletcher makes the point that 'it is a gross breach of the etiquette of the sea life, and a shocking exhibition of bad manners and low inquisitiveness, for passengers to visit unasked the quarters of an inferior class.' The 'inferior classes', as he calls them, should have their rights respected by the 'superior class'.[56] People in 'inferior class' cabins were themselves regarded as 'inferior' or second-class citizens next to those in 'superior class' category staterooms. Definitions applied to cabin space were being extended to include the occupants' social status.

Spatial divisions between the classes were obvious once people were on board. Each class had its separate entranceway, set of public rooms, and deck space. First Class was allocated the preferred mid-ship space while Second, Tourist Third Cabin and Third Classes had to rest content with the less desirable forward and aft areas, which were affected more strongly by the often tumultuous weather on the high seas. First Class passengers especially resented the frequent visits of the 'inferior' classes into their public space. A character in Sutton Vane's play, *Outward Bound*, perfectly captured the indignation of the 'superior' class at the prospect of having to mix socially with the 'inferior' classes. The passengers, who are on an unknown ship with an undisclosed destination, are all dead but unaware of it. Mrs Cliveden-Banks, described as a 'disagreeable woman, very judgmental and class-conscious', assumes that her secretary has booked passage for her in First Class, but is faced with the probability of sharing public space with Mrs Midget, a 'poor cockney charwoman'. Horrified at the very thought, Mrs Cliveden-Banks demands that the steward 'take the good woman back to her proper place immediately. She's been wandering. She's on the wrong deck, she's in the wrong class,' indicating that Mrs Midget belongs in Steerage. When she is told that there is only one class on board, Mrs Banks is near panic: 'How am I to know who are the ladies and gentlemen, and who are not?...Well then – if she eats – and if there's only one class – she will eat in the same place as we shall. It can't be done. I shall disembark immediately.'[57] While Vane was clearly poking fun at such class snobbism, many flesh-and-blood First Class passengers could well identify with Mrs Banks' disgust at having their paths cross with social 'inferiors' on board a deluxe luxury liner.

Class consciousness extended even to the realm of animals. Pets whose owners had booked First Class accommodations were decidedly better off on board ship than Third Class travelers. The French reputation as animal lovers made TRANSAT a favorite choice for pet owners. In contrast, a voyage with Cunard Line meant six months' quarantine for the animal once the ship had reached a British port. French Line took great pains to pamper both pet and owner. A special '*menu de Toutou*' was printed daily listing the superb cuisine a pet could expect that evening. Company rules regarding the keeping of pets in the ship's kennels were routinely ignored, 'if the little companion was well-behaved and calm'. A dog would often spend the day with newly acquainted 'friends' on deck in the kennel area, supervised by a qualified staff member, and return to the master's cabin at night, as at home. Company publicity brochures boasted that, 'It's a lucky dog whose master travels French Line!' (See Figure2.) Despite restrictions placed on animals by the government, Cunard-White Star made every effort to make animals feel welcome on board its vessels. Stewardess Edith Sowerbutts noted that she had once served breakfast to two dogs who were staying in their owner's suite of rooms on the *Olympic*: 'I have never seen bacon and eggs gulped down so quickly as by these two dogs.' Treated as VIPs, the dogs slept on two separate beds – 'one had a sable coverlet' while the other 'had to be content with ermine.'[58]

Shipping company executives had a difficult balancing act attracting new customers while not alienating their veteran travelers. At the 16 July 1930 Cunard Line executive committee meeting, an unfortunate incident on the *Franconia* consumed much of the time of the board members. Several members of Tourist Third Cabin entered First Class quarters under the pretext of having to make inquiries at the purser's office. It was recommended that a small Tourist Third Cabin purser's office be set up on 'D' Deck.[59] An October 1935 voyage report of Henry Villar, chief purser of French Line's new flagship *Normandie*, comments on the complaint of First Class passengers regarding the 'invasion' of their class by Tourist and Third Class Jewish passengers who came for Sabbath service to the First Class children's dining room (where the Torah was placed). The 'synagogue' was transferred first to the Tourist Class children's playroom and then to the Third Class smoking room.[60] While this objection would appear to reflect class snobbism, there are clearly implicit shades of racism in such remarks.

By the 1930s, ultra-nationalist, fascist groups were a reality in many parts of Europe. Their programs often included an anti-Semitic agenda and appealed to populations that had seen their countries' power and prestige abroad and stability at home severely weakened by the devastating effects of a global war and a worldwide depression. France had the most vigorous fascist minority in Western Europe. There were no fewer than five right-wing nationalist leagues, including François Coty's Solidarité Française, Jacques Doriot's Parti Populaire Française and Charles Maurras' Action Française, which had been organized before the First World War. England was not exempt from ultra-nationalism. In October 1932, Sir Oswald Mosley founded the British Union of Fascists (BUF) as a bold and decisive remedy for unemployment. Before long, the targets of his Black Shirts' venom fell on unassimilated eastern European Jews who had settled in the East End of London. Mosley's party was largely discredited by 1936. Similarly in many eastern European countries, fascist groups, newly formed, chose Jews as the principal scapegoats for their societies' economic woes. Many Jews became alarmed at increasing tendencies towards anti-Semitism and sought to immigrate to America. Even on their voyage across the Atlantic, they could not escape the blatant prejudice of their fellow passengers. On the other side of the Atlantic, Jews also faced prejudice from an American public that had little sympathy for their plight. The American action in turning away over 900 Jewish emigrants on the ill-fated voyage of the *St Louis* in 1938 is one glaring example.

The mixing of classes was such a problem that Henry Villar reported in July 1937 that special printed notes were being left in all cabins reading: 'The Company's regulations prohibit Passengers from passing from one class to another. Passengers are therefore kindly requested to refrain from applying for this privilege and to keep within the confines of the class in which booked.' When Third Class passengers did not comply, Villar proposed that spiked gates be installed.[61] Cunard Line's general manager expressed a similar concern to ships' captains in April 1930, suggesting that 'suitable notices should be displayed on board indicating the class of passenger allowed in the various parts of the ship.' Captains were instructed to make 'reasonable efforts' to prevent passengers who are traveling in the 'lower classes' from making use of the 'higher class' public rooms and deck space.[62] Cunard's board of directors even discussed the need for fitting a screen on the *Berengaria*'s 'A' deck and two doors on 'B' deck for the express purpose of separating Tourist and First Class passengers. The directors added that this would 'give the Departments the same favorable opportunity for securing tourist passengers as now possessed by the *Leviathan* and *Majestic* – two other ex-German ships.'[63] They believed that they were just following common practice in constructing a physical barrier to separate classes.

Tourist Third Cabin passengers themselves complained about the invasion of their private space by the Third Class passengers. On the June 1933 *De Grasse* crossing, Tourist Third Cabin passengers voiced concern about the promiscuity of the Third Class passengers on board. Their objection, however, had more to do with racial prejudice than with class consciousness. The Tourist Third Cabin passengers (mainly French) resented being mixed with the Third Class (mainly Spanish) travelers whom they described as 'always a little disorderly'. Chief Purser Louis Mallet suggested that in order to achieve peace, the *De Grasse* should only accept Tourist Third Cabin passengers when the ship called at Plymouth and Third Class passengers only when it stopped at Spanish ports.[64]

Racial prejudice was also seen in the treatment given to sixty black artists from New York's famed 'Cotton Club', who were traveling Tourist Class on board the *Lafayette* as 'goodwill ambassadors' to the 1937 Paris Exposition Internationale. American passengers from the southern states expressed their dismay at having to sail in the company of blacks. The ship's personnel took great pains to appease their bigoted guests: 'We have endeavored to correct their initial impression by giving them extra-special treatment.' The 'Cotton Club' artists gave two performances for the passengers, the majority of whom were delighted. Once again, the same American passengers complained that the black performers were too visible on board the ship. To avoid further problems, a special sitting was organized in the Tourist Class restaurant to segregate the Americans.[65]

Tourist Third Cabin passengers also resented being on display for First and Cabin Class passengers who enjoyed 'slumming' through Tourist Class public space during the voyage. Instructions to the ship's captains from Cunard Line's general manager expresses the concern that 'many of the passengers traveling Tourist Third Cabin naturally resent the idea of having the passengers from superior classes surveying their quarters in this manner.'[66]

Segregation of classes exceeded mere social snobbery. Mixing of classes, as White Star Line saw it, could bring serious health repercussions. The company thus ordered that communication among classes be discouraged 'to avoid any annoyance or delay to the First or Cabin Class passengers on arriving at their destination, for should it become known to the Health or Quarantine officers ... that such communication had existed on a voyage in the course of which any contagious or infectious disease had occurred, First or Cabin Class passengers who might otherwise have been allowed to land, would probably be made subject to quarantine.'[67]

Tourist Third Cabin passengers objected to having the same curfew as Third Class passengers. Cunard's general manager notified captains in April 1928 that the '10 p.m. off the decks rule' should not apply to Tourist Third Cabin passengers. This 10 p.m. 'lights out' policy was a practice instituted for immigrants during the height of the steerage trade, and an extension to 11 p.m. was now recommended for Tourist Third passengers. Company rules for 1927, however, specifically stated that an inspector make rounds to see that all Third Class female passengers were in their cabins by 10 p.m.[68] The rationale for the curfew reflects the company's concern that such women might be 'night-walkers' who were on the promenade looking for prospective 'clients'!

Ships sought to monitor the moral conduct of their passengers with ships' masters often cast in the role of surrogate fathers. 'Ship's Notices' posted on board White Star Line's *Doric*'s 'Scholars' Summer Cruise' through Scandinavia in August 1933 stated that the captain had issued a 'no-smoking' policy for students and had set bedtime at 10 p.m. when 'the bugle will be sounded', with lights out at 10:30 p.m. Pool hours would be regulated (according to sex) and living quarters were to be segregated: 'The corridors on Deck B will be out of bounds to boys. No girls will be permitted on Deck D.'[69]

The curfew for Third Class passengers was finally suspended in 1932 'in view of the limited emigrant traffic now moving. Although there is a definite movement of other types in the Third Class, it has been decided that the rule relating to passengers' retiring hour be suspended until further notice on both Westbound and Eastbound voyages.'[70] Implicit in this comment is the perception of steerage passengers as riffraff rabble-rousers.

Disorderly conduct was directly linked to overconsumption of alcohol on board, and during the Prohibition era in the United States, shipping companies like Cunard Line imposed strict regulations on the sale of alcohol for its Third Class passengers: 'In view of the representations which have been made, it has been decided that spirits may be sold in Third Class bars on Eastbound voyages only. They must not be provided under any circumstances on westbound voyages.'[71] This rule had less to do with the Volstead Act than with the company's fear of rowdy behavior on westbound crossings from Third Class passengers, many of whom were emigrants. [72]

Bootlegging presented a particular problem to companies like French Line, which issued special notices to passengers warning against 'attempting to conceal any wines or liquors in their baggage or about their persons.' There had previously been instances when people were solicited immediately after landing by a person posing as a ship's steward to purchase wine. The notice advised passengers that these were 'bootleggers' and that their wines were 'manufactured counterfeits of poor or dangerous quality'.[73] In a meeting of the executive board, Cunard's general manager noted that a suit had been filed against the company in America by the Neptune Association of Masters and Mates, an association of merchant seamen, seeking to prevent the company from 'bringing liquor into the United States on board their vessels under seal'.[74] Instructions to captains in February 1926 mandated that 'the outside doors of all bars should be locked and the keys, as well as the keys of the cellar immediately delivered to the Purser on arrival of the ship' in all American ports. Even with such precautions, crew members managed to smuggle liquor ashore and, in the process, supplement their income. The general manager instructed the captain 'to organize unexpected and thorough searches of different parts of the ship each voyage' to curb crew smuggling.[75]

The prospect of unlimited alcohol was especially attractive to Americans during the Prohibition era of 1920–1933. White Star stewardess Violet Jessop correctly observed that Prohibition in America 'had revolutionized its people's morals'. One great incentive for Americans to travel by ship was 'as a means of circumventing what they had voted for'. She expressed her dismay for this new breed of tourist: 'All Americans aimed to travel some time in their lives, but here were people unused to voyaging, surrounded by ostentatious splendor, pathetic in their arrogance and not in the least embarrassed to be known as "bootleggers".' Jessop found the 'ultra-fashionable' to be the most pathetic, as they used the ship voyage as an excuse 'to replenish their cellars ... [H]ere were people of every class and walk of life who were taking a holiday from their national conscience.'[76] If the Volstead Act accomplished little else, it did contribute to a new transatlantic stereotype – the noisy, argumentative, drunken American, who transformed smoking rooms into drinking rooms, to the horror of the steamship companies' veteran passengers.

French Line especially geared its ads to attract the thirsty would-be lawbreaker by describing their ships as 'the longest gangplank in the world' to Prohibition-free Europe. Once aboard, brochures promised, you were already in France and thus free of American law and so let the party begin: 'As you sail away, far beyond the range of amendments and thou-shalt-nots, those dear little iced things begin to appear, sparkling aloft on their slender crystal stems ... Utterly French, utterly harmless – and oh so gurglingly good!'[77]

Raoul de Beaudean, who made his career with French Line, rising to the rank of Commander of the *Ile de France*, speaks about the behavior of passengers on a 1929 voyage of the *Flandre*, which sailed between France, the Antilles and the Panama Canal: 'Following an old custom we invite the most notoriously priggish and stuffy passengers on the list to a cocktail party. College de France professors and other notable personages in very formal attire and wearing starched collars to boot, despite the dog days, accompanied by their severely dressed and sacrosanct wives, pompously pile into the officers' mess.' [78] What first resembles a 'grim church gathering' soon changes gears after several rum punches and 'the most horrible words begin to fall from these same distinguished lips', and when at last they take their leaves, 'the passages are hardly wide enough to permit their descent to the dining room ...'[79]

Normandie's Commander Pierre Thoreux likewise comments on the decline in the quality of passengers coming from America during the Prohibition era who were 'rather low class', and 'attracted by French wines and spirits', which they consumed in great quantity once outside of American territorial waters. 'For many of them,' he writes, 'the ports of call were secondary,' and upon leaving New York, they spoke of 'the good time' they were anticipating on board.[80] Passengers increasingly looked to the ship's staff to keep them occupied with around-the-clock activities. When the concept of 'pleasure cruising' began to take off in the 1920s and 1930s, a social staff (cruise director, assistants, social hostesses, etc.) was brought on board to plan a daily program of leisure activities. One of the few references to a 'cruise staff' is found in a *Franconia World Cruise Log Book* for 1927, which lists both a cruise director and a hostess as being in charge of passenger entertainment and activities.

On early transatlantic steamers, ships' pursers were multi-faceted individuals who were both administrators and social hosts who planned a program of activities for their passengers. French Line began including a daily program, '*Chronique du Bord*', which listed the day's events in the pages of its on-board magazine, *L'Atlantique*, in 1925.[81] In keeping with the tradition of providing refined and intellectually stimulating programs on transatlantic crossings for their First Class passengers, steamship companies included enrichment lectures in their activity schedules. On its westbound crossing in October 1929, the *Ile de France* announced a lecture by Captain H. A. White, leader of the Field Museum Expedition to Abyssinia and Central Africa, who was returning by ship after a year of exploration on the continent.[82] Lectures were also given by professors, government officials, industrial magnates, and other distinguished personalities on the passenger list. Companies often hired an orchestra for their ships, but little other entertainment was provided. R. A. Fletcher writes that in 1913, the ship's band was often recruited from the crew – mainly stewards – whose ordinary duties were lightened somewhat in exchange for sharing their musical talents with the passengers. Passengers were left largely to their own devices for nightly entertainment and chose a social director from among their ranks to act as master of ceremonies for the evening's program. Captain E. G. Diggle recalls that on one memorable occasion, the Prime Minister of England took the chair.[83] Passengers planned fancy dress balls and talent shows, which often featured celebrities traveling on board. Not only did the company get great free publicity, but such passengers also provided free entertainment! Celebrities like Tullulah Bankhead and Gloria Swanson were frequent travelers on board the transatlantic steamers. Marlene Dietrich met Ernest Hemingway on the *Ile de France*, a particular favorite with film stars. Maurice Chevalier was a regular on the *Ile de France*, and Arturo Toscanini would sail on no other ship. In some instances, an entire theatrical company would stage a production with all proceeds given to the Seamen's Fund. Passengers were also known to take up collections for relatives of deceased crew members. After the war, the *Aquitania*'s purser's office ran a 'Daily Sweepstake' with 10 per cent of the receipts going to seamen's charities and prizes reaching as high as $9,000.[84] After hours, enthusiastic passengers, like those on the *Berengaria*, were known for bringing out their own gramophones to provide dance music.

The purser's staff would also plan a variety of deck sports to keep their passengers happy. This was especially the case with the transition to Tourist Third Cabin Class when there was an increased demand from middle-class audiences for non-stop activities. The staff organized boxing, wrestling and fencing championships, bridge tournaments, treasure hunts and rifle, pistol and pigeon shooting contests. Other deck sports included deck tennis, deck croquet, deck golf, ping pong, horse racing (with passenger contestants urged on by girl 'jockeys'), shuffleboard (the oldest and most popular deck sport), and quoits.[85] The *France* even had an open-air bowling alley. (See Figure 3.) Boxing, wrestling and fencing matches featured crew members, but sometimes passengers saw the real thing when actual champions traveling on board delighted passengers with demonstrations. Former amateur heavyweight world champion, Eddie Eagan, crossed the Atlantic three times on French Line ships with the American Olympic team.[86] Cunard Line organized a Sports Day, on which passengers joined in all kinds of juvenile competitions: potato and bucket races, egg and spoon contests, pillow fights and tug-of-war teams (between officers and passengers). (See Figure 4.) Sports Day ended with a gigantic carnival dinner dance in which all passengers wore fancy dress.[87]

To encourage physical fitness, the shipping companies hired a gym instructor who was a permanent member of the crew and conducted separate 'physical jerk classes' for men and women. Eagan was a frequent contributor to *Gangplank*, French Line's English language publicity magazine, writing exercise tips for passengers during crossings. He believed that the main requirement for a passenger's happy traveling experience was to be in good physical condition. Consequently, shipboard was the perfect place to keep in shape and to train 'with the fresh, tangy, salt air'.[88] Shipping company executives were always keeping tabs on their competitors and tried to be the first to introduce new activities and facilities for passengers. In this climate, Cunard Line executives unanimously decided to install a miniature golf course (very much in vogue in the 1930s) on board the *Aquitania* since White Star's flagship *Majestic* and French Line's *Ile de France* already had such courses.[89]

Roydon Freeman describes the lengths to which passengers would go in amusing themselves, often at the expense of their own pride and dignity: 'With hands tied behind our backs, we snapped at buns hanging on strings, and when the chewed fragments fell on the deck we knelt down and inelegantly gnawed at them until every crumb was swallowed.' The ship was the one place where the great men of industry and other 'notables' could let down their hair and engage in almost infantile behavior. Freeman describes another shipboard favorite – 'cock-fighting' – among passengers trussed up like chickens: 'Reduced to that position of almost helplessness, squatting with knees drawn up nearly to his chin and with a broomstick between them, and his wrists tied to that, anyone is liable to lose his debonair manner.' The two trussed men were picked up bodily and deposited within the chalk circle and thus 'the contest began with much wriggling for position, each trying to push the other out of the ring by thrusts with his stockinged feet, without himself losing his balance and being pushed helplessly over.'[90]

Ship life was pure escapism for both passengers and crew. On board, a passenger could let down his guard. During a 1934 *Samaria* cruise to Portugal, North Africa and Spain, men were requested to wear the tops of their bathing costumes when away from the pool. This became necessary since the film *Tarzan* made bare chests so popular![91] Freed somewhat from business concerns, passengers lost all of their inhibitions and engaged in role-playing in ceremonies that resembled medieval charivari rituals.[92] For crew, there were opportunities to reverse roles as well, imposing their dominion over passengers in the famous 'Crossing the Line' ceremony on all ships which crossed the equator during the world cruise. This ritual, as old as the sea itself, was an elaborate spectacle in which King Neptune and his courtiers (ship's officers and crew) were received by the captain, who then asked permission for the ship to cross the equator. Neptune granted the request on condition that 'all who had not crossed before must do homage to the king and be thrown overboard as a sacrifice to the fishes.' As a gesture of goodwill, Neptune commuted the new initiates' severe sentence to a good dunking in the ship's swimming pool. The passengers then came forward and one by one dropped on one knee, swearing allegiance to the god of the sea and promising 'to go to bed early and not to make any noise or disturbance likely to keep the fishes awake at night.'[93] Stewardess Rose Stott recalls one such proceeding on the 1923 *Samaria* world cruise: 'The prisoners ... sat on a spring box with backs towards the swimming pool ... [F]aces were lathered with soot and shaved with a large wooden razor ... [L]adies' faces were done with flour by the manicurist and then each one was pushed backwards into the pool where four sea-bears were waiting to receive them and duck them three times.'[94] Among those 'initiated' in such elaborate ceremonies were British Prime Minister David Lloyd George, US President Herbert Hoover, the editor of the *Chicago Herald*, and actor Douglas Fairbanks.

Such round-the-clock activity did not appeal to all passengers' tastes. While attracting new passengers, shipping companies had to reassure their Old World clientele that only people 'of a congenial type' would be accepted as their shipboard companions: teachers, college professors, serious students, clergy, and business professionals. The United States Line boasted that included in its list of Tourist Third Cabin passengers for one ship's voyage in 1923 were thirty-seven members of Phi Beta Kappa, a further guarantee of the legitimacy of this new class of travel.[95] *L'Atlantique* continued to satisfy the tastes of its more traditional passengers with articles on fashion, the arts and travel, as well as advertisements promoting motor tours on the European, African and Asian continents that featured, of course, the hotels of French Line. First Class passengers were entertained with features on the Grand Prix races in Monte Carlo, an account of the French Olympic Games (1924), and exclusive articles like 'The Secret of Chic', 'Why I Play Golf' and 'The Way to Smoke a Cigar', the latter written by a 'connoisseur' who divulges his secrets:

Cigar smoking is a drama with a prologue and three acts: you choose your weed; open the end; you light up, you smoke. Simple! say you. On the contrary. Here, we have a ritual bungled at each stage alarmingly by vulgar people, correctly done from first to last by a mere handful of the cognoscenti. How many of the new rich, for example, persist in choosing a cigar by its colour![96]

It proved to be a tough balancing act, however, for steamship companies to satisfy at the same time both a new lively class of travelers out for a good time and the more sedate veteran passengers. There was a great reluctance on the part of both veteran passengers and ships' officers to embrace this new breed of tourist. One captain found the behavior of these interlopers abominable. 'There is a limit to frivolity and I fancy it has nearly been reached,' he said, commenting on the around-the-clock party atmosphere on board and what he perceived to be the decline of moral standards, especially evident in the 'highly objectionable' style of dancing wherein 'they hold each other familiarly, sometimes with heads together'. An aristocratic bluestocking, Edith Somerville, was equally distressed by such developments as the 'fat-legged flappers, who squeal in companies, walking arm-in-arm', or the sight of 'harassed stewards, with their intellectual faces, bringing trays of tea to long silent rows of mummies in chaises longues'.[97]

Another veteran American traveler complained that an ocean voyage had become nothing better than a holiday at a luxury hotel: 'the dear, picturesque portholes are gone, and the plate glass windows try to deceive people'. Gone too was the peace and quiet one used to be able to enjoy on deck, replaced now with 'universal "doing something noise"' of an infinite variety of organized deck sports. She lamented that 'the real rest of a sea voyage is gone forever; every disturbance and disaster in the whole world is reported by wireless.'[98]

Daniel Boorstin speaks about these changes as signaling 'the decline of the traveler and the rise of the tourist'.[99] The word 'travel' comes from the French *travail* or work, a word derived in its form from Latin *tipalium*, a torture instrument consisting of three stakes designed to rack the body. According to Paul Fussell, before the development of tourism, which he traces back to nineteenth-century England, 'travel was conceived to be like study, and its fruits were considered to be the adornment of the mind and the formation of the judgment.'[100] Boorstin distinguishes between the traveler and the tourist, the former being an active person at work, the latter a passive being who 'expects interesting things to happen to him. He goes "sightseeing", he expects everything to be done to him and for him'.[101]

Boorstin has quite succinctly described the appeal of a 'pleasure cruise'. This new type of passenger, the tourist, was ready and willing to travel abroad, but had precious little experience. Venturing out into the unknown presented a formidable challenge to amateur tourists. Happily for them, major travel organizations, like American Express, Thomas Cook and Raymond Whitcomb, had anticipated their needs and offered organized, hassle-free tours for the somewhat intellectually curious but thoroughly inexperienced novice adventurer. (See Figure 5.) Although the concept of 'pleasure cruising' dates back to the late nineteenth century, it was only with the creation of this new breed of mass tourist who traveled Tourist Third Cabin that cruising itself became an option for the middle classes.

As with crossing, cruising too began to lose the 'exclusivity appeal' that it once enjoyed among wealthy veteran passengers like Edith Somerville. She would undoubtedly have preferred to hold on to the 'good old days' when cruises were not open to the general public, as was the case in 1867 when a paddle-wheeled steamer, the *Quaker City*, made the first extensive cruise by an Atlantic passenger liner to the Holy Land. As Mark Twain recounts in *The Innocents Abroad*, all prospective cruisers had to submit applications to a selections committee. Personal interviews were scheduled with those who made the first cut before final selections were made. Twain was one of 'the chosen', but far from a happy sailor. He found the cruise to be 'a funeral excursion without a corpse' in which days at sea repeated a routine of 'solemnity, decorum, dinner, dominoes, prayers, slander' with saintly and boring companions, exactly the type of voyage that Edith Somerville would have enjoyed.[102]

Pleasure cruising began to catch on with the wealthy in the early 1890s due to the efforts of Albert Ballin, who saw the possibilities of pleasure cruising as a means of making up for the loss of company revenues during the slack season (winter) for ocean crossings. The line's 8,000-ton *Augusta Victoria* departed from Hamburg on 22 January 1891 with 241 passengers on a two-month Mediterranean adventure. Soon, other companies followed suit, tapping into what was becoming a lucrative market for passenger travel in the winter months. When cruise activity to Europe stopped (as did transatlantic travel) with the outbreak of the First World War, shipping companies organized tours for Americans to the Orient, South America and the West Indies. After the war, attention turned back to Europe as the first tourists escorted by American Express crossed from New York in 1919 on the *Mauretania*. Tours were organized for visits to the First World War battlefields of the western front, including one that transported the American Legion delegation in 1920. This relationship with American Express proved to be a fruitful one for Cunard Line, especially after the early 1920s when the steerage market dried up.[103]

Early cruises were purposely designed to cater to an older, more affluent clientele with plenty of time and money to spare. Particularly appealing to such an audience was the introduction of the world cruise, the first of which was a 130-day global odyssey, offered by Cunard Line's *Laconia* and chartered by American Express in 1922. This was the first continuous circumnavigation by a passenger liner, tracking the route of Magellan's fleet 400 years earlier.[104]

Throughout the 1920s, 'pleasure cruising' remained the preserve of Fortune 500 types. Cruise fares were priced accordingly to assure prospective passengers that they would be sailing with their social equals. This situation is replicated today when small, exclusive cruise companies, that depend for their survival on the 'superior class' clientele who frown on the 'inferior class' passengers traveling on 'bargain basement' ships, engage in advertising promising would-be clients unlimited Moët & Chandon and beluga caviar served at the pool if they so desire.

In 1923, American Express chartered Cunard Line's flagship *Mauretania* for a Mediterranean jaunt that was popular with the passengers. This trip, however, was exclusively designed for the wealthy; American Express had arranged for prices to be so prohibitively high that passengers could proudly boast 'I was in the *Mauretania* when she was the millionaire ship.'[105] Cunard Line introduced its *Franconia* in 1923 as a ship attuned to every rich man's dreams. It was equipped with a swimming pool, racquetball courts and a state-of-the-art gym so passengers could keep fit while enjoying suites of rooms that rivaled those in the most luxurious hotels ashore. At the same time, they had enough public space to move about and have access to wireless service in order to keep in touch with the rest of the world. What more could the wealthy want?[106]

The construction of the *Franconia* and *Laconia* represented a tremendous advance in shipbuilding regarding passenger comfort. For instance, they were the first ships to have hot and cold running water in every cabin. The *Franconia* was specifically designed for world cruising, being equipped 'with a system of ventilation that makes her admirably adapted to a voyage in the tropics.'[107] Brochures for the *Franconia* world cruise of 1929, organized by Thomas Cook & Son, quoted prices starting at $2,000 and advertised an extensive cruise staff on board to cater to the passengers' every whim. An elaborate daily program of activities was organized to satisfy peoples' desire for utterly frivolous distraction. Guest lecturers were close by to provide historical commentary on the culture and society of ports visited, thus assuring passengers that they were in fact engaging in some form of intellectual activity. As a company executive at one of today's exclusive shipping lines put it: 'It doesn't matter if they attend the lectures or not; we just have to show that we offer them!'

By the late 1920s, shipping companies had identified another potential lucrative cruise market – the middle class, which, with the inception of Tourist Third Cabin Class, increasingly was attracted by the possibilities of leisure travel. White Star Line was in the forefront of the new cruise industry with its publicity magazine advertising fares within the budget of the middle class for Mediterranean cruises in its upcoming 1928 season on the *Adriatic* and *Laurentic*: 'A luxury cruise at a price that will bring it within the reach of people of limited means is an innovation which the White Star Line is introducing during the coming season ... When the winter season commences, economic travel will now be made possible at a price never before offered on the Atlantic for cruises of this nature. The accommodation available for this purpose is the Tourist Third Cabin, a class which has attained tremendous popularity in the North Atlantic service since the White Star Line introduced it in 1924.'[108]

Once again, the wealthy were under siege. Their exclusive floating sanctuaries were being threatened by an invasion of the 'inferior classes'. One White Star passenger, William Postlethwaite, a farm laborer more than seventy years old, fulfilled a dream of a lifetime when he embarked on a *Mediterranean* 'pleasure cruise' in October 1932. For years he had set aside a threepenny bit towards a super-holiday. When he had collected 1,000 threepenny bits he booked passage on White Star's *Doric*.[109] Imagine Edith Somerville's positive horror at the prospect of sharing a table with a farm laborer!

Brochures targeted this middle market, advertising cruises to suit any size budget, provided one had the time to spare. As pleasure cruising became more popular, companies expanded cruise itineraries into the summer months. A twenty-two-day itinerary to Canada and the United States could cost as little as $190 for the Tourist Class passenger or $310 for First Class accommodations.[110] (See Figure 6.) By the 1930s, even time did not matter. White Star Line's publicity magazine in July 1931 announced the inauguration of weekend cruises to nowhere from New York on its luxury liners *Olympic*, *Britanic* and *Majestic*: 'These American cruises have been planned with the idea of catering for those who do not wish to be away from home for any great length of time of whom there appear to be large numbers in the United States at present.' [111] Six-day cruises from New York to Nassau on the *Homeric* were also initiated.

To reach the general public, shipping companies used elaborate displays in department store windows to promote pleasure cruises. (See Figure 7.) One example was Messrs Lewis of Manchester, which in 1933 transformed its Great Hall into the Sun Deck of the White Star liner *Georgic* and presented four shows daily. Mannequins displayed cruise wear (a boost to department store receipts) while others worked on 'electric horses' and 'cycles', recreating the atmosphere of the gym on board. Announcements described the Mediterranean ports included on the itinerary. At the close of every performance, people rushed to the travel agencies with inquiries about the cruise. This proved to be a successful partnership for the shipping company and the department store, both of which attracted potential customers. (See Figure 8.) Cruise wear became a major focus of department stores, which benefitted from articles like those of Jane Gordan, special fashions writer for the *News Chronicle*, who counseled women travelers about what to wear to be the best-dressed woman on the cruise. Red, white and blue became a popular colour scheme.[112]

A 1937 issue of *Vogue Magazine* offered its readers advice on appropriate travel attire for winter cruising and identified the three general types of cruise wear as 'active sports clothes, spectator sports frocks, and dinner or evening dresses'. It counseled that before packing shorts, 'look at your figure and make your choice'. The good news, *Vogue* tells its readers, is that women whose figures have altered over the years could wear the new shorts, which are a 'longer, and kinder length ...'[113]

While Emily Post called practical one-piece knit dresses 'ideal day time clothes' for cruising, only the 'shingle-thin' can consider wearing one, she warns: 'One who is inclined toward plumpness should NEVER wear a knit dress without a sweater coat, a coat, moreover, which hangs loose enough not to cling around the line of the equator across the back!' She also discouraged women from wearing loud colours, a real temptation 'set against the vivid background of a tropical, Caribbean scene', and warned that a woman who contemplates wearing anything flamboyant 'should remember that in any public place to be the most conspicuously dressed is all too apt to be the most vulgar.'[114]

Repeat customers were a shipping company's greatest source of publicity. One White Star passenger, Alan M. Nichols, wrote of his positive experience on a *Doric* cruise in the company's publicity magazine: 'From the moment one boarded the boat, one felt at home; all the stewards were on duty and when you met your cabin steward you had found a friend ... One is astonished by the fact that all amusements are free.'[115] Nichols applauded the democratic 'ONE-CLASS-ONLY' system and called the trip a real bargain at £10 for thirteen days.

The stock market crash of 1929 had reverberated throughout Europe by the early 1930s and seriously damaged the transatlantic trade. Shipping companies offered greatly reduced fares to attract customers on their monster ships, which were sailing half empty. Seafarers lucky enough to keep their jobs resigned themselves to wage cuts in order to ride out the storm. 'Bargain basement' cruising became the shipping companies' salvation in these lean times. Cunard Line's *Berengaria* became famous for its $50 'booze cruises' from New York to Nova Scotia. Waiter, Dave Marlowe, described such short cruises as 'whoopee cruises' whose passengers 'were out for a good time and got it. "Sugar daddies" and their inevitable blondes were plentiful.'[116] White Star Line's *Olympic* was sent on one-day bank holiday cruises from Southampton.[117]

In the summer of 1932, 100,000 British people went pleasure cruising, which was described as a bargain, a 'carefree' vacation. An article by a self-professed 'shipping expert' that appeared in *The Daily Mail* in April 1933 explained that the monster liners of the shipping companies, temporarily idle due to adverse business conditions, had found a new source of employment as they 'now go sauntering off in search of sunshine'. The article notes that the number of sun worshippers and pleasure cruisers had increased dramatically – from 24,000 carried on sixty-eight cruises in 1930 to 175,000 carried on more than 250 cruises in 1933.[118]

The *Mauretania* was not only stripped of her Blue Riband, but was painted white (which to some critics resembled a wedding cake, as with the monument to Victor Emmanuel in Rome) and used for pleasure cruises rather than as a transatlantic steamer at the end of her career. Occasionally on a Bahamas cruise, she would do 31 knots for an hour to show her passengers that she 'still had it in her'.

Rates for West Indies and South America cruises on the *Mauretania* started as low as $80, 'the answer to a maiden's prayer'. On the cover of the cruise brochure was 'Marge', a girl in a one-piece bathing suit who tells her friend that 'this is certainly going to be a grand vacation! ... I want a change. I'm tired of being an old stick-in-the-mud.' Posters advertising upcoming pleasure cruises lured prospective passengers with the promise of 'stepping for a while into a new world – a world of sunshine, color, romance and laughter'.[119] Love was definitely in the air judging from the number of engagements announced during Mediterranean cruises. In fact, many mothers took their daughters on cruises in the hopes of finding some dashing, eligible beau, and shipping companies eagerly publicized their success by calling themselves 'Cupid's agents'.

For many, the ship was the destination, with the ports of call becoming incidental. French Line sent its flagship *Normandie* on a twenty-two-day cruise to Rio in February 1938 promising passengers that this would be 'the most notable event of any cruise season'. The company guaranteed non-stop activity: 'there will be something going on every minute.'[120] John Malcolm Brinin notes that one consequence of cheap and easy travel to Europe was a marked change in the general purpose of travel itself:

> Suddenly overseas travel lost its character as an adventure with hazards and became an extended outing under the leadership, perhaps, of a professional guide from Atlanta or Minneapolis and, in any case, watched over by American Express. Instead of being regarded as a scene of new and challenging experience, Europe tended to become a place for fun ... Americans began to go to Europe on the pleasure principle – for the chance to drink when, where and what they please, to live on a scale beyond anything they could imagine in Kansas City or Pittsburgh.[121]

Brinin correctly observed that even shore excursions would be designed to insulate the passenger 'from the weird, grubby or outrageous reality of any one place in favor of exposing him to polite glimpses of its military establishments, its bazaars and the night clubs where natives entertained him with show-biz parodies of themselves.'[122] Sea days came to supersede shore excursions as the highlight of the passenger's trip, with many commenting more on the fancy costume parade than on the diverse ports visited.

Pleasure cruising found converts even among the most skeptical intellectuals of the age. In an article written for *Harper's Bazaar* in 1930, Evelyn Waugh defends the new style of travel while at the same time poking fun at it. Commenting that every Englishman 'assumes himself to be a traveler and despises his fellow countrymen as tourists', and confessing himself to be 'a slave to this particular snobbisme', he humbly concedes that 'the moment I went on board the *Stella* [*Polaris*] I should have crossed that very imaginary line … I was frankly and wholly a tourist.' Even Waugh came to see that 'pleasure cruising has its advantages'. Chief among them was that it offered an end to the luggage problem:

> The satisfaction of unpacking my trunk once and for all and pushing it under the bed, of arranging ties and shirts and handkerchiefs in a chest of drawers, hanging up my suits in a wardrobe … and knowing that I was settled for a month, made up for the romance of a great deal of promiscuous adventure.[123]

There was no hassle with passports, for on a pleasure cruise, 'one simply hands in one's papers to the Purser and he does all the necessary bribery.' Still, such benefits did not prevent his snobbism from surfacing in his description of the new middle-class tourists returning on board after a day on shore:

> I do not think these happier travelers are ever disappointed in anything they see. They come back to the ship from each expedition with their eyes glowing; they have been initiated into strange mysteries, and their speech is rich with the words of the travel bureau's advertising manager; their arms are full of purchases. It is quite extraordinary to see what they will buy.[124]

He concludes with a positive endorsement:

> Cruising is a pursuit entirely of its own kind ... an entirely
> new sport, with its own aims and rules. One sets out
> primarily for rest and change of scene and comfort and one
> certainly gets that, and one's recreation should not be the
> study of foreign places and people but the study of one's
> fellow-passengers among foreign places; and to the right-
> minded person that should be a source of exquisite and
> abiding delight.[125]

What was clear was the different character of the individual
traveler. Paul Fussell has characterized the various features
of tourists (contrasted to travelers) as corresponding to the
increasing emergence of mass-consumer society. As the globe
became more connected and remote parts more accessible, the
exotic experience of explorers faded into the background and
mass tourism developed as another phase of consumerism.
Individual travelers still existed and experienced some remarkable
moments, sometimes recreating them in fascinating books, but
they were the exception, decreasing in number with the passing
of the years. As American Express, Thomas Cook and Raymond
Whitcomb took leading roles in providing organized tours, the
age of travel as discovery became a relic.

Individuals still roamed around on deck; writers, politicians
and movie stars added the aura of celebrity-hood to the liner's
particular maritime personality. Luxury suites were still in
demand, more people were crossing the Atlantic to conduct
business, and others still were uprooting their lives and
emigrating abroad. The latter would soon be joined by those
seeking refuge from increasingly ominous political and social
conditions in Europe.

The type of passenger on transatlantic crossings changed
dramatically with the heightened political tension in Europe in

the late 1930s. Once again, shipping companies had to respond to the needs of the moment in order to survive. As early as November 1933, Cunard managers discussed the possibility of enlarging the kosher kitchen on the *Aquitania* in response to the 'increased share of Jewish business in the Atlantic'. Cunard anticipated that such an addition would 'secure considerable Jewish bookings to and from Palestine for the *Aquitania*'s two Mediterranean cruises'.[126] Percy Bates received a request from F. H. Samuel of the *Jewish Chronicle* in 1937 to offer a direct British passenger service to Palestine.[127]

The Compagnie Messageries Maritimes informed the minister of the Merchant Marine in February 1939 that it would station its ships, *Patria* and *Providence*, in the port of Marseilles to receive wounded and sick refugees from the civil war that raged in Spain. The liners would temporarily serve as hospital ships. A company letter included a cost breakdown for the government's requisitioning of its ships.[128] French Line and Cunard-White Star Line both participated in the evacuation of members of the Abraham Lincoln Brigade from Spain after Franco's victory.

Cunard-White Star stewardess Dorothy Scobie recalls a sailing in the summer of 1939 from Liverpool, which carried a sizeable number of refugees from Germany, Hungary, Russia, Latvia, Austria and other Central European countries:

> These people had embarked in Liverpool and none of them had big trunks. Always they counted and recounted their dozens of suitcases and brown paper parcels. Hat boxes, string bags and attaché cases. Most of the men had briefcases which they never let out of their arms ... What sorrows had they left behind? Indeed, whom had they had to leave behind? What traumas had they already witnessed in their short lives?[129]

Frank Mortimer, who joined Cunard-White Star's *Aquitania* in 1935 as a kitchen porter, spoke about Eastern European immigrants sleeping on the deck, refugees who were escaping the Hitler regime and had Jewish sponsors in America. 'Most of their belongings were in carpet bags,' he observed, and none had brought with them any changes of clothing, 'fleeing the Nazis with only the clothes on their backs.'[130] Sponsors were required by the steamship company to fill out an 'affidavit of support' identifying their employment and yearly income as well as value of savings and other possessions before passage could be secured for their relatives.

Normandie regular Ludwig Bemelmans described one such passenger whom he encountered while traveling back to the United States in Third Class during the 1930s:

> There was a man in a sweater and a cap who had left his home, his business, and a fortune of several millions behind when he was dragged out of bed in the middle of the night by the Gestapo. He still hid himself behind ventilators and sneaked along the corridors ... He was still followed by ghosts. He clung to the side of the deck-house, when he walked outside, or stood alone on the deck. He seemed to apologize for his own presence. He was afraid that it would all end and from somewhere a hand would seize him and drag him back into his misery. Slowly he began to heal ... The last day, I saw him look up. He smiled.[131]

The *Normandie* played an unofficial role in transporting German Jews to safety in December 1938. Two bridge officers on watch discovered a group of twenty stowaways fleeing Hitler's Germany. The refugees had paid two crew members handsomely to be smuggled on board. They were hidden in a seldom used passageway leading to the banquet room, in the back of the First Class dining room in a space 8 m by 8 m, which for them was a safe haven from Nazi atrocities.[132]

In the early days of the Second World War, shipping companies continued to carry refugees from Eastern Europe to safety in North American ports. Ships' staff were instructed to treat all of their passengers with respect, not only for humane reasons but because French Line officials speculated about the possibility that fair treatment would result in increased revenues for their company once the war was over: 'Many refugees, even those traveling in Third Class, are former merchants, bankers or industrialists who occupied important positions in Germany and Austria and who will become lucrative passengers for us in the future. We want them to take away a good memory of their voyage with TRANSAT, and despite their current financial position, we think that it will be good politics to treat them well now.'[133] Cunard-White Star Line was also eager to tap into this new market of refugees from Eastern Europe who preferred to sail on non-German ships. In a letter to the Secretary of the Department of Overseas Trade, company executive Robert Crail warned that unless something was done to protect their position, their competitors would dominate the refugee trade.[134]

As in the First World War, major shipping lines contributed their transatlantic steamers to their government's war effort. Once again, ships played an integral role in transporting troops, functioned as floating hospitals, and, after the conclusion of hostilities, transported soldiers and war brides back to America. By 1948, ships had been reconverted back to luxury vessels and re-entered service to embark on a series of cruises throughout Europe and the Caribbean. Although the days of transatlantic travel by ship were numbered, a thriving cruise business was begun, which was symbolized by the introduction of Cunard-White Star's *Caronia*, the first ship designed exclusively for pleasure cruises.

Chapter Three

'The Soul of a Ship': Experience and Life of Below-Deck Personnel

Perhaps the sea water really does get into the soul.
Whatever the reason, you just keep coming back for
more and always threatening to leave the sea. Sometimes
one does leave it and what a glorious feeling of achieving
what others have only talked about. Yet there is a dull
ache and one is lonely and something is lost. People ashore
don't speak your language any more ... So you found yourself
back again whilst the sea had a last laugh as it beckoned you
with its soapy fingers and whirled you back with promises of
distant shores.[135]

Many seafarers who have sailed on the great passenger liners share this love/hate relationship with the sea that Cunard-White Star Line stewardess, Dorothy Scobie, describes. They are drawn to the sea because of the adventure, glamour and fantasy lifestyle it promises. Yet they resent the demands and rigors of shipboard employment, the loss of the sense of the individual, and the subordination to an officer hierarchy on board that seems more powerful and exacting than any authority ashore. They spend half their waking hours at sea planning their 'escape' from what they perceive to be a 'floating jail' and yet once ashore feel as though they are alone in a foreign land unable to communicate with the people around them. The sea becomes their only refuge from this ambiguously perceived world and they keep going back, contract after contract, year after year, to a paradise/jail-like existence, to be sure, but a place that, for them, is home.

Following the First World War, all European nations sought to return to the 'normalcy' of the prewar years. With post-war recovery came a renewed sense of promise and progress for the future. As we've seen, Cunard Line, White Star Line and French Line eagerly adapted to the new age by converting their ships from coal- to oil-burning vessels, making the switch from steerage to Tourist Third Cabin Class, introducing the more democratic one-class and classe unique ships, and increasing the frequency of cruise itineraries for eager but cautious travelers.

Such developments meant new opportunities for the companies' seafarers. The stokers of the grand prewar liners became obsolete. To accommodate the changing nature of tourism, many new positions were introduced as more services were made available for passenger comfort. The number of medical staff, shop attendants, bath attendants, hair dressers, and cruise staff personnel all increased during the interwar years.[136]

A French Line brochure described the men and women who worked aboard their vessels as 'the soul of a ship', without whom 'the most gigantic, most lavishly decorated and most costly steamer ever fashioned ... would be but a lifeless, helpless, aimlessly drifting iron hulk.' TRANSAT attributed its success in attracting and retaining 'a large and high-class clientele', largely to 'the men and women who, through a sense of duty and devotion to it, breathe life into its ships'.[137]

New and bigger steamers were being built that promised employment for many a would-be seafarer from Liverpool, Southampton, Le Havre, Marseilles, and other port towns in England and France. The decision to leave one's family to spend a life at sea, for most people, was purely a financial one. Although not bringing in great wages, a job at sea (especially one that opened up the possibilities for gratuities) proved far more lucrative than a similar position ashore. Earning potential was far greater on the high seas than in the port towns at home, especially during the Depression years of the 1930s. On board these luxury liners, seafarers detached themselves from the grim poverty ashore and yet felt secure in knowing that their work was helping to improve their families' economic situation at home.

The average age of a young man who 'signed on' with one of the shipping companies was between fourteen and twenty (See Figure 9.) In many cases, he would remain at sea until he retired unless he was dismissed, injured, or died while in the company's service. Many crew members began their careers at sea as 'mousses' (bellboys) or page boys and then progressed to positions including stewards, waiters, or assistant cooks. Even experienced crew joined as apprentices so as not to 'destroy the esprit de corps of the service', as Cunard Chairman Thomas Royden explained to Lady Lettice Shepard, who, in April 1923 wrote inquiring about a steward's position for her footman.[138]

On any given ship, an average of 96 per cent of the seafarers were male, and many signed on at a very early age. Most came from families having long maritime traditions – fathers, uncles and brothers had sailed before them. Dave Marlowe recalls that 'the smell of my father's sea-chest always fascinated me. It reeked of ship's tobacco, fruit, and that strange indefinable odor … always associated … with the sea and ships.' After the First World War, he got his opportunity to 'sign on' and marveled at his good fortune: 'Not for me were the homely jobs that my schoolmates had favored. Errand-boys, shop assistants, milkmen, paper-boys … I was going to sea!'[139] Frank Severini, who joined White Star Line's flagship *Majestic* in 1924 as a page boy at the age of fourteen, on the other hand, was not enthusiastic about the prospect at first. All of his family worked on ships, and one uncle had been lost on the *Titantic*. His father, a chef on the *Olympic*, used his influence to secure a position for his son. Only the money attracted him and he recalls that 'I cried my eyes out' when he first went to sea but soon 'got used to it and loved it.'[140] Jack Dempsey (not to be confused with the famous boxer), joined Cunard Line's *Mauretania* in 1934 at the age of fourteen as a bellboy. He had first been captivated by the idea of becoming a seafarer while serving an apprenticeship at a laundry in Southampton: '... the monotony of several days removing stains, cleaning and pressing was relieved by a visit to the docks ... to collect uniforms from the *Leviathan*.' He describes his adventure on board in finding himself in crew quarters:

> Before long I was surrounded by members of the American crew, and a few British, discarding their uniforms and tossing them in my direction! Turn the pockets out, I had been told and so I did. 10 cent pieces and larger coins cascaded to the deck. I tried to give them back, a gesture which was greeted with laughter and a dismissive chorus of "keep it, son." The day's lucrative takings had set me thinking. This is where I should be, not in a factory, but how?[141]

Dempsey's persistence landed him a job on the *Mauretania*. Once on board, he was dazzled by its opulence: 'Never before had my eyes observed such splendor. All that paneling, large ornate doors, tables wet with silver cutlery, flowers and waiters in wing collars with black bows and neat waistcoats bustling around – it was magnificent.'[142] Such wealth could easily be contrasted against the background of the Depression-ridden Southampton docks. Others, like Edwin Praine, a waiter on the maiden voyage of the *Queen Mary* in May 1936, expressed the same sense of wonder upon entering the almost make-believe world of the great floating palaces, finding it 'strange to see the crew drinking champagne and smoking Havana cigars'.[143]

The initial impression of another young man, who joined the *Queen Mary* in 1937 as a bellboy, was one of astonishment: 'It was a different world from what you had been used to … there was stuff that you never knew existed … there was stuff on the menus that you never knew … such as turkey … all sorts of magical things.'[144] After a while, crew members became accustomed to such luxuries and ate from the same menu as the passengers, although most were obliged to consume their food standing up in the galley while on duty. 'It is quite astonishing how very quickly most of us can get used to expensive living, food and drink – even exotic living at second hand,' commented stewardess Edith Sowerbutts. Many who were indulging in lobster, caviar, oysters and the like 'might have been brought up on bread and dripping and porridge.' But she too had to acknowledge that 'meals on the run did not taste so good.'[145]

Once on board, life for the ordinary seafarer was less than idyllic. 'Below the decks' in crew quarters, a world very different from the splendid life on the Promenade, was being played out simultaneously. Long hours (usually from 7 a.m. until 10 p.m.), hard work and extreme discipline awaited the would-be seafarer. John O. Wann comments that in the early days, the *Queen Mary* 'was not popular among seamen' because working on board such an enormous floating palace was intense, the accommodations were 'mediocre', and the crew bar, the Pig & Whistle, 'was nearly a quarter of a mile from our quarters.'[146] Dave Marlowe had a similar experience and agreed that for crew, 'the *Queen Mary* holds no illusions'. Sightseers who 'swarmed over the ship in hundreds' to admire its grace and beauty 'never saw the glory hole' which he shared with twenty-four other 'tired-eyed and weary' boys who put in long days scrubbing decks, polishing brass and furniture 'until everything was immaculate' and the ship was ready to 'hold court' with its admiring public.[147] Marlowe also writes about his participation in the chain-gang on board. During eastbound sailings when the ship was only half full, crew members were kept busy painting cabins, checking over crockery, cleaning silver and other odd jobs.[148]

Still, for the working poor of Liverpool, Southampton and Le Havre, ship life, with all its drawbacks, was more tolerable than what they had known at home. One man, who joined Cunard-White Star Line's *Homeric* as an engineer's steward in 1934 aged twenty, acknowledged that he was lucky to secure a job during a time when unemployment figures for seafarers was at an all-time high. His Roman Catholic connection worked for him when an Irish steward friend was able to get him the job. 'Every man on Deal Street was a seafarer,' he said. The children of seafarers were so poor that they had to wear clogs instead of shoes. One person on the street had a 'bungalow bath' (portable) on which you could sit. When the husband was at sea, the bath was loaned around the street.[149]

Liverpudlians in search of work would gather at Dock Tavern, which was the hiring place for seafarers. Company representatives went to the tavern to get 'hands' for the next trip. There was no contract for ordinary crew, and thus no job security. At the end of each voyage, one would have to 'sign on' again for the next trip. Since the British shipping companies did not pay for crew uniforms, a great initial expense was made by the family with no guarantee of long-term employment. This situation contrasts to the practice of French Line, which did supply its crew with uniforms. Each member kept a *carte d'habillement* that recorded the date and type of clothing that had been replaced. Additional requests had to be approved by the *maître d'hôtel*. Joining Cunard Line's *Aquitania* in 1935 at the age of twenty as an assistant cook, Frank Mortimer had to provide his own knives. 'Anything you had to use for the job, you had to supply yourself,' he said, '... nobody could touch your knives ... you were responsible to keep them sharp and in good condition.'[150]

Cunard Magazine described each of its company's ships as 'a floating town' and likened the captain to the chief magistrate and the chief officer to the chief constable. The chief engineer was compared to the borough surveyor, and the purser became the town clerk, a sort of 'jack-of-all-trades'.[151] *Aquitania*'s Captain E. G. Diggle referred to a ship's master as lord mayor of the city and his officers as city councillors.[152] As 'chief magistrate' of this 'floating town', the captain was responsible for keeping every crew member 'up to the high standard of discipline and efficiency usual in the service'. A TRANSAT brochure described the captain as both a 'perfect host' to his passengers and 'a stern but affectionate father' to his crew. He inspired both fear and respect among the crew, although some captains were more popular than others. A rigid, stern, inflexible master might run a tight ship, but it was unlikely to have been a happy one. The master of the vessel was set apart from the rest of the crew and even had his own personal servant, a special boy steward who was referred to as the 'captain's tiger'.[153] The captain conducted a daily inspection of the public rooms to ensure that 'cleanliness is at all times maintained on board'. At the onset of each voyage, an inspection of crew uniforms was made to make sure that every button was in place. Cunard Line reminded its captains that 'a man who does not take any pride in personal cleanliness, habits, and/or dress, seldom takes pride in his occupation or duties', and made clear that if they and other officers took 'greater pains in demanding that their subordinates pay more attention to their personal appearance, the result will be reflected in a corresponding degree in the general bearing and smartness of the whole of the ship's company.'[154]

Management periodically issued guides like *Useful Hints for Stewards*, *Rule Book for Crew*, and *Reglement des Etats-Majors* to ensure that the sterling reputation of the company remained untarnished. Crew members who committed infractions against company policy were severely punished by the master of the vessel. White Star Line told its stewards that 'the traveling public tell us a well-trained English Steward is the best in the world. Please endeavor to maintain this good reputation.' It also reminded them that a 'courteous and interested service is profitable both to the Company and yourself.' *Useful Hints for Stewards* further counseled stewards to take care in maintaining a neat appearance since 'passengers will not be attracted by untidy servants', and that hands and fingernails should be cleaned before each meal with care to 'remove cigarette stains, if any'. Stewards were advised to refrain from idle conversation with passengers and warned not to talk 'about the passengers, the crew, the steamer, or the Company's business'.[155]

In such a competitive business, shipping companies took passengers' comments seriously. A memo to Cunard Line's general manager in June 1922 regarding transatlantic crossings of the *Berengaria* stated that passengers found the cuisine and service to be below the standard of quality desired. The memo referred to 80 per cent of the saloon (First Class) waiters as 'third rate' and suggested that the dining room staff be strengthened 'in order to attain for *Berengaria* that high mark of proficiency necessary to the reputation she now deserves' and more important, not to lose out to any of Cunard Line's competitors.[156] Many crew received 'on-the-job training' once on board. Bridge officers gave sailors lessons on the handling and navigation of lifeboats. *Cours du Soir* were offered on board French Line ships daily between 4 and 5 p.m. at the *Ecole Hotelière* and provided intensive language classes to mousses (bellboys) whose English was not adequate to deal with the largely American audience. French Line also maintained a school for the education and training of young men about to enter its hotel and stewards departments in Le Havre at which they 'are given a thorough grounding in the theory and practice of their future jobs.'[157] This rigorous course of instruction was supplemented by compulsory physical training with the gymnastic instructor planning a daily physical fitness program designed to keep mousses and young commis-waiters (apprentices) fit and up to the demands of the job.

Shipping companies dealt harshly with those crew members whose behavior threatened to damage the reputation of the line. In May 1938, the French Line vessel *Lafayette* caught fire while in port in Le Havre. A *femme de chambre*, Mme Poure, came forward with evidence implicating a crew member, Claire Unterneh, and her boyfriend, M. Levieux, head cashier in the purser's office, with the theft of the cash box on board ship. On the morning of the fire, Mme Unterneh gave Mme Poure a packet of love letters to safeguard for her. She claimed that the letters were from an earlier lover, and that her new friend now demanded that she destroy them. She refused saying that he must marry her first. Mme Poure became suspicious of her friend's story, opened the packet and found 52,800 francs (both in American and French banknotes), the exact amount of money 'lost' in the fire on the *Lafayette*. Although she refused to implicate her lover, both Mme Unterneh and M. Levieux were found guilty and imprisoned. A series of thefts of passenger belongings took place on board the *Lafayette* earlier in the year. The captain's report to the secretary general of TRANSAT warned that the bad publicity that such incidents could cause the company would be used against them by their competitors. He suggested that great care be taken in the recruitment of new crew members and that the French Line should be careful to avoid embarking 'questionable elements' as members of their staff.[158] Other petty thefts involved items from the ship's kitchen or the ship's liquor storage room that were sold ashore (an especially lucrative business during Prohibition in the United States), all of which met with stringent penalties. One chief steward of Cunard Line was arrested and charged in court with smuggling diamonds into the United States. This publicity was not the kind Cunard appreciated. Equally embarrassing to the company was a case of an indiscreet bellboy who was caught peeping through a hole in the bulkhead of the bathroom that a Second Class passenger on the *Samaria* was vacating. The aforementioned bellboy's services were promptly dispensed with on his return to England.[159]

Fraternization was expressly forbidden between passengers and ordinary seafarers. Aside from fulfilling their duties in the public rooms or on deck, crew members did not venture out into public space on the promenade. Passenger space, in fact, was completely off limits to crew. Company rules also prohibited crew members from soliciting gratuities from passengers or smuggling liquor off the ship. Either offense, if caught, meant immediate dismissal. Smoking in staterooms or alleyways met with the same penalty.

Fernand Brossard, a French Line employee, had a close call, his services nearly being terminated. He escaped dismissal because of a unique talent he possessed and which French Line exploited. Sent to sea at the age of twelve, Brossard began entertaining the crew with the Guignol puppet show he had been performing since he was four years old. After the First World War, he returned to sea with French Line. He began entertaining the passengers in Third Class incognito as Charlot (as the French affectionately called Charlie Chaplin), and was invited to the First Class lounge. When Brossard was called to the purser's office, he thought he was being discharged. Instead, the positive response from the passengers convinced TRANSAT to give Fernand a full-time job producing a First Class Guignol theater on board. He joined the *Ile de France* when she was launched in 1927 and was promoted to the new *Normandie* in 1935. Brossard became something of a celebrity, being invited, between sea-trips, to perform in Baltimore, Philadelphia, and even in Columbia University's Hall of Philosophy. Although he was not the inventor of the art, Brossard was responsible for bringing Guignol to American audiences.[160]

Other crew members, without Brossard's special talents, learned early on to submit in silence to the powerful officer hierarchy. Dave Marlowe recalls an incident that caused his demotion from serving in the First Class dining room to waiting on tables in the stewardesses' mess. His misfortune was to tell a troubled passenger that the chief steward had found the half cuff-link that he had lost at dinner the previous night. Little did he realize that the chief steward had no intention of returning it. As a consequence, he was chastised and punished for his honesty by his superior.[161] Marlowe later switched to an American ship on advice from a friend who painted a more positive picture of life on board for crew: 'We eat in the room after the people are gone, we don't do stores, we scrub out with mops, not on our benders [knees], and we get better pay. What more can a guy ask?' Marlowe found American officers 'to be more human, more laid-back, not hung up on rank like their British counterparts.' Even the crew behaved differently, 'for they all seemed so sure of themselves … They spoke quite respectfully to the officers, but more as man to man, often omitting the "sir", a thing that would have brought sharp rebuke on a British ship.' The work went on just the same, he said, with everyone doing their job, 'and it certainly produced a far more harmonious feeling between officers and men.'[162] He earned more money, did not have the additional expense of buying a uniform, and shared the 'glory hole' with only five other men as compared to the twenty-four with whom he had to bunk on the *Queen Mary*.

Though Cunard-White Star Line ship brochures boasted of the plentiful space and posh accommodations for First Class passengers, there was no mention of the glory holes Marlowe describes, those large rooms at the aft end of the ship which served as home for ten to twenty or more young men who were stacked along the bulkhead in steel bunks and shared their accommodations with cockroaches and other equally undesirable roommates. Though the *Queen Mary* may have dazzled its passengers, crew were far more critical. While conceding that the tips were good on board the *Queen Mary*, they found the work grueling and although the food was great, Marlowe says, 'at the time when, exhausted, I was standing up to eat, I did not notice the flavour.'[163] Sowerbutts comments that such practices frequently led to digestive troubles which were common among crew who routinely put in 13-hour days and that the 'only difference between these men and horses was that horses would be left in peace in their stables while they munched, whereas stewards and stewardesses could be summoned by a bell or a light for passenger service.'[164]

French Line was the only company to publicize the crew accommodations. In announcing the debut of its new flagship, *Normandie*, in 1935, The *Nautical Gazette* explained that the 1,300-member crew had not been neglected. 'The crew quarters, the 'forecastle' of ancient days, strikes a new high in the wonder ship from France,' the article stated. Crew bunks were 'of steel frame construction, enameled and designed for genuine comfort ... All bunks are provided with comfortable mattresses, blankets, and sheets. The same perfect ventilation that serves the passengers is carried out in the crew quarters.' Crew accommodations were well lighted, had steam heat, and contained individual steel lockers.[165] In short, they were spartan but clean. French Line, quite predictably, paid a good deal of attention to the cuisine served to its crew on board. The maritime law of 20 July 1910 greatly improved the quality of life for French crew. The ration of wine was augmented by 50 per cent. Crew members were entitled to fresh fish at least once per week, and menus were to be varied. There was also much discussion relating to weekly allowances. Sample menus were submitted for approval of the unions. Crew members even complained about the quality of the *vin ordinaire* and requested a Tunisian wine that was *plus leger*.[166] This was in stark contrast to the Peninsular and Oriental Steam Navigation Company, which issued memoranda to pursers that no 'grog' allowance was to be issued to stewards, who would instead receive a sum of 5 shillings per month as compensation. So concerned was the company about drunkenness among its crew that barmen were instructed not to sell liquor to any crew member not on the authorized list.[167]

Although hardly acknowledged, the work of the steward/stewardess was often the most gruelling on board. From early morning until late at night, these workers were kept busy cleaning public rooms, serving morning tea and coffee to passengers in their cabins, and preparing the dining room for meals and cleaning up afterwards or tending to cabins. They scrubbed floors, polished brass, made sure all cutlery, plates and linens were kept in good order, and were at their passengers' beck and call nearly 24 hours a day. They worked seven days each week, had little shore leave, and never received overtime. Male stewards were looked down upon by fellow crew members as not 'proper seafarers'. Jo Stanley's interviews with former crew members suggest that 'they were not even seen as "proper men" – especially as so many were homosexual' and they performed what was considered 'soft work'.[168] In her memoirs, White Star Line stewardess Violet Jessop writes of this denigration of male stewards in her first encounter with Ned Tracy, a junior fifth engineer: 'I found he hated stewards unreasonably. There was something vital about him that rebelled against their passivity. He despised their cupidity, their lack of manliness, their submissiveness, and that they mostly subsisted on tips brought forth his bitterest scorn.'[169] Jessop, however, saw the stewards' timidity in the face of authority as a response 'to their restricted life since boyhood or to the cringing fear of sudden dismissal without opportunity for redress.' They were 'handicapped by the scantiest education' and received little training on board. She blamed the employers who compeled stewards to grovel to and ingratiate themselves with passengers in order to subsidize the 'starvation wage' they earned 'for intolerably long hours'.

While their monthly wage of £8 ($41) might be meager, that was little indication of what their yearly income with tips might average. Although Frank Severini was only earning 12 shillings a week as a page boy on the *Majestic* in 1924, he considered it a 'top job' since he made good tips and was able to meet celebrities like Johnny Weissmuller (*Tarzan*), who, having been paged at the pool, gave Frank a substantial tip. He recalls that the largest tip he received was from an elderly millionaire, a famous Hollywood film producer who gave him $50 for returning his lost wallet.[170] One of the most coveted positions on board was that of chief smoking room steward, whose annual income might be as much as £3,000 ($15,000), chiefly from tips. A cabin steward or stewardess in the First Class section of a luxury liner could easily make £600 ($3,000) including gratuities, or four times what they would earn ashore. Dining room stewards routinely tipped the kitchen staff for speedy service so as to keep them in good stead with the passengers.

In his book on sea travel, Roydon Freeman includes guidelines on appropriate tipping. While the suggested gratuity for a five-day crossing for a cabin/dining room steward was $2.50, a chief steward could hope to collect up to $5 from rich passengers. No wonder then, that 'at the home port of a giant liner you are quite likely to see a chief steward met at the quay by his chauffeur and limousine, while the Captain walks off towards an omnibus, for the Chief Steward's income is often twice the Captain's.'[171] This may, in fact, explain Ned Tracy's resentment of stewards who obviously were financially far better off than he himself. Crew members were generally a resourceful lot. Some augmented their incomes by turning their hobbies into lucrative sidelines. Barbers and members of the orchestra often moonlighted as amateur photographers, selling passengers mementos of their excursions ashore. Others made model ships and clocks, which passengers purchased as souvenirs of their cruise. The barber's shop on board doubled as a 'general store' where all practical necessities, including remedies for seasickness, could be purchased. This enabled the barber to supplement the meager income he earned at his trade.

Like Ned Tracy, officers generally did not mingle socially with the crew and regarded them as a class apart. Commenting on the dining room staff, Sir James Bisset, commodore of Cunard-White Star Line and wartime captain of both the *Queen Mary* and *Queen Elizabeth*, admits that 'we on the bridge had no special interest in them except that they kept us fed.'[172]

Violet Jessop observed that aboard ship, 'there was too much regimentation and too little consideration for the dignity of the individual.' Officers and engineers regarded stewards with undisguised contempt. Although stewards 'seem like an agreeable fraternity, circumstances make them utterly indifferent to one another, unless they need something.' Jessop comments on the breakdown of any camaraderie as soon as crew members were promoted to superior positions and 'forget their less fortunate brethren, whose lives they often make hell in order to maintain their own precarious place.' Stewards were generally a passive lot whose 'individual initiative has been quashed' through long years of continued regimentation. 'One rarely heard them complain that they found their work ... monotonous and distasteful,' she said. 'They never realized that the very monotony had eaten like a canker into their souls, killing ambition and leaving them content to get along without exerting their minds.'[173]

As Jessop astutely observed, a class system was clearly at work even within the crew ranks. First Class stewards regarded themselves as superior to their Third Class counterparts. Not only were the gratuities higher but a boost in social status came with serving the rich and famous. This 'upstairs, downstairs' mentality was very prevalent on board the 'floating palaces' of the interwar years. Stewards working in First Class sections of the ship believed that their self-worth had increased because of their close contact with celebrities and powerful businessmen – even if they only cleaned up after them. Interviews with former seafarers always include mention of the many 'important' people they met while working on board, as the many scrapbooks of celebrity photos, which they have meticulously cared for over the years, would indicate.

Edith Sowerbutts writes of meeting noted celebrities including Robert Taylor, Gary Cooper, Marlene Dietrich, Doris Duke, and Douglas Fairbanks Sr. While she acknowledged that Erich Maria Remarque was an important writer, she described him as 'a cynical type', and remembers him mostly for 'the mucky state of his wash-bowl'. One favorite passenger with the crew was another familiar face on board the *Queen Mary*, Paul Robeson, whom Sowerbutts describes as 'every inch a gentleman'. Robeson was one of the few celebrities who had more time for the crew than many of his fellow passengers, frequently entertaining male crew members in the Pig & Whistle. He treated the crew as valued individuals and always remembered their names.[174] As a black actor and socialist, Robeson understood the realities of prejudice and discrimination and was especially sensitive to the plight of crew who, aboard ship, were treated like second class citizens both by passengers and the officer elite (and by a few fellow crew members who had managed to rise to the rank of petty officers).

Relations between officers were generally friendly, although when Captain William Eldin Warwick joined Cunard-White Star Line in 1936, he recalled friction between the officers of Cunard Line and former White Star Line as a result of cutbacks in staff caused by the 1934 merger, which was referred to by some White Star people as the 'submerger'. Warwick, assigned to the *Scythia* as junior third officer, aged twenty-four, found that the next youngest officer was forty-nine years old because of a hiring freeze. Commodore Geoffrey Mar likewise recalls that when he joined Cunard Line in 1936 as a junior officer, many of the other junior officers were twenty years older than him.

Officers on both French and British ships were held to a high standard of conduct. The captain and all chief officers were required to file voyage reports with the general manager of the company commenting on any personnel problems. 'Character books', which were annual reports on officers' conduct, were also kept. Officers were rated on overall intelligence, sobriety, education, conduct, initiative, health, job suitability and qualifications for promotion. Negative comments from a superior officer could result in the termination of an officer's contract or a denial of promotion. An officer referred to as 'reliable and sober' or as 'a total abstainer' was guaranteed a long career with the company. Anyone described as 'a man of vile temper not accustomed to discipline' or 'a capable chief steward, but hot headed and tactless' would have a harder time convincing the company hierarchy that he deserved a promotion. Other negative comments, including characterization as a 'very affected and conceited' individual or, 'a gambler', or as suffering 'from nervous exhaustion and unfit for duty' could jeopardize a person's career altogether.

One captain reprimanded an officer 'who does not realize the dignity of his position, inasmuch that he consorts with any member of the crew', something that was frowned upon on all ships. The officer was also accused of insobriety which led to the rationing of his 'wine bill' during the next voyage. Additional comments about his personal appearance led the captain to conclude that he was 'unsuitable to wear his officer's uniform.' Perhaps the most damning charge against this officer, however, was that he 'has a very disturbing influence among the Juniors. [He] is very radical in his views.' Such an accusation could mean immediate dismissal, as was the case of an engineer aboard French Line's *Alaska* in 1925. Although he had been with the company for three years and had already received a promotion, he was dismissed on the grounds that he had a 'clear tendency towards communism' and had insulted his superior officers, thereby being a bad influence on the crew.[175]

Bridge officers and engineers working on British liners were expected to refrain from having much direct contact with the passengers and discouraged from even frequenting the public rooms. While the British sought to maintain a polite but formal distance between passengers and staff, Americans expected a more friendly reception from the officer elite on board. The rules expressly forbade the captain, bridge officers, engineers and all other officials (other than the purser and surgeon), from receiving passengers in their rooms. They were also instructed to refrain from participating in the amusements of passengers – games, concerts, deck sports, and so on – and 'while courteously replying to any questions which may be put to them by passengers, [they] will not seek conversation with them'.[176] By contrast, French Line officers were not only encouraged to mix with passengers but socializing with their guests was part of their job description. When not on duty on the bridge, officers were required to mingle with passengers in the public lounges and even take a few women traveling alone for a spin or two around the dance floor! As Raoul de Beaudéan, captain of the *Ile de France*, wrote: 'This courtesy, rare on transatlantic liners, tacitly involved the obligation to dance with all the ladies and particularly with the plainest and clumsiest ones ...'[177] French Line officers became most popular with the passengers, particularly Americans, who eagerly sought to hob-nob with the ship's officer elite during their voyage and perhaps even find a little romance.

Fraternization between male and female crew was clearly not encouraged by the shipping companies. The Pig & Whistle was off-limits to women, who were largely confined to their tiny, cramped quarters for socializing with friends. Men and women had separate crew messes. Companies purposefully did not hire young women as stewardesses so that male crew members could keep their minds on their work. Stewardesses, however, generally did not seek out fellow workers, for they had higher stakes. Like young female department store clerks ashore, stewardesses dreamed of bettering themselves socially and economically by marrying 'the boss', in this case, one of their superiors in the officer class. Even when friendships did develop, it was difficult to sustain a normal relationship. Violet Jessop recalls that once on a cruise stopping in Jamaica, she and Ned went out for a drink at a famous hotel that was crowded with passengers. 'They appeared somewhat surprised to see us,' she said. 'I learned from later experience that passengers generally are surprised if you use the same public buildings they do.'[178] As a general rule, only an officer would even consider patronizing a restaurant frequented by passengers.   Crew members found themselves equally confined both on board ship and on shore. Even if they married, a practice not encouraged by the steamship companies, spouses were rarely assigned to the same ship. While John Patrick Mullins sailed on the maiden voyage of the *Queen Mary*, his wife, Helen, was a nurse on another Cunard Line ship.[179] Delia Callaghan met her husband while working on the *Berengaria*. While they were 'allowed' to marry, she never saw him very much, only in port on occasion.[180]

Captain William Eldin Warwick fondly recalls meeting his wife, who worked as a 'barbareen' (a nickname for a female hairdresser), on the *Carinthia*. Their budding romance captured the attention of his crew, half of whom 'would line up to see what she was wearing when we went out.' Once married, she left her position altogether and thereafter sailed occasionally. When asked if she wanted to leave her job, Captain Warwick replied, 'Being a man, I never asked her!'[181] At least he was honest!

In order to keep up crew morale, which frequently needed boosting, social and athletic clubs were organized on all Cunard and French Line ships. (See Figure 10.) Such accessibility to sports activities was a reflection of the opening up of 'leisure' to members of the middle and working classes which began in the interwar years. In his memoirs, *Aquitania* purser, Charles Spedding, writes that 'shipowners themselves have never given much, if any, thought to this side of sea life.'[182] A crew committee, headed by the captain, organized football, cricket, bowling, billiard, swimming and boxing matches when two ships were in port. Before the war, most lower-, middle- and working-class people had little exposure to most sports.[183] The steamship lines organized social events including dances, concerts and cinema viewings for their crews on board as well as picnics and shore excursions in American ports of call. Cunard Line presented each of its passenger liners with a handsome challenge cup, for which different departments of the ship would compete in rowing matches. Cunard attributed the 'high standard of efficiency which exists' among its crews in the manner of manning lifeboats to the 'keen competition among departments to possess the cup.' A silver medal was presented to each member of the winning team.[184] Company executives rightly calculated that a happy crew would result in positive ratings from passengers who would be likely to choose Cunard for a subsequent voyage.

The social and athletic association had its own crew publication, *The Commodore*, for each Cunard Line ship, and the July 1930 issue published for the *Aquitania* included various practical columns: 'Repair Queries', advice on caring for one's garden at home, fashion tips, and suggestions for touring while in a foreign port. There were updates on various upcoming sports events and results of matches with other ships. Crew members contributed poetry and other literary articles. A notice from a department store, Austin Reed Ltd, solicited help from the crew to increase business in their on board shop. Awards of credit notes for £5, £3 and £1 were given as prizes for suggestions regarding the most popular items demanded by passengers. Advertisements for radios, gramophones, furniture, flowers, ladies' silk hosiery and underwear, laundries, sports goods, steamship trunks, ship uniforms, engagement rings, furs, car hire service, and the YMCA also appeared on the pages of *The Commodore*.[185] Such ads reveal that the working classes were quickly becoming mass consumers in the interwar years and that various merchants were actively competing for their business.

Despite long hours and often tedious labor, seafarers had their own lives and the money for some of the luxuries that would never have been possible if they worked ashore. Articles on spring and summer gardening and home decorating tips indicate that crew members sought to maintain two lives simultaneously. They wanted the security of having their own private space ashore to which they could retreat and plant their gardens when ship life became too restrictive. At home, they were their own masters. But they maintained a separate identity on board that provided an added degree of comfort because they also saw themselves as part of the ship family. There was a strong camaraderie among the crew that revolved around a ship's social and athletic association, and the net effect of this social bonding was to create a more amiable work atmosphere and, therefore, a happy, more contented crew that was loyal to the company.

Sports were similarly used in the 1920s and 1930s to unite youth at home behind even the most unpopular governments in Europe. Léon Blum's Popular Front government in France was the first to create a Subsecretariat for Leisure and Sports, or the Ministry of Idleness as it came to be known. Its director, Léo Lagrange, set as his goal 'the improvement of the race', using methods promoted by the Nazi Strength through Joy leisure and sports organizations.[186] Competition in sports had the effect of deflecting attention away from a nation's social problems and rallying the people around the flag of patriotism. In the same way, shipping companies encouraged sports competitions between crews of different shipping lines in order to neutralize discontent and engender a feeling of loyalty to one's company.

There was an intimate relationship between a ship's crew and its home port – generally where the families of crew members lived. An article in *Cunard Line Magazine* spoke about the interest that the people of Southampton took in their crews when a ship was in port. It acknowledged the town's indebtedness to their sons and daughters who work on the ships which 'mean so much to the life of the town'. On one occasion, the crew of the *Aquitania* was honored by the mayor who arranged a gala for their benefit. A repeat performance was held for the crew of the *Mauretania*. Not only did the ships bring business to the port of Southampton, but they also brought employment to its inhabitants, thereby contributing to the economic well-being of the port.[187] The British Sailors' Society arranged to have seafarers entertained at Christmas at more than 110 homes and hostels affiliated with the society in 1932.[188]

Life for families of seafarers was often difficult. Although seafarers' wages made their families financially more secure, the absence of a husband, wife, sibling, or child had a negative effect on the family. Economic security came at a price, as Captain William Eldin Warwick found out. On one of his visits home, his youngest son, who had hardly seen his father, was puzzled when introduced to him and asked, 'What's a dad?'[189] Flora Ackroyd recalls the changed atmosphere at home when her father, an engineer with Cunard Line, was in port. 'The sky was the limit,' she said, remembering his treating them to fish and chips and a concert.[190] Those were happy times, but the periods in between were lonely and often anxiety-ridden. Her father was senior second engineer on the *Lusitania* when it was torpedoed. He was pulled out of the water hanging on to an overturned lifeboat. Many other families were not so fortunate.

To address the retirement needs of Cunard Line staff, a Superannuation Fund was established in 1925, which made 'all permanent male employees of the Company over 21 years of age in the United Kingdom' members of the fund. Employees' contribution of 2.5 per cent of their salaries would be matched by 7.5 per cent from the company. The widow of a deceased Cunard employee would receive a yearly pension according to her age, ranging from £36 to £100, and all children under the age of seventeen would receive a yearly allowance of £25. Although officers benefitted from this fund, seamen and firemen were not eligible to join as they were not on the 'regular salary list.'[191] Cunard Line board minutes from 1911 mention the existence of a type of pension fund for long-term employees (including stewards, stewardesses and firemen) with fifteen-plus years' service that provided a weekly retirement allowance of 5 shillings.[192] The fund was discontinued in 1930 as the full effects of the Depression were felt in England.

Times had not changed that dramatically for crew since the days when Charles Logan sailed with Cunard. Having served the company faithfully for twenty years, he contracted lead poisoning on the job as a 'lamp trimmer' and, when he developed paralysis, was subsequently discharged as 'a total wreck' from the *Lusitania* in 1912. Since he did not qualify for workmen's compensation, the company gave him £25 and promised him a 'light job', which he never received. He died seven and a half years later, in 1919, leaving behind a widow and child. Through the intercession of the mother, the son obtained a position aboard a Cunarder as a bellboy but was made to work with 'a drunken Chief Steward' and some 'uncultivated boys who made his life intolerable'. When he was let go, Annie Logan wrote to Cunard Chairman, Sir Percy Bates, complaining that she had to live on a meager widow's pension. Bates reluctantly agreed to reinstate the son in 1935.[193]

Cunard generosity had its limits. When a steward on board the *Carinthia* met with an accident in July 1928, he was examined by specialists who found that he was suffering from Bright's disease and diabetes and had a short time to live. Having worked for Cunard for thirty-two years, he put in an insurance claim for £450 for the support of his wife and two children. Although not related to his illness, the accident caused him the loss of his finger which was amputated in October. Upon advice from the company's lawyers, Cunard admitted liability but was only willing to consider a £200 settlement, £100 short of what was suggested by the lawyers.[194]

French Line provided a range of social services for the families of its crew. In 1913, a maternity fund, La Layette Transatlantique, was established with the goal of helping pregnant wives of men in French Line service for at least six months. This provision applied to both shore and seagoing staff. The fund provided medical attention and a layette for the baby and sought 'to look after the general welfare and happiness of the mother, keeping up her courage and giving the newborn infant a fair start in life.' It was personally administered by ladies' visiting committees in the four principal embarkation ports of the company – Le Havre, St Nazaire, Bordeaux and Marseilles. Auctions and special concert programs were held aboard TRANSAT ships, like the Fête de Bienfaissance, the proceeds of which went to several benevolent institutions, such as the French and American Seamen's Fund.[195]

As a result of the severe economic consequences of the Depression, shipping companies adopted a policy of austerity in order to survive. On 1 May 1931, Cunard Line reduced all sea/shore staff salaries by £10, not restoring them until April 1937.[196] Letters of dismissal were sent to crew members of shipping companies whose liners were sailing half empty and could no longer support a full staff. French Line terminated the services of many of its crew in 1932 with two weeks' notice and an indemnity of three months' salary.[197]

Once economic recovery began, TRANSAT established a Service Social to work with the needy families of company employees in 1936. In June 1939, French shipowners grouped together to create a national association, the Union Sociale Maritime, which was headquartered in Paris. Its work included finding placement for orphans in foster homes and the sick in convalescent centers, aiding wives of enlisted men, and securing work for 'company widows'. TRANSAT organized a workshop for the fabrication of woolens for the Army Service Corps that provided work for 300 wives of mobilized seamen during the winter of 1940. The efforts of the Service Social and the larger Union Sociale Maritime were cut short by the bombardments of Le Havre in the spring of 1940. An eleven-page report, dated 16 May 1941, addressed French Line workers' housing and living conditions. French Line managers examined company activities and proposed necessary measures to aid the maritime population of Le Havre. The Service Social researched the names and addresses of crew members who were prisoners of war and helped families to send them packages. The children of these prisoners under the age of fourteen received 100 francs.

Disaster relief was made available for mobilized seafarers' families who were victims of the English bombings of Le Havre. The Service Social provided clothing and temporary shelter for homeless families. It also worked to facilitate the relocation of women and children to other regions in case of renewed bombardments, and sought to provide treatment in the proper sanatoriums to seafarers' family members inflicted with tuberculosis. In making aid available to its needy employees, French Line wanted to ensure that families would use it wisely. The company's paternalism was transparent in choosing to give relief in the form of goods rather than money to avoid the 'bad practice of getting the unemployed used to receiving handouts.'

Once shortages and rationing limited TRANSAT's ability to help families send parcels to POWs in Germany, the company appealed to its workers to aid their imprisoned colleagues. To facilitate the Service Social's efforts, French Line appointed a committee composed of liberated POWs to make suggestions regarding the particular needs of prisoners who remained in Germany.[198] The managers expressed the concern that seafarers, like their counterparts ashore, might have a tendency to blame the employer for all their misfortunes. Thus, the company sought to be prudent in distributing aid according to what they deemed appropriate. Seafarers played no role in this decision. While showing its compassion for needy employees, TRANSAT also feared and distrusted its workers whom it often viewed as potential anarchists and troublemakers.

The fear of anarchism and communism and other forms of 'trouble' predated the outbreak of the Second World War. The paternalism of the shipping companies was most strongly felt in the discipline they exerted over those employees whom they considered disloyal or untrustworthy, particularly those who deserted their posts to join in strikes called by their unions. In such cases, the full wrath of the father towards his wayward children was demonstrated by the letters of dismissal sent to crew members who were considered 'dangerous agitators'. Shipping companies' general hostile attitude to labor organization among their crew is best revealed in the comments of pre-First World War writer R. A. Fletcher, who describes a labor organizer as a 'sea lawyer' who is 'not a solicitor whose taste for a nautical life has induced him to slip before the mast, but a sailor who combines a discontented disposition with a passion for grumbling, an uncanny knack of finding something to grumble at, the gift of gab, and an elementary knowledge of a few of the legal points which may arise under the articles.'[199]

After the First World War, diplomats at the Paris Peace Conference called for an 8-hour day/48-hour workweek as an ideal to be achieved by all nations. At the 1919 Washington Conference, a convention was adopted that the 48-hour week should be applied to seamen of all member states of the League of Nations. This question was discussed further at the Genoa Conference organized by the League's International Labour Office which was held 15 June–10 July 1920 and attended by members of the International Shipping Federation and the International Seamen's Federation. In preparation for the conference, a memo to Cunard Line managers warned of the increase in crew (mainly in the catering department) which would be necessary if such a measure were adopted. The 833-person crew aboard the *Mauretania* would need to be increased to 1,239, while the *Caronia*'s 470-member crew would number 754.[200]

Returning from the Genoa Conference, Cunard Line Chairman, Sir Alfred Booth, stated that it was impossible to establish an international convention regarding hours of labor at sea and intimated that if 'such a system were adopted ... foreign nations, having no surplus sea labor available, would find it physically impossible to carry it out. They would interpret it elastically, and fall back in the payment of overtime, thereby escaping the heavy burden which increased complements would impose on the British shipowner.' Contrary to seamen's expectations that the 48-hour workweek would eliminate unemployment, Booth was convinced that the unemployment rate would rise dramatically and that some ships 'would not go to sea at all; some would be laid up undergoing expensive alterations; others would be sold ... [T]here would be a serious check to the building of new tonnage and shipbuilding would come almost to a standstill.'[201]

Fearing a dramatic increase in crew expenditures, the International Shipping Federation failed to accept the draft convention proposed at Genoa regulating work hours at sea. Meanwhile, the seamen believed that they had the right to apply the principles of the Washington Convention. Since the two sides had reached an impasse in negotiations, the establishment of international legislation was postponed to a later date. The International Seamen's Federation asked Albert Thomas, Director of the League of Nations' International Labour Office, to organize another conference and act as arbiter in the dispute between shipowners and seafarers. If no arbitration was permitted, they indicated that they were prepared to call for a 48-hour strike in all ports.[202]

The purpose of the conference was to find an acceptable balance between the proposal of the seamen which called for an

8-hour day and a 48-hour week and the more modest concession of the shipowners for a 56-hour workweek for the Engine and Deck departments and a 70-hour week for the Catering Department (excluding France and Holland where the 48-hour week was already law). After considerable delay, the conference was convened in Brussels in October 1921 and was followed by a second session of the Joint Advisory Commission to the International Labour Office in Paris on 7 March 1922. The commission consisted of five representatives for shipowners, five for seafarers, and four members of the governing body of the International Labour Office.

By 1922, the Genoa Conference's recommendation that all countries adopt systems of unemployment insurance for crew members was accepted by seven countries. The hotly contested issue concerned the recommendation for the 48-hour workweek. The French government indicated that, to keep competitive, it would drop its own law providing for a 48-hour workweek at sea if the proposal was not universally adopted. After much discussion, the manager of the International Shipping Federation, Cuthbert Laws, acting on behalf of the shipowners, stated that the 48-hour week was a 'lost cause'. Though the International Labour Office could act as mediator in the dispute, the shipowners alone had the power 'to adopt whatever attitude they considered right when such a proposition is brought forward.'[203] At the end of the day, the seafarers went home empty-handed. French seamen lost the rights they had, and the British seafarers' representative, James Havelock-Wilson, was absent from the conference to avoid responsibility for the failure of the International Seamen's Federation to achieve its demands.

While negotiations for an international regulation of labor at sea were continuing, the Cooks and Stewards' Union, founded in 1909 by Joe Cotter, was engaging in strike activity against Cunard Line, opposing a wage cut of £2.10 per month agreed to by the National Maritime Board that was to take effect on 6 May 1921.[204] This reduction was £2 less than the cut requested by the shipowners for sailors and firemen and £3 less than that which was requested for catering personnel. The *Liverpool Echo* reported that, of the 598 stewards on the *Aquitania*, 590 of them went on strike, with stewards voting six to one against wage reductions. The paper noted that several strikers from the ship were survivors of the *Lusitania*. 'Cotter's Union', as the Cooks and Stewards' Union was commonly called, saw no reason for wage cuts during a time when the company was making huge profits and followed the example of Swedish and American seafarers who refused to accept similar cuts. Cunard Line's justification for the wage reduction was that the shipping industry was going through a depression.[205] This is a curious comment from a company that was in the process of launching five new ships between 1920 and 1925 and that was benefitting from the post-war acquisition of Germany's *Imperator*, which would sail under the Cunard flag as the *Berengaria*. The more plausible explanation for the company's tight budget for staff salaries is that it sought to pass on to its seafarers the high costs of converting coal- to oil-burning vessels and of transforming steerage space into more comfortable Tourist Third Cabin quarters.

On 14 May, 300 Cunard Line home office volunteers crossed the picket lines to take the place of the strikers, and the *Aquitania* sailed for New York from Southampton, according to schedule. This happened despite Joe Cotter's threat that sailors and firemen would refuse to take the ship out with 'black leg' labor. All 3,000 passengers were promptly embarked, and the general manager afterwards awarded bonuses to the volunteers. Despite company fears, 1921 did not become a replay of the violent 1911 strike known as 'Bloody Sunday', which had been led by 'Explosive Joe' Cotter.[206] 'Cotter's Union' all but collapsed and eventually merged with the British Seafarers' Union to form the Amalgamated Marine Workers' Union (AMWU) in January

1922. The AMWU continued until it was gradually absorbed in 1927 into the newly constituted National Union of Seamen (NUS), which was led by J. Havelock-Wilson.[207] Despite the wage cut temporarily imposed on seafarers during the most severe years of economic depression in the early 1930s, the NUS achieved important concessions from the shipowners in the years preceding the Second World War. Significant progress was made in the improvement of crew accommodations, and, in a stunning policy reversal, the shipowners agreed to revisit the issue of a limited workweek for the catering department. With the outbreak of the war, however, all such discussions were put on hold.

Strike activity in the maritime industry was especially visible in France in the decades preceding the Second World War. One of the most important strikes of the French Merchant Marine occurred in the summer of 1912. Fearing a strike, which would paralyse its fleet in all French ports, French Line managers voted to increase crew salaries in response to the rise in the cost of living. The unions, believing the increase to be too little too late, ordered its members to go out on strike on 9 June. All major French ports were affected, and in Le Havre the *France*, *Touraine*, *Rochambeau*, *Savoie* and *Provence* were laid up for fifty-five days. The strike was finally settled on 3 August, when the state intervened to force the company to grant a modest salary increase. The *Lorraine*, which was in dry dock undergoing refurbishment, was tied up for 182 days, which resulted in great financial expense to TRANSAT.[208]

In the decade preceding the First World War, French Line extended existing social laws to its seafarers by increasing salaries and pensions, establishing disability insurance, regulating hours of work and payment for overtime, and providing vacation pay. This came at a significant financial cost to the company. The resolution of the 1912 strike increased the company's expenditures by 500,000 francs, which made it more difficult to keep up with its competitors, especially the British shipping companies, who provided far fewer benefits to their employees.[209] Many of the strikes in the interwar years were related to the application of the law of the 8-hour day in France. Strikes on individual ships were also caused by personnel problems, as in the case of crew members aboard the *France* who deserted their posts in 1925 to protest the reassignment of an unpopular maître d'hôtel to the *Paris* after they demanded his dismissal from the company. A twelve-day strike by the engine room crew over wages affected the *Ile de France*, *Paris* and *Rochambeau* in the summer of 1928. Few concessions were made by TRANSAT. 'Agitators' were dismissed, and legal proceedings were initiated against strikers for breaking their contracts, as was the case with strikers on the *Paris* and the *France* who abandoned ship in October 1922.

All strike activity was coordinated by union leaders and their representatives on board. The union representing the kitchen staff in May 1936 demanded that crew cooks, butchers and bakers receive a raise because their work had become more complex. Since TRANSAT had upgraded the quality of the cuisine for its seafarers, short-order cooks were no longer sufficient. Cooks in the crew mess needed more skill and experience and demanded adequate compensation.[210] A letter from the unions to the company managers, dated 7 August 1936, expressed crew members' outrage that a recent brochure advertising a cruise to Canada on the *Champlain* commemorating the 300th anniversary of Champlain's explorations mentioned that gratuities were included in the price of the ticket. This was a hotly contested issue for crew members as tips were their bread and butter, and this announcement threatened to result in a work stoppage. In addition to standard demands for better wages and benefits, unions argued for upgraded menus and higher quality wines, both serious matters of the heart to the French.

The most publicized of the interwar years' maritime strikes in France was a ten-day standoff in 1938 between the Fédération Nationale des Syndicats Maritimes and the Ministère de la Marine acting in concert with the French shipping companies. This struggle centered on the battle over the 40-hour week. France's first Socialist-led coalition government, the Popular Front, which grouped together Socialists, Communists and Radical Republicans, took power on 4 June 1936 under the leadership of Léon Blum. What brought these divergent political groups together was the common fear of Fascism. In the first days of its existence, the Popular Front was threatened by a wave of strikes from the left. Through the Matignon Agreements, workers were granted substantial concessions, including the principle of collective bargaining, a two-week paid vacation, an average 12 per cent salary increase, and a reduction of the official workweek from 48 to 40 hours without loss of income. Bending to pressure, Blum's government acted imprudently, and his social program, however well intentioned, backfired. Although the average national wage increased by 47.5 per cent, the effects of the implementation of the 40-hour week undermined workers' gains as the cost of living rose 46 per cent between May 1936 and May 1938. Blum's position was indeed precarious as he tried to steer a moderate course in extreme times when racism was on the rise, and segments of the French, lured by the many right-wing nationalist movements, began to subscribe to the fascist belief of 'Better Hitler than Blum'. The government was forced to turn its back on its campaign platform and devalued the franc three times between 1936 and 1938. When Edouard Daladier replaced Blum in April 1938, the Socialists had already left the government, and workers' suspicions were raised that it would now cooperate with the employers to renege on the implementation of the 40-hour week.[211]

On 30 November, the local maritime unions, conforming to directives received by the leadership of the Confédération Générale du Travail (CGT), ordered their members to cease work, thereby delaying the departure of the *Wisconsin, Ile de France, Paris,* and the *De Grasse.* The strike was called to protest the laws of 12 November 'which forecasted a negative development concerning the forty-hour week...These laws also anticipated a 2 per cent contribution of crew members' salaries toward benefits provided by the company. TRANSAT had delayed the application of the law of 40 hours, which was to have taken effect on 8 June 1937, and officers were asking for compensation for overtime work.[212] The November laws hinted at the suppression of the five-day workweek/8-hour day in favor of organizing work on a daily basis of 6 hours and 40 minutes.

Anticipating a work stoppage, the French government, through its Minister of the Merchant Marine, M. de Chappedelaine, issued the law of 28 November 1938 which requisitioned the personnel of all French shipping companies subsidized by the state. Such an action brought a sharp exchange of letters between former Prime Minister Léon Blum and Edouard Daladier over the legality of invoking the law of 1877 to apply to the present situation. Daladier had claimed that the government was just following the example of Blum who used the law of 1877 (modified on 21 January 1935) requisitioning maritime personnel outside of mobilization for his own purposes on 6 June 1936. In both cases, Daladier insisted, France was in a state of crisis justifying extraordinary action by the government.[213]

Crew members reported to their posts as scheduled but refused to work. On the afternoon of 30 November, the secretaries of the unions called a meeting at the Salle Franklin in Le Havre, and union members of the *Ile de France* left the ship to attend. They were quickly slapped with a penalty of 50 francs and had one day's pay withheld for deserting their posts. *Normandie* arrived on 1 December and was scheduled to depart on its transatlantic journey to New York on Saturday

3 December. Among its passenger 'celebrities' were Anthony Eden, Gary Cooper and Douglas Fairbanks Jr. The union called a 'general strike' for 3 December to protest the actions taken by the government against the strikers on 30 November. The crew of the *Normandie*, which had also been requisitioned by the government, joined in the strike. As a consequence, passengers scheduled to sail on 3 December were rerouted to Cherbourg to board Cunard Line's *Aquitania*. One indignant French passenger commented, '[T]his ship which serves the prestige of France does not merit today such an unjust humiliation.'[214] French Line filed complaints against those crew members who had technically broken their contracts. Union organizers and others identified as agitators promptly received letters of dismissal from the company, which was drafting blacklists for each ship of those seafarers who were to be fired for their role in the strike. Those placed on the 'index' were mainly men from Le Havre, between the ages of fourteen and forty-nine, with the average age of the strikers being between thirty and thirty-two. Those seafarers thought to be of 'questionable character' – that is, suspected of being either 'communist revolutionaries', 'dangerous agitators' or 'drunkards' – were dismissed. [215]

On 5 December, Henri Cangardel, French Line general secretary, gave the order to man the *Paris* with TRANSAT-loyal crew and newly recruited shore personnel along with merchant marines for engine and bridge personnel. The government promised protection against reprisals from strikers to those crew members who wished to join their ships. The *Paris* departed from Le Havre at 11 p.m. on 7 December and arrived at Cherbourg at 3 a.m. the following day without incident and embarked 489 passengers. Among the Third Class passengers who boarded the ship in Cherbourg were 150 members of the Abraham Lincoln Brigade returning from the Spanish front where Franco's forces were virtually in control.[216] On 9 December, 2,000 union members met in the Salle Franklin and voted nearly two to one to continue the strike (1,300 for to 700 against). The secretary-general of the Central Committee of French Shipowners appealed to M. de Chappedelaine to have station police readily available at the quais should they be needed by ships' captains if crew members became violent and provoked an insurrection. Captains were instructed to bar any union representative from coming on board and were given authority to 'lock out' any crew member thought to be an agitator. Worker solidarity began to break down with news of crew defections. As early as 8 December, the crew of the *Cuba* secretly voted against the strike. Desperate appeals from the Fédération Nationale des Syndicats Maritimes to support its fight to uphold the law of the 40-hour week continued: '[E]ach time that the workers defend their right to maintain their livelihood, it is said that their struggles have a political character to them.' The union blamed the press for biased coverage of the strike. It accused the press of having been 'hired' and 'bought off' by big business, and demanded the release of imprisoned union organizers. It unsuccessfully pleaded with its members to remain firm: 'Unity in our ranks is essential, Comrade Marines, so that we may respect ourselves today and will conquer tomorrow.'[217]

On 10 December, 2,800 navigators presented themselves to the company for work while 900 strikers were meeting at the Salle Franklin. At the end of the day, the strike was over with seafarers having made no gains. By the spring of 1939, crew were protesting against what they saw as 'revenge' on the part of French Line. Substantial cuts had been made in seagoing personnel, beer allowances were reduced, and discipline was more strictly enforced. A poster distributed on board the *Normandie* warned crew that the captain expressly prohibited the distribution of any kind of political journals. Apparently this was not viewed as a contradiction to Republican freedoms. This notice was posted after the captain had discovered that two members of the crew were circulating copies of *Verités*, the journal of the CGT, which contained articles criticizing the Minister of the Merchant Marine Chappedelaine.[218] Once the Second World War began, the company discontinued all accessory wages (which made up 40 to 60 per cent of their earnings) including cost-of-living supplements, allowances for laundry, tobacco, alcohol and overtime pay, and for the duration of the war, the 40-hour week dispute was put on the back burner. As a result, strike activity ceased.

In 1944, an international conference of seafarers was held in which representatives from the twelve maritime countries present adopted a series of demands that became the International Seafarers' Charter. Its main goal was to secure recognition of uniform minimum standards. The charter was the main agenda for a special maritime session of the International Labour Organisation held in Seattle in 1946. The principal features of the charter were manifested in a series of conventions and recommendations which provided for an instrument that recognized the seafarers' right to an international minimum wage. Much of the credit for this success belonged to the new general secretary of Britain's National Union of Seamen, Charles Jarman.

Sixty years later, seafarers were voicing many of the same complaints of crew members of the 1930s. In an extensive exposé of the cruise industry, *New York Times* reporter Douglas Frantz examined working conditions for seafarers on the new mega-ships at the close of the twentieth century.[219] The 'migrant workers of the oceans' (as Frantz calls the thousands of people from Third World countries who 'sign on' as unskilled labor – dishwashers, assistant cooks, cabin cleaners and the like) were putting in 18-hour days, seven days a week, for little more than $400–$450 a month. Yet they remain at sea, just as their predecessors did, because wages, however meager, are much better than they could ever hope to earn at home.

Just as in the interwar years, legislation governing the industry is often ignored. Despite the call for a 70-hour week from the International Labour Office (an affiliate of the United

Nations), crew members routinely put in 80- to 90-hour weeks. Unions had thus come full circle. After all the discussions in the interwar years for a 48-hour week, today's seafarers are routinely putting in the same number of hours as did crew in the 1880s, for whom an 84-hour workweek was the rule. While in theory entitled to receive sick leave and disability payments, seafarers sometimes find their services with the shipping line terminated when they become ill or meet with an accident. Cruise staff are generally considered independent contractors and thus receive no vacation pay or pensions and little in the way of medical coverage, even those who make a career at sea. While outside advocates note that working and living conditions on board have dramatically improved in recent years, they acknowledge that 'improvement' must be measured by the position a seafarer holds in the company.

Society on board ship (both for those on the promenade and 'below the decks'), is still highly stratified. Although technically one-class ships, the megaliners of today have a vast array of passenger accommodations ranging from tiny, cramped inside cabins to luxurious suites with balconies larger than the average condo or townhouse ashore. The same class/caste system prevails in crew quarters. The officer elite and skilled seamen continue to enjoy better living and working conditions than the 'migrants' who clean the kitchens and cabins. Unlike its superiors who enjoy many passenger privileges, this invisible workforce cannot venture into the public space of passengers and is confined to crew quarters 'below the decks'. The International Labour Office has become more modest in its demands on the cruise companies than it did sixty years ago. Rather than a 48-hour workweek, the ideal now to be achieved is a 10-hour day and seven-day workweek that would bring a monthly minimum wage of $435. One extra roadblock that seafarers of the 1930s did not have to confront when looking for a job on board ship was the need to go through an intermediary and pay a hefty placement fee, as is the practice today. Recruiting agencies charge up to $500 for ship placement. Workers have been reluctant to complain about this practice for fear of being blacklisted. Frantz notes that maritime laws to protect seamen have been on the books since the thirteenth century in recognition of the fact that seafarers form a social underclass easily exploited by both shipowners and officers.

John Maxton-Graham, who has edited Violet Jessop's memoirs, suggests that the reader should regard Jessop's comments in chapter nineteen about the evils of shipboard employment and their long-term negative effect on the individual as 'a rambling diatribe' of a jaded middle-aged woman. The chapter, he explains, was written in the 1930s 'long after the earlier events and colored by a dour recapitulation of her career thus far at sea.' Margaret Meehan, one of Jessop's nieces, concurs, describing this chapter as 'one long moan' and completely uncharacteristic of her aunt whom she described as 'sweet natured'. Neither, having worked at sea, can reconcile the two Violets presented here. Indeed, they cannot understand that the two Violets are, in fact, one and the same person. Jessop's words strike a chord with many a seafarer today. Violet's love/ hate obsession with the sea is common to all seafarers, both past and present. While being seduced by the extraordinarily unique lifestyle shipboard employment promises, enabling one to live outside the norm of society, seafarers still experience a loss of the sense of the individual. The paternalism of the company and the officer caste, the restrictions placed on the individual, the extreme regimentation of the work itself have the cumulative effect of making the seafarer submissive. As Jessop writes:

They had come to accept the limitations of their life, the struggle for existence, the everlasting uncertainty, the lack of humanity and minimum of consideration most companies afforded them. Both employers and passengers exploited them, though the latter, having paid exorbitant fares, no doubt felt entitled to willing slaves, making demands they wouldn't dare on their own servants ashore.[220]

The sea, which offers the individual freedom from the conformity of life ashore, demands another kind of conformity, altogether more stifling and exacting. It is perfectly understandable that Jessop, while maintaining a 'great zest for life' and thoroughly enjoying her experience at sea, still felt the limitations and self-sacrifice that ship life entailed. These two feelings – exhilaration and confinement – seem at odds with each other but are essential to understanding the complex character of seafarers. They are a rare breed, often misunderstood. Perhaps because they do not fit comfortably into either world – at sea or on shore – their observations seem confused to us.

The lure of the sea is still a powerful force which influences some crew members to come back contract after contract. Like Violet Jessop, Dorothy Scobie and others, young men and women today sign on as entertainers, disc jockeys, cruise staff, stewards/stewardesses, and waiters 'to explore distant shores', but still for many, the 'traveling palace' becomes more of a floating jail wherein the inmates impatiently serve their sentences, anxious for the day when they will be free to leave and resume their life ashore with greater economic security.

Chapter Four

'Traveling Palace' or 'Floating Sweatshop': The Experience of Women Seafarers

A career at sea has traditionally been viewed as a male preserve. When one thinks of ships, the image conjured up is decidedly masculine, from swashbuckling pirates and big, burly, menacing stokers to Captain Ahab types. Rarely does that image include a female presence.[221] Shipboard employment was seen as unseemly and unnatural for women for all of the reasons that went into constructing the 'cult of domesticity' ideal of true womanhood in the nineteenth century. And yet, as we have seen, women were spotted on passenger liners on occasion; they constituted 4 per cent of the crew on some ships. Their presence would increase in the interwar years. What made women desire a life at sea? Was it just another job or did they see it as a means of liberation from predictable lives ashore? Did it offer upward social mobility and high adventure? Was ship life a radical departure from their world at home or did it offer continuity with that life in providing women with a safe shelter, a substitute home? Was this yet another form of 'sweated' labor – in this case, the sweatshop being a 'floating palace' on the high seas? These are some of the questions this chapter will address.

The First World War has been described as a great social leveler that brought tremendous change to the lives of Europeans, specifically in their perceptions and expectations of their place in society. Among these changes was the notion of a woman's 'proper place'. The war opened up opportunities for women in the workforce which went beyond the traditional avenues of employment. Prior to 1914, European working-class women in search of an income were generally concentrated in those fields which closely resembled domestic work – textiles, confection of ready-made clothing and alimentation. Although the variety of work remained constant, the locale in which the work was executed shifted. Work that had been performed in the home was now transferred to the factory setting. Another common occupation sought by young single women was domestic service, which was seen as an apprenticeship for marriage. With the coming of industrialization, married women were presented with a special challenge. Now that home and workplace were no longer under the same roof, they found it difficult to juggle successfully their dual responsibilities of wife/mother and co-breadwinner. Many took on piecework in the garment trades and became the 'orphans' of the industry, untouched by unionization and consigned to sweatshop-like working conditions, which Charles Kingsley and others have graphically described.[222]

Educated women of the middle class fared no better than their working-class sisters. They were forced into the role of 'angel of the house', with their exclusive role in life being an attentive wife and mother, making the house a safe haven for her husband and children – in short, the ideal Stepford wife.[223] Those women who rebelled against the cult of domesticity ideal met with adversity and condemnation from society and were labeled 'unnatural' women. People like Florence Nightingale were complete anomalies to their peers. Rather than accept the comfortable lifestyle awaiting her as a 'lady of the leisured class',

Nightingale was determined to find her own serious work and in the end paved the way for the professionalization of nursing. Other middle-class women who had not been snatched up by some dashing, eligible beau were destined to fend for themselves. As society's 'left-overs' or 'odd women' they sought employment as teachers and governesses. Others became involved in social work – not the 'lady bountiful' types castigated by Nightingale, but women committed to changing the social welfare system in their countries who became the first social case workers.

The First World War temporarily changed the status and variety of women's work. Now they began to infiltrate that masculine holy of holies – heavy industry – taking over the jobs the soldiers left behind in munitions factories and automotive plants, and working as riveters in shipbuilding and as streetcar conductors, work that before the war was deemed unsuitable for women and beyond their physical and intellectual grasp. After earlier being told 'to go home and keep quiet', a Scottish woman doctor finally persuaded the British War Office to allow her to organize fourteen hospital units staffed by women doctors by 1917.[224] Women nurses on the battlefield were both hailed as patriots for their heroism and castigated as 'bitches' for the power they appeared to exert over the mutilated, emasculated soldiers. The oft-quoted verse of Nina MacDonald captures the sense of impending doom on the part of traditionalists who feared that gender roles were being dangerously blurred and that androgyny might be the drastic result of such unorthodox behavior: 'Girls are doing things/They've never done before ... All the world is topsy-turvy/Since the War began.'[225]

Where would it all end? Happily for the traditionalists, the conventional family of husband, wife and children was reestablished after the war, and women were edged out of lucrative jobs back into traditional low-paying employment to make room for the returning veterans. Propaganda in 1919 was artfully used to bully women back into the home just as in

1914 it was used to bring them into the war effort. Posters with jingles like 'Shells made by a wife may save a husband's life', were replaced with advice to, 'Get a hold of pots and pan and broom and you'll sooner find a groom', or counseling that, 'A job will not bring happiness near. The home alone is your proper sphere!'[226] In his massive study of modern France, historian Theodore Zeldin wrote that 'the war of 1914 did not produce any radical change in female attitudes, largely because it did not make all that much difference to the women.'[227] Perhaps in the short term this might be the case, but the effects of the temporary liberation from routine domestic drudgery were to be felt for generations to come.

Women had at long last disproved the masculine construct of female physical and intellectual inferiority – a myth created in the classical and early Judeo-Christian worlds and reinforced in the eighteenth and nineteenth centuries by such noted intellectuals as Jean-Jacques Rousseau, Joseph Pierre Proudhon, Jules Michelet and others. Some women's attitudes towards work had, in fact, changed. Even among the middle and upper classes, there was a discernible perception that women had the right to fulfill themselves outside of the bounds of matrimony and motherhood. As a result, they eventually began to venture into the public sphere, armed with marketable skills gained from the possibilities presented by higher education, which was increasingly available to them. Mary Wollstonecraft's vision of an educated sisterhood was becoming a reality. However, women were going beyond Wollstonecraft's vision of the educated mother able to teach her children. There were no longer attempts to justify higher education for women. As Carrie Chapman Catt had once remarked about suffrage, she didn't know what it was, a right, a duty, or a privilege, but that 'whatever it is, the women want it'.[228]

No longer would women mask their desire for self-fulfillment through education by the argument that an educated woman made a better mother. They sought an education to become better individuals. Thus we see the creation of the 'new woman' of the 1920s – the androgynous flapper who ventured into bars and cabarets once thought taboo for 'proper' women.[229] Women infiltrated the hallowed halls of such male bastions of higher education like Oxford and Cambridge. Women began to limit the size of their families by use of birth control and engaged in free unions with men. These actions were seen as assaults on the nuclear family. Freud's sexual revolution opened up the discussion of a woman's right to expect gratification as an active participant in sex rather than as a docile receptacle of a man's desires. Women actively sought employment in the public sector. In many countries, women gained the right to vote. Traditional society was nonplussed and saw nothing good coming from these changes and agreed with Oswald Spengler's pre-war forecast that Western civilization was in decline.

Were their fears justified? Now that women had begun to assert themselves, was the patriarchal world, as it was known, coming to an end? The short answer to the question is 'yes', but change would come about gradually. In countries like France, which had a strong women's movement in the nineteenth century, suffrage was granted only in 1944. Traditions die hard. The campaign for women's rights, launched in earnest in the nineteenth century, is still going on two centuries later and in some areas of the world may require another two centuries to be won. The interwar years were crucial ones for Western women's self-development. Many shared Nora Helmer's need to educate herself and recognized that there were duties 'just as sacred' as motherhood – a duty to one's self.[230] Nevertheless, society was still caught between the traditional ideal of 'true womanhood' and the modern concept of the 'new woman'. Though pioneers were breaking new ground, the majority of women continued to observe the dictates imposed upon them by patriarchal society.

Here, we look at this transformation from 'odd' to 'new' woman in the experiences of women seafarers in the interwar years. Since the eighteenth century, women found employment on transatlantic steamers, mainly in the catering department – as stewardesses, conductresses, shop assistants, bath attendants and hairdressers.[231] In steamers carrying laundries on board, women were hired to fill such low-paying jobs. Most of the work women did on board ships corresponded to the traditional occupations of women on shore – domestic service. However, the locale they chose to pursue this variation of otherwise traditional domestic work was a ship on the high seas.

This investigation builds on an earlier study of women engaged in sweated labor in the Parisian garment industry in the late nineteenth and early twentieth centuries.[232] Like the homeworkers in the Parisian garment trades, ships' crew members formed still another hidden labor force, left largely unprotected from company economic exploitation. The writer George Gissing noted that in Victorian society there were more than 500,000 superfluous women destined to be left alone to support themselves for lack of a husband – the so-called 'odd women'. Many of the women joining a ship's crew would fall into this category: the average profile of a stewardess in the early twentieth century was a middle-aged single or widowed 'odd' woman. The latter group, the 'company widows', were left destitute by the death of their husbands and had no other means of survival, and often no other recourse but to send their children away to convents. As there was no financial compensation given to widows whose husbands had died in service, the shipping company provided them with a safe shelter as well as a job on board one of their liners. One notable exception to the 'odd woman' rule was Violet Jessop, the famous *Titanic* and *Britannic* survivor who joined Royal Mail Line's West Indian service in 1908 at the age of twenty-one and spent the next forty-two years at sea.[233] Her mother, a 'company widow', worked as a stewardess for a time but had to resign because of frail health. Violet interrupted her studies and assumed the role of principal breadwinner. During her interview, she was warned of the pitfalls of sea life for a woman – especially an attractive young woman. The warning issued from a mix of paternalism and self-interest: the righteous bureaucrats of the shipping lines feared that the stokers and mates would be too easily distracted in their work by the presence of a young woman who would most certainly lose her virginity in the face of such temptation.

By the 1920s, as hemlines rose and women started doing daring things once frowned upon in polite society, the complexion of female personnel on board began to change. Younger women were now joining the ranks of stewardesses, conductresses and so on. Besides, by this time, those menacing stokers had left the scene! Ship life was attracting even middle-class women who chose a life at sea. Their decisiveness stood in contrast to the 'company widows' who continued to depend on the paternalism of the steamship company and resigned themselves to a life at sea as a means of survival.

Here we get a glimpse of the 'new woman' of the modern age who defied convention and went to sea not only out of financial necessity but increasingly by choice, lured by the prospect of independence and the possibility of seeing the world, to be the maker of her own destiny instead of assuming the expected role of 'angel of the house' or 'lady bountiful'. The oral histories of these women are rich in detail and reveal a complex subculture that existed 'below the decks' on the passenger liners of the interwar years. For some women, ship life continued to provide a means of economic security, but for many others, it became a passport to liberation:

I had a youthful dream of Empire – that British Empire
on which the sun would never set! Or so we thought.
I wished to see the wide, open spaces in our Dominions

beyond the seas which offered great opportunities to those with a spirit of adventure.[234]

Edith Sowerbutts represents one such 'new woman' who was lured by the sea's promise of distant shores and was ready for 'adventure and pastures new.'[235] Born into a working-class background and raised in a single-parent household, Edith learned very early on that she had to rely on herself. Although she completed commercial college, she was more drawn to social work and spent several years in Australia working for the Commonwealth Migration and Settlement Office before joining Red Star/White Star Line in 1925 at age twenty-nine. She worked both as a conductress and stewardess for the ships of White Star Line and Cunard Line and spent twelve years at sea. Hers is the typical story of women seafarers in the interwar years.

Prior to joining Cunard-White Star Line as a stewardess at age twenty-five in 1937, Liverpudlian Dorothy Scobie had hotel experience and, like Sowerbutts, came from a working-class family with dreams of a life of adventure on the high seas.[236] It was on the great passenger liners that she made her home for the next twenty-three years. She was lured by the call of the sea from a very early age, as she explains:

> As a small girl I had often accompanied my mother on her visits to the office high up in the Cunard building on the waterfront. In the vast corridors I would gaze in wonder at the models in their glass showcases. I seem to have been, all my life, deeply stirred by the sea and men who sail on it. The glamorous trade of merchant shipping for what colour and life it conjours up of past history and glory.[237]

Sowerbutts and Scobie were young women in their twenties who sought out a life at sea not only for financial security but also for the adventure it promised. Shipboard employment

133

was very competitive as indicated both by the many letters companies received and inquiries in women's magazines asking for advice about how to apply for a post on board. Many shipping companies employed a 'lady superintendent' to oversee the placement of female personnel on board their steamships. Oftentimes, people made direct appeals for work to the chairman or company secretary. Cunard files include many employment enquiries made by women or by male relatives speaking on their behalf. One man sought to secure a stewardess position for his sister as her husband was killed during the war while in the company's service. Another recommended his sister to the company on the basis of his family's long association with Cunard Line. His father worked for more than twenty years at sea. After his death, the company found a position for his mother, which she held for fourteen years. His sister, who had earlier given five years of service to the company, wished to return in 1922 as the brother could no longer bear the financial burden of the family. Women often spoke up for themselves. One war widow, age twenty-eight, described herself as 'thoroughly domesticated and energetic' for shipboard employment.[238]

The chairman received one request in September 1929 from a 'company widow' whose husband had died at sea the previous year. After the lady superintendent rejected her application, she took the liberty of writing directly to Percy Bates. She appealed to Bates' sense of company loyalty explaining that her husband had served Cunard faithfully for twenty years. Learning that her neighbor recently secured a position without having any family connection with Cunard, the woman complained that she, as a 'company widow' should be given first preference, especially since she had two children to support. She had already written to Bates in 1920 on behalf of her husband who sailed as chef on the *Carmania* during the seamen's strike and was later not permitted to sign on for the next voyage. Her husband had also sailed on a ship that was torpedoed in 1917. In the end, Bates upheld the decision of Mrs Hatfield, the lady superintendent, who believed that the woman was not suited for the position of stewardess or bath attendant and added that her husband 'was tolerated' only![239]

As early as 1904, company guidelines stressed that stewardesses must be physically up to the challenge and that preference would be given to those with hotel experience.[240] Women remained a tiny fraction of the crew of passenger liners through the 1930s. For example, French Lines' premiere ship *Normandie* employed twenty-five stewardesses and 686 stewards in 1935, and White Star Lines' *Olympic* carried twenty-four stewardesses and 562 stewards.[241]

In their publicity brochures, shipping companies spoke of their staffs as highly trained professionals whose families had a long maritime history. A Cunard-White Star Line promotional brochure for the Queen Mary speaks about adherence to a 'British Tradition':

> The way the stewardess lays out milady's clothes for dinner is an instance of it ... well might she be an old retainer in a British manor home. The mother, father and grandfather of the stewardess have, in all probability, all served in the Cunard-White Star Line ... and think how much more welcome will be that forenoon cup of hot bouillon, when it is served by a steward who regards this service as a life-long career.[242]

This, in fact, was Kathleen Smith's orientation to a life at sea. Although she was not excited by the prospect when she took a job with Cunard in 1937, she was continuing a long family tradition – her father and uncles had all gone to sea. She would follow in their footsteps and make the ships her home for the next thirty years.[243]

A TRANSAT brochure praises its crew as being 'the soul of a ship'. Among female personnel featured were the stewardess and governess-nurse, who were described as integral members of the crew. In addition to the stewardess's many fine attributes – 'discriminating', 'feminine', 'courteous' and 'efficient' – the stewardess also 'possesses the valuable quality of human understanding', allowing her to assume the role of confidante and amateur psychiatrist to 'Madame' as well. (See Figure 11.) The governess-nurse was hailed as the 'most important member of each shipboard personnel' and the ideal 'little mother'. In addition to her 'sweet and understanding nature', which made her popular with the children, she was also a linguist who could converse with youngsters of many nationalities.[244] Such stereotypes reflect the mentality of the age, which the women used to their advantage.

The stewardess was becoming a more respected member of the ship's crew even before the First World War. In 1913, R. A. Fletcher wrote that there was

> a decided change for the better from the incompetent and lazy stewardess so common at one time, whose sole idea was to collect tips and do a minimum of service in return, to the clean energetic stewardess of the modern liner who takes charge of the weary travelers and makes them as comfortable as she can even in the democratic third class.[245]

As stewardesses catered exclusively to the needs of female passengers traveling alone, stewards looked after cabins occupied by married couples.[246] While stewardesses on British liners served all classes, French ships appear to have carried *femmes de chambre* only in First and Second Class.[247] An article in the TRANSAT publicity magazine, *Gangplank*, 'Why Women Choose The French Line', speaks of the pampered service a female passenger receives at the hands of the *femme de chambre*, whose sole *raison d'être* is 'to make her passage a happy present and future joyful memory.'[248]

Other opportunities for women on board passenger liners included hairdressers, shop girls, bath attendants and laundresses (on ships carrying laundries), but the majority were employed as stewardesses and/or nurses. Because nursing paid poorly on shore, many nurses took jobs at sea as stewardesses. In fact, the policy of Union Castle Line was to recruit only nurses as stewardesses on its South African run.[249]

A wage differential existed between male and female stewards aboard French liners, but British stewards and stewardesses earned roughly the same.[250] Roydon Freeman comments that on large luxury liners in 1930, women serving First Class passengers could earn up to £20 ($100) in tips per month.[251] Given the fragile economic state of many European countries at the time, this was a considerable wage, and crew members felt themselves to be part of a privileged class. Not all seafarers were so lucky, however. At the 1930 Annual General Meeting of the National Union of Seamen, General Secretary Robert Spence reported that there were 20,000 unemployed seafarers. By 1932, that number doubled as the full effects of the Depression were felt.[252]

Once a woman had secured a position at sea, what was she to expect? Stewardesses' responsibilities extended far beyond what Cunard Line's company guidelines indicated. According to the 1904 regulations, stewardesses were to be occupied with the care of women and children exclusively, and would be able to enjoy leisure time when the ship was in port and the passengers were off on tours as 'no cleaning is required ... very little work is done.' That promise never matched the reality, and in time, the promises changed. The Cunard Line *Rule Book for Crew* in 1913 stipulated that 'when the ship is lying at any foreign port, the stewardesses are to be constantly employed, and every opportunity must be taken by them to keep the ship's linen in order.'[253] To be sure, very few stewardesses ever found themselves in the position of having too much time on their hands and, as Freeman observed, although women took jobs 'to see something of the world', very few were allowed to go ashore at foreign ports.[254] One stewardess whom Jo Stanley interviewed commented that there was 'no freedom at all. You'd never even think to just go off and spend the night off the ship.'[255] Stewardess Anne Smith's experience on the *Laconia*'s world cruise (1922/23) was very different from passenger Joel Burdick's, whose account describes many exotic and enticing foreign ports. She was not permitted to go ashore in places where the ship had to use tender service, which was reserved exclusively for the use of passengers. 'One gets positively fed up with being stowed on board so long altogether,' she complained. Though ship life was far from being 'rosy and fair' for her, she concedes that 'hardly anyone's life is that so must not grumble and on the whole I must be pretty lucky.'[256]

Most transatlantic steamers did not carry laundries on board. Only on special cruises would TRANSAT install a portable laundry for the duration of the voyage for the convenience of passengers. As early as the 1930s, French Line pursers made repeated appeals to the company to install a permanent facility on board. Until then, passenger laundry, when not done by local women while the ship was in a foreign port, was left to the *femme de chambre*, who received little in the way of financial compensation for her effort. Smaller vessels, like the *Cuba* and the *Colombie*, carried only two stewardesses on board, and they were too busy with routine duties to handle the added burden of passenger laundry.[257] Nevertheless, as the *Cuba*'s purser reported, to keep passengers happy one *femme de chambre* was given charge of all the washing and ironing of passenger laundry. Out of necessity, she paid a sailor 5 francs to do the washing while she was left with the task of pressing. To avoid disappointing the passenger, the *femme de chambre* was thus obliged to work overtime, in addition to her normal overtime hours. *Ile de France* purser Roger A. Raulin, noted the great success of the temporary laundry installed on board for the Easter Caribbean cruise of 1938. With a staff of eight, the ship's laundry needs were met at a substantial financial savings to the company. Raulin recommended the permanent installation of a laundry on board, which could be run by a relatively small number of laundresses – a small financial investment which would yield great returns to TRANSAT.[258]

Passengers were often very demanding. Anne Smith once had nine passengers in her charge and resented the 'one old lady still in bed' who kept her 'hanging around' the ship all day, preventing her from going ashore in Naples to see Vesuvius.[259] Exacting passengers often rewarded stewardesses for their service with souvenirs from excursions ashore. Rose Stott, who served aboard the 1923 *Samaria* world cruise spoke of a gift from 'one of my ladies'. As she could not get ashore in Calcutta herself, a lady passenger brought her a small figurine of an Indian woman watercarrier.[260] Violet Jessop initially did not have a very complementary view of American travelers and wrote that intermixed with their 'subtle ingenuity and good nature is a streak of selfishness'. She was to learn firsthand that people are not often what they seem. Far too often had she 'trudged on aching feet and nerve-racked back up and down stairs ... sweltering in unbelievable heat, to satisfy the gastronomic exactitude of some noted woman.' Although described by the press as 'an angel of benevolence', the passenger 'never hesitated to demand of me what she wanted, no matter how her request upset my daily routine, and in spite of the fact that she liked me' and declared to all that Violet 'was so sweet'. One woman, who expressed concern that Violet looked exhausted and urged that she take a rest, added: 'Before you go, I know you will leave me some cracked ice and some sandwiches in my room, and, oh yes, some oranges too.' Violet concluded, however, that the 'one thing that I had to keep reminding myself of was the fact that I should not be needed in my job if she and her kind did not travel', and she later acknowledged that generally, Americans, 'however exacting, do consider you a person first, rather than a servant, and that makes a world of difference.'[261]

Passenger appreciation was often expressed by letters the companies received praising the service rendered by particular crew members: 'We, the undersigned, ... are indebted to Mrs Davies ... for a very large share of the comfort we have experienced while we have been onboard ... She has done a great deal beyond her own particular duties to contribute to our comfort ... and [we] wish to place ... our appreciation of her services.'[262]

As shipboard personnel were expected to project the proper image of the company to the passengers, much care and attention was given to the seafarer's appearance. Standard uniforms were worn by crew which differed according to rank, season, and the class of ship on which one sailed. Black shoes and stockings were to be worn by female staff regardless of the season. No jewelery was permitted and skirts had to be no more than 8 inches from the ground.[263] Cunard Line and White Star Line made no provision for uniforms. This often turned out to be a great obstacle to those seeking employment on board the passenger liners as a large expenditure was required before a crew member actually set sail. As job security did not exist on the high seas, there was no guarantee that a person would be signed on for the next voyage. French Line was more generous with its employees in this regard. Each seafarer had a *carte d'habillement* which recorded uniform requests. Application for new clothes was submitted to the secretary of the chief maitre d'hôtel for approval.[264]

Throughout the 1920s, new opportunities that carried more prestige than the position of stewardess became available for women. Edith Sowerbutts credits the lady supervisor for female seagoing personnel of Canadian Pacific Line, Mrs Andrews, as being 'a woman ahead of her time', who took the lead in 1925 to introduce female stenographers to the purser's office.[265] In fact, as early as 1924 Cunard Line's *Scythia* included mention of a typist on board, a Ms Woodworth, and in 1926, a Ms Harrison, (formerly a typist on the *Carmania*), held the position of junior assistant purser – Grade J on the *Berengaria*. By the late 1920s, typists were typically listed in the 'miscellaneous' column. Since such women were clearly breaking new ground and remained outside of the traditional crew structure, no one knew where to place them on the crew manifest. [266] By 1932, Cunard Line advertisements for the *Aquitania*'s cruises to the Mediterranean boasted that 'a thoroughly experienced Lady Stenographer and Typist is carried on the steamer', a particular selling point for passengers who sought to combine business with pleasure.[267] In her memoirs, Sowerbutts describes herself and other female seafarers as pioneers: 'We, of my generation, comprised the thin edge of the wedge. Women would eventually be signed on for seagoing positions once considered to be male preserves.'[268]

On particular chartered cruises, a cruise staff which included a social directress, an assistant social directress and a bridge instructress (all of whom enjoyed passenger status), would be brought on board. Such was the case with the 1937 *Franconia* North Cape–Russia cruise planned by the American company, Raymond Whitcomb.[269] Cruise staff, in fact, were seen as a selling point for Cunard-White Star 'pleasure cruises'. A publicity brochure, 'Introducing the Staffs', announced the cruise staff for the upcoming 1938 season. Among the 'Charming Social Directresses' introduced were Miss Dorothy Mason, a former dance and drama teacher at Cornell University, and Mrs George Hawley, a graduate of Mount Holyoke College and prominent in Detroit social circles. Mrs Edna J. Weeks, billed as a 'bridge expert' on the *Georgic* cruise season, was a noted bridge teacher at a time when women experts on the game were 'practically non-existent'.[270] (See Figure 12.)

Clearly 'new' women were emerging on the passenger liners in the interwar years. Evidence suggests that male crew were not totally supportive of their female colleagues and were, in fact, even threatened by each advance they made. In a voyage report of the *Normandie* crossing dated 7 June 1937, Captain Pierre Thoreux noted a conflict with the beauty salon personnel who threatened to go on strike in protest of the replacement of the head coiffeur with a woman.[271]

A position which brought much more prestige and status (but less money than the position of stewardess) was that of conductress. Mr Mitchell, personnel officer for the International Mercantile Marine Company, made it perfectly clear to Edith Sowerbutts that he would not tolerate a woman being promoted to the rank of officer on board.[272] His objections, however, were silenced by the Canadian government, which insisted that all female immigrants be supervised by a female officer at the expense of the steamship company. That officer was a conductress, a new position that carried privileged officer status. As a conductress, Sowerbutts was entrusted with the welfare of unaccompanied women immigrating to Canada.[273] Her prior experience working with the Commonwealth Migration and Settlement Office in Australia made her especially suited for this position.

When Sowerbutts joined Red Star Line's *Zeeland* in 1925 (run by White Star Line and owned by the International Mercantile Marine Company of New York), she was given passenger status and was not required to wear a uniform. She enjoyed an idyllic life, dining and sipping champagne with passengers and playing bridge and deck tennis with them in the afternoons. Her name appeared on the Cabin Class passenger list with a notice informing passengers that she was on board for the benefit of all ladies traveling alone. Conductresses reported to the purser on board. Their job description included interviewing and listing all unaccompanied women who were resettling in Canada. Canadian immigration authorities insisted that all ships carrying immigrants from Europe have in their employ permanent welfare officers. Most of the immigrants were single women, but some with children were joining their husbands in Canada, and all 'seemed both surprised and delighted to see another woman dealing with them.'[274] Conductresses often found that children traveling alone were placed in their charge. Shipping companies sought to assure parents that they could 'put a girl in the care of a Conductress at the start, and at the finish you may collect her with as much confidence as you yielded up the charge of her. The danger is that the young lady will have been so well looked after, that she will be reluctant to return to ordinary control.'[275] In the end, however, this might have proved problematic to her perspective employer in Canada, who was expecting a docile domestic servant.

Among her varied responsibilities, Sowerbutts helped the ship's doctor during his medical checks for all women and children in Third Class since Red Star Line ships did not carry female nurses on board until the 1930s. In her capacity as conductress, Sowerbutts looked after many foreign unaccompanied women including Poles, Ukrainians, Yugoslavs, Greeks, Italians, Romanians and Germans. Many young women from south and central Europe were recruited for domestic service in Canada. There was, unfortunately, a great deal of racial and social prejudice against these women, even on the part of the crew. Sowerbutts recalls a Third Class Belgian chief steward's remark that 'They're only Polaks,' when she objected to having two women share a shower. The officer dismissed Sowerbutts as 'half-witted' although well-intentioned 'to regard those emigrant girls as ordinary, decent human beings entitled to good standards.'[276] To this officer, such women were examples of the *untermenschen* that Hitler's Nazis would later vow to exterminate.

Edith was not a typical conductress, most of whom were elderly and motherly women who sought out this position because it was considered an easy job. Restless with too much time on her hands, Sowerbutts took on extra work: 'I have often in my long life been accused of having too much energy, mainly by male colleagues.'[277] Because she was able to type, she assumed responsibility for the ship's daily newspaper. In her leisure time, Sowerbutts helped the purser, who was in charge of the social program, organize deck tournaments and sports events. She also served as 'captain's hostess', as no social hostesses were employed on the transatlantic passenger liners at the time. Edith even passed the necessary examination to get certified as a 'lifeboat man' and was able to launch a lifeboat in an 'abandon ship' situation. She was the third woman to gain a 'lifeboat ticket'. When she began her career at sea, Sowerbutts admits, 'I was in love with life. I still had stars in my eyes ... I didn't realize it at the time, but I was about to crash against one of the bastions of well-entrenched masculinity – for the sea was still predominantly a man's world, and still is.'[278]

Although her base salary paid more than that of a stewardess, £12 per month, she received no tips from her immigrant charges and, therefore, found herself broke at the beginning of each new voyage: 'I liked to spend, needed clothes and enjoyed life in port ... such is youth.'[279] With the Depression came the end of Canada's 'open door' policy on European immigration. Ship's conductresses' services were dispensed with as soon as their ships arrived at the home port. Sowerbutts finally secured another position at sea in 1934 when she joined Cunard-White Star's *Olympic* as a stewardess. Her sister, Dorothy, had begun service in 1927. 'We were glad of our seagoing employment, my sister and I,' Edith says. 'We had never in all our lives seen so much money, nor had we been able to spend so freely.'[280] While the money was good, Sowerbutts admits that she never worked so physically hard in her life as she had during the next five years in service at sea as a stewardess, commonly putting in 13-hour days.

After the merger of Cunard and White Star lines in 1934, there was often friction between the two crews, who now had to work together and resented the extra responsibilities they were made to assume. On Cunard Line ships, stewardesses always handled chamber pots, a practice that appalled White Star's female crew. The phrase 'Cunard chambermaids, White Star ladies' was coined at the time of the merger. Cunard insisted that its stewardesses wait on all ladies. It had always been customary for White Star stewards to take charge of cabins of married couples unless the wife expressly requested a stewardess. After 1934, Cunard rules were to apply, which meant extra work for the former White Star stewardesses, much to their dismay.

Shipboard employment for female crew members offered few advancement possibilities. Stewardesses on British liners started in Third Class and advanced their way into First Class cabins. While this might afford a boost in status, the base salary remained the same. The difference was in the tips, but there was never a guarantee that First Class passengers would be overly generous. Many commented that royals were worst in this regard. The general perception was that Americans, to quote stewardess Kathleen Smith, 'were worth going for.'[281] Many crew members' oral histories reveal a common concern: lack of job security. When one signed off, there was no guarantee that you would be reassigned to the same ship. Everyone sought the larger transatlantic liners, like the *Queen Mary*, which was known to be 'a good money maker'.[282]

Cunard Line offered its female crew one possibility of advancement with the introduction of the position of 'leading stewardess' on all their ships, a 'leading lady' who was responsible for all female staff at sea, and who had the privileged position of taking care of First Class lady passengers. There were 'perks' other than financial compensation that came with being assigned to First Class cabins – such as good food secured from the pantryman who was tipped handsomely for his service.

Another coveted position that carried added incentives with it was that of 'special stewardess'. Cunard introduced a special rate of £20 ($100) for a passenger to engage a personal steward or stewardess for the duration of the voyage.[283] Cunard saw this primarily as a public relations strategy, and in a memo to pursers in 1931, the general manager advised that 'while every effort will be made to collect on the above basis respecting the service of a special stewardess, it may be found necessary, at times, to accept a slightly lower figure rather than lose the business.'[284] In this manner, stewardesses came into contact with a number of celebrities. One 'special stewardess', Nora Roberts, was assigned to the Duke of

Windsor and Mrs Simpson aboard the *Queen Mary* as well as to Greta Garbo, who presented her with a doll in appreciation of her service at the conclusion the voyage.[285] Delia Callaghan, who worked at sea for thirty-five years as a stewardess, acted as a decoy on the *Queen Mary* for the nanny of the Lindbergh baby. Her friend was entrusted with the safekeeping of James Mason's Oscar.[286] Kathleen Smith, whose career at sea totaled thirty years, kept an autograph book of First Class passengers whom she served including celebrities like James Stewart and Rita Hayworth, and commented that the Duke and Duchess of Windsor were 'exceptionally nice'.[287] Violet Jessop spoke fondly of her acquaintance with Anatole France 'who told me he was on a brain holiday. His magnetism and two-edged humor made it always a pleasure to pass the time of day with him; he would remind me that it was good for my French to talk with him.'[288]

In interviewing numerous stewardesses who sailed on British liners in the interwar years, Jo Stanley concludes that these women regarded themselves as very much superior to ordinary crew members and that

> these stewardesses saw their passengers as ladies and themselves as ladies. There is a sense that stewardesses were determined to believe that they were every bit as good as their passengers – even though they belonged to the group who mopped up the products of seasickness.

In reality, however, stewardesses inhabited a vastly different world from the 'ladies' whom they looked after, and as Stanley correctly observes, 'stewardesses were really pushed to find enough time in the day, whereas the passengers' chief interest in time was to kill it.'[289]

On board a ship, bonds of friendship develop much more quickly, with greater intensity than on shore. Stewardesses often became confidantes and friends to their female passengers, an artificial friendship usually restricted to the duration of the voyage. Violet Jessop recalls one passenger with whom she believed she had formed a close bond who 'clung to me during the entire voyage while she recovered from a personal calamity, glad of my sympathy and understanding.' The woman invited Jessop to visit her in New York: 'She could never, she said, do enough for me in return for the long hours of my off-duty time which I had spent at her side, or for the moral support I had given her.' As the woman left the ship looking 'full of poise', she chatted with 'some equally elegant women of her set'. Violet could hardly believe that the 'intimate and soul-revealing talks had taken place at all between them'. Months later, Violet decided to take the woman at her word and visited her at her hotel in New York. The woman had no clue as to who this person was who had appeared on her doorstep: 'In a flash, I saw that she had completely forgotten me,' and though she attempted to make Violet feel welcome among her guests, 'I knew she had not the faintest idea who I was.'[290] On board ship, social barriers dissolved when this New York socialite needed Violet to get through a personal crisis. Back in New York, however, the social distance between the stewardess and the socialite was reestablished and Violet understood then that the two could never be friends, as they inhabited vastly different worlds.

Despite Jessop's cynicism about friendships with passengers, lasting attachments were formed on board ship. Edith Sowerbutts recalls how the pianist, Dame Myra Hess, became genuinely fond of Janet Austin, her stewardess on board the *Queen Mary*. Upon her retirement from Cunard Line, Ms Austin went to live with Dame Myra, who had made a small apartment for her in her home, 'thus ensuring a continuation of their friendship', and of her services, no doubt. Several shipmates, she notes, were remembered generously in the wills of wealthy passengers.[291]

Generally, female seafarers enjoyed better accommodations than their male colleagues, usually sharing a cabin with one other woman rather than bunking in a 'glory hole' with thirty-plus crew members. However, there were great restrictions on their freedom. They had very little public space to call their own. They inhabited a largely enclosed world 'below the decks' and were not allowed in passenger space except when cleaning cabins. Even in crew quarters, space was limited. Since crew bars like the famous Pig & Whistle were off limits to female seafarers, the women did most of their socializing in their tiny cabins. The chief diversion of stewardesses whose day began at 7 a.m. and ended only at 10 p.m., notes Kathleen Smith, was to sleep when off duty. With no days off while the ship was at sea, the best one could hope for was 2 or 3 hours free in port.[292] Privileged governesses/nurses had meals in the passenger dining room, but only with the children. Very little fraternization between male and female crew ever occurred as each had their separate mess. Still, stewardesses, who were often skilled nurses or trained teachers, had high social aspirations, and preferred to socialize with the officers rather than the ordinary crew.

Stanley refers to a sisterhood that was sometimes formed on board ships between female seafarers who would look out for each other, helping a fellow mate through an ordeal such as sexual harassment, covering up for an addicted stewardess's alcoholism, and in one instance procuring an abortion for a friend in trouble. And yet there is evidence also of bad blood between some women. Mme Talbot, *femme de chambre* on the *Champlain*, in June 1938 made a formal complaint against her roommate, Mme Rivoal, whom she charged with stealing a winning lottery ticket from her purse which was left in the cabin. She also cited an earlier instance when Mme Rivoal stole 200 francs from her pocketbook.[293] Stanley comments that while women seafarers could be viewed as a group/company, they were individuals with different attitudes to the job and 'were more united in other peoples' eyes than in the stewardess's subjective experience.'[294] In fact, women often found themselves competing with each other for a higher status position. One angry woman wrote to Cunard's general secretary, Thomas Royden, that the lady superintendent demoted her to Steerage Class because she had complained that less capable women with less seniority were being promoted to Cabin Class. 'I can see that influence is everything,' she wrote, 'even for a stewardess and those who have no need to go to sea at all such as sea captains' daughters with fathers [who] get the promotions.'[295] Even among the crew, within the ranks of the stewardesses, a rigid social hierarchy was firmly in place.

Unions admitted women but were not overly enthusiastic about their competing for jobs with male seafarers. The first union to recruit women nationally was Joe Cotter's Liverpool-based Cooks and Stewards' Union, founded in 1909. Since unions primarily represented the interests of male workers, women interlopers were not taken seriously. Experiences were parallel on shore, where unions also generally excluded or were indifferent to women. Time often ran out at meetings when women had anything to say. Although the men pressed for equal pay for women in the catering department, they gave only lukewarm support to female colleagues. Dorothy Scobie was soured by the National Union of Seamen, which, she said 'didn't do us any good', and she complained that there were no special representatives for women. Although women were made to sign on as members, Scobie felt that the NUS was not pro-women's rights, that it was designed specifically for men, and that its chief interest was in collecting dues.[296] Delia Callaghan's experience on board the *Queen Mary* in 1938 was somewhat different. She received two weeks' vacation for which she credits the union that 'stood up for us then'.[297] And yet, after thirty-five years of service at sea, Callaghan never received a pension from Cunard-White Star Line and had no one to argue her case, even though the Royal Seamen's Pension Fund claimed that women workers were eligible after fifteen years of service.

Sailing without contracts, crew members had to 'sign on' after each voyage. This gave the officers, who made such determinations, extraordinary and sometimes sinister power over the crew. Participation in strikes often met with immediate dismissal. In the blacklists of crew members kept by TRANSAT following a major strike in November/December 1938 are found the names of several *femmes de chambre* and nurses, the two important positions that French Line brochures earlier had boasted of as being 'the soul of the ship'. These women abandoned their posts on the *Paris*, *Ile de France*, *Champlain*, and *Normandie* in an act of solidarity with the male crew. Like many of their male colleagues, they received letters from French Line dismissing them. One *femme de chambre* on board the *Ile de France*, Henriette Smeyers, was singled out among the women in an officer's report as 'an agitator and promoter of disorder' – in short, an anarchist![298]

Some female crew members were in a particularly vulnerable position when faced with an officer who sought to exert his power by making unwanted sexual advances. Sexual harassment was not recognized as such by company officials, and the officer's word always carried more weight than that of the female crew member. Violet Jessop describes one such experience with a new captain on the Royal Mail Line who was considered a philanderer and who made sexual overtures to her. Jessop understood her superior's power over her and knew that 'because of his position, much that he did was ignored.' To make matters worse, his wife was a shareholder in the company. When Jessop disregarded notes and chocolates left in her cabin and rejected his advances, the captain began to find fault with her work and made her life difficult. In another incident, the purser came into her cabin one night while she was recovering from malaria: 'I lay awhile marveling at these men. The effrontery of them! The captain, the purser, many others who had positions to maintain, groveling and sniveling like dogs. Yet they would be my judges, should I or the likes of me make one false step on board; in their power lay our very existence. I was revolted.' She concluded that 'sea life was not the setting for a normal woman, however it might afford her a living. Assuming she was normal, it would be a terrible strain on her to remain so, and keep her personality.'[299]

Shipping companies strictly regulated women's workplace behavior and were quick to terminate the services of stewardesses whose conduct was considered 'unseemly' for women. Under that category fell insobriety, sexual 'misconduct', and disobedience or rudeness to passengers. Termination of service because of 'illness' sometimes implied that a woman did not have the right sort of temperament suited to a competitive, stressful workplace. This, in fact, was the reason given for Ms Emily Coleman's departure from Cunard in 1929. Having worked as a Third Class matron for nearly two years on board the *Antonia* and *Lancastria* and as a nurse in 1926 on the latter ship, she was now judged to be 'too temperamental' by the surgeon. Her letter to the chairman of the board further indicates that Cunard thought her too demanding and believed that she had threatened to resign. As a result, they decided to replace her. She denied these allegations and asked to be reinstated. In a memo to the chairman, the lady superintendent, Mrs Hatfield, acknowledged that Coleman 'was a conscientious worker' but said that she was not suited for life at sea and that the surgeon wanted no part of her. End of story![300]

A similar predicament befell Mary B. McNaught, a trained nurse who made one trip as matron of the *Aquitania* in 1926 when she came up against a male supervisor. The night before landing, the chief steward gave her a dressing down for committing a series of infractions against ship's policy – an accusation which she vehemently denied. He cast aspersions on her moral character, charging her with having 'visitors' in her cabin and frequenting the cabins of men. When she appealed to the staff captain to intervene, the chief steward 'suddenly discovered that my work was not satisfactory.' She wrote to the people at the head office, she said, to make them aware of the harassment to which women crew members were subject by their male overlords and requested to be reinstated on board the *Aquitania* 'if only to prove Mr Powell's insults groundless.' Rather than hold the chief steward accountable for his inappropriate conduct, the company chose to find another position for her.[301]

In the Peninsular and Oriental Steam Navigation Company Stewards Registers for the interwar years are found similar cases of such women, like thirty-two-year-old stewardess Mrs Edith Holdstock, who, although given a 'very good' for conduct, was termed 'unfit for the Company's service' by the chief steward. In passing this judgment, he cited the doctor's report describing Holdstock as having a 'neurotic temperament aggravated no doubt by a recent operation performed a few months before joining the Company' and, therefore, judged unable to perform her shipboard duties. Another P&O stewardess, Mrs Mabel Evans, aged thirty-nine, was dismissed on the grounds of being 'very hysterical, bad tempered, not amenable to discipline.' In short, her services 'were not required here.'[302] In each of these cases and in countless others, there is no record of union intervention on behalf of any of these women. All simply had their services dispensed with and were cast aside with no further comment.

Mme Planteau du Maroussem, nurse on board the *Normandie*, was denied a promotion in 1936 despite recommendations from both the seamen's union and the doctor. The request, which would have given her officer rank and an increase in salary, was denied on the grounds that Mme du Maroussem was 'incompetent', although she was acknowledged on board as a first-rate professional nurse.[303]

Ship life for crew was far from the glamorous picture painted in company advertisements and promotional brochures or concocted in the imagination of working-class women who sought shipboard employment as a means of expanding their horizons. As Sowerbutts discovered, behind the romantic ideal lay a reality of hard work that required daily sacrifice. Yet many made a career at sea if afforded the opportunity. Two considerations weighed heavily in their decision to go to sea: economic earning potential and the ability to explore 'distant shores'. As Sowerbutts writes: 'Most of us had one main interest: keeping our jobs, earning good money, looking after home commitments. We thought it an impertinence for anyone to enquire about our private lives, our behaviour ashore,' as lady superintendents did.[304] Since female seafarers had little opportunity for a social life on board, they took advantage of shore leave, as in the case of Delia Callaghan and her mates, who would go out for a meal, or catch a film at Radio City whenever the ship was in New York.[305]

From the memoirs of Sowerbutts, Jessop and others, we see a decidedly 'new woman' emerging on the passenger liners of the interwar years – a self-sufficient, independent individual who was on her own with no male protector. Despite the rigorous work schedule, many women ventured off the ship during their free time in port and were intellectually curious and insightful observers of the many cultures and peoples they encountered. Sowerbutts speaks of the café life in Antwerp, Brussels and Paris and about her fascination with New York and the opera: 'I was accustomed to getting around by myself, and well able to look after myself too,' she proudly states.[306] Jessop was excited by the prospect of her first world cruise: 'All those places that from childhood I had longed to see, Japan, China, Siam, Java, represented history, mystery and love.'[307] Though some women were clearly interested in shopping and sipping tropical drinks on Caribbean beaches (a sharp contrast to the grim reality of life in Liverpool during the Depression), others were true adventurers, exploring the local culture and history.[308] On the *Laconia* world cruise (1922/23), Anne Smith and two female companions were so struck by Honolulu – 'the most beautiful place I have ever seen' – that they nearly missed the ship and 'one woman did have to climb up a rope ladder.' Smith lamented the fact that she did not have much time to explore Yokohama because of her work schedule but 'beggars cannot be choosers and we are learning a little more geography each day.' She complained that 'we hear very little about the place we visit; that's the worst of not knowing one's history and geography well, the passengers have lectures before every place they visit, but we don't have that privilege.' Anne Smith was an intelligent young woman who had the innate curiosity of a real traveler. Her letters make reference to the colorful flora and fauna she observed in India. She was impressed with Bombay, which she described as 'a fine European city', and became interested in the burial customs of the Parsees in the Tower of Silence and Indoos.[309]

Rose Stott made good use of her time in port on the *Samaria* world cruise (1923), noting the customs of local peoples and the unique flora and fauna of areas she visited. She became acquainted with eastern religions and thought of Buddhism as 'a religion of kindliness, of compassion and self-sacrifice – a tender, womanly faith.' Stott greatly admired the Japanese people, their culture and society and especially the religious practice of Shintoism. 'Of the malignity of religious hate, of the bitterness of religious persecution, the Shinto faith knows nothing,' she wrote. 'It has been to the people the familiar friend and the comforter.'[310]

On a 1937 North Cape cruise, Sowerbutts, after listening to a female Intourist guide who had been appointed to give a city tour of Leningrad, commented that Russia 'sounded like a country without a soul.' This is an insightful observation of a country which was then caught up in the craze of Stalin's purges.[311] No heart or soul was to be found there; only fear and suspicion in the eyes of a terrorized people.

New York made an indelible impression on Dorothy Scobie on her first trip there. She was overwhelmed by the Statue of Liberty, the Empire State Building, Wall Street and the

Brooklyn Bridge as the ship sailed into New York harbor. She describes the magic of Broadway and Fifth Avenue, places about which she had long dreamt but never thought she would see. She writes with a child-like simplicity and sense of amazement about everything that New York had to offer: 'I liked to eat at the Automat in Times Square and just watch the crowds ... I liked to put my nickels in the slots and see the great boxes being filled with huckleberry pie ... lemon merengue and strawberry shortcake ... Shells of roasted nuts and people chewing gum seemed to pervade the entire atmosphere. All the women were clothes conscious ... Mostly, however, I was impressed by the smartness of the older women, who looked years younger than the same age group at home.'[312]

Home to most of these women were the industrial port towns of Liverpool, Birkenhead and Southampton in England or Le Havre, Cherbourg and Marseilles in France, where huckleberry pie and strawberry shortcake were luxuries out of their reach.

At sea, women could live out their dreams and forget the economic hardships faced by their peers at home for a while. Despite its many drawbacks, life at sea offered women an escape from the mundane, grim reality of depressed port town existence and a glimpse into high society living on board the magical floating palaces. Regardless of all of the complaints about excessive discipline and hard work, 'the sea gets to you,' explained Scobie, who admits that although she never liked her job, she would always return to 'give it another whirl.'[313] Despite Violet Jessop's cynicism about life at sea, she too came under its spell: 'Though seamen crave leave at home, that steel beehive – as someone once described *Aquitania* – is their other home. Inside it, they are linked to their shipmates by profound bonds, inhabitants of a coherent, shipwide community into which no passenger, however esteemed or frequently booked, is ever admitted.'[314]

Kathleen Smith and Edith Sowerbutts describe their experience on the *Queen Mary* on its last transatlantic voyage before war was declared in 1939. Sowerbutts notes that 'every nook and cranny had been adapted for extra beds and bunks; she was crammed from stem to stern with over 2,300 passengers,' many of whom were forced to make do with baggage alcoves as accommodations.[315] Regular passengers, who still occupied First Class staterooms and suites on main deck, refused to make any concessions in their demands, regardless of the state of imminent war. To persuade passengers to vacate their cabins early on the morning of the ship's arrival in New York, Sowerbutts greeted them with the news that on 4 September, the first ship of war, the *Athenia*, had been sunk by an enemy U-boat on its Canadian run. 'That news reduced the breakfast orders to a minimum,' she recalls. 'It got people moving.'[316]

They stayed on the ship for three weeks in New York, packing up glasses, crockery, silver and the like, which all went ashore to a warehouse on the dock. The *Queen Mary* went to Australia to take up its wartime role as troop carrier. As the ship sailed out of New York harbor with an all-male crew aboard, Smith could hear the men singing 'There Will Always Be An England'.[317] Female crew were transferred to the *Georgic*. Sowerbutts describes the tense journey back home: 'Normal passengers, of whom there were a few, seemed delighted to have the *Queen Mary*'s crew aboard; we seemed to inspire confidence. The blackout at sea was absolute. Gas masks were given to all.' There were many lifeboat drills. Passengers wore their jewels in case the ship went down. Sailors were assigned to extra submarine watches. Sowerbutts was told to purchase a half bottle of whiskey at one of the ship's bars, in case they had to take to the lifeboats, just as a precaution – 'under the heading of first aid'. She carried along with her a 'personal ditty bag' which contained bandages, cotton, safety pins, aspirin and the like. No one was allowed to light a cigarette or smoke on the open decks. A gala concert was given in the Tourist Class dining room by the male crew of the *Queen Mary* with the most popular act being 'a really wicked impersonation of Hitler'. The crew was 'signed off' upon arrival in London, thus ending Sowerbutts' career as a merchant seaman: 'I had swallowed the anchor for good this time.'[318]

Other women sought to continue in service during the war years. In her Second World War scrapbook, Dorothy Scobie, who worked during the war in the Women's Royal Naval Service (WRNS), included an undated article, 'Women Want to Go to Sea Again'. The author comments that 'many of them came from long lines of seafarers, and feel more at home afloat than ashore.' The article quotes Miss Edith Hughes, the only welfare worker for seafaring women at the Mersey Mission to Seamen, in an interview with the *Daily Mirror*. 'These women are magnificent,' she says. 'Many nearing middle age have still a boy's love of adventure, and are upset at having to give up their old jobs. The few who still go to sea are heroines and the envy of them all.'[319] Many of these women resumed their life at sea along with a new group of female seafarers once hostilities in Europe were brought to the end in 1945 and prewar 'normalcy' was established. As ships were updated and modernized, so too did the complexion of the female crew begin to change.

The world of women seafarers was still very much a closed one in the mid-1970s.[320] Women still made up but a tiny fraction of the total ship personnel. There were new opportunities for women mainly in the cruise staff – as international hostesses, bridge lecturers, arts and crafts instructors, social directresses, youth counsellors, entertainers, and aerobics instructors. Women worked in and managed shore excursion offices on board. There were a good number of hairdressers and shop attendants and nurses. One new non-traditional avenue of employment that opened to women was the position of croupier in ships' casinos. Stewardesses on the ships of Holland America Line were replaced by men from the former Dutch colony of Indonesia – a source of cheap labor. Female officers were as rare as the Hope Diamond!

By the mid-1980s, that picture of limited possibilities for women at sea had dramatically changed. In 1989, we sailed with our first female cruise director and were introduced to a female chief purser whose staff included a number of female junior officers. Women had made their debut as dining room and wine stewards and were back cleaning cabins, but the average profile of the stewardess was a young, often college-educated woman who was eager to explore the 'distant shores' that her foresisters had earlier described.

Work on board is considered temporary for most young women today, who generally 'sign on' for one or two contracts to do something different, for a change from their routine lives ashore. The average age of female crew is between twenty and thirty-five. One twenty-four-year-old aspiring dress designer signed on as a stewardess to get 'inspiration for my work', she explained. In addition to exploring new cities, she was busy observing the colors, shapes and designs of women's fashions worldwide, using the ship and its ports as a laboratory for her work.

The 'new' woman of the interwar years prepared the way for the 'modern' woman of the new millennium. Women seafarers have finally broken the male monopoly of power on board the great passenger liners. Ships now carry female security officers on board, another non-traditional avenue of employment for women. Women today attend officers' meetings and hold important decision-making positions. They have even managed to secure a few stripes on their uniforms for their efforts. Most women, however, are realistic about the limitations of making a career at sea. One Italian chief housekeeper said that she had advanced as far as was possible for a woman and doubted that women would be promoted to the prestigious position of hotel manager any time soon. 'It'll be a long time before shipping lines allow a woman to supervise a crew of three hundred or more,' she said. But less than a decade later, women have broken through that barrier and now serve as hotel managers on the ships of Cunard, Holland America, and Royal Caribbean lines, although they are still the exceptions to the rule .

The new millennium also saw women invading that 'holy of holies' – the bridge – as deck officers, the last bastion of masculine power at sea. On a trip on Cunard Line's then *Caronia* (ex-*Vistafjord*) in 2000, I was cheered to find a female deck officer in training. Undeterred by hard and grimy work, this junior officer was immersed in all the details of deck maintenance and supervision. She, along with a small group of women engineers, were paving new ground for women seafarers. The efforts of Edith Sowerbutts, Dorothy Scobie and others were finally beginning to pay off. Victoria Drummond, goddaughter of Queen Victoria who realized her ambition of becoming a ship engineer in 1924, did not endure ridicule or sacrifice in vain.[321]

A 1923 *Cunard Magazine* illustration speculates about the prospect of lady 'skippers' (see No. 13). What seemed like a far-fetched idea then would become a reality in the next century with Royal Caribbean's announcement in 2007 that Karin Stahre-Janson had been appointed to the master's helm. Other lines were soon to follow Royal Caribbean's lead. In 2010, two of the oldest and most distinguished shipping lines in the industry, Cunard Line and P&O Cruises, made the historic announcement that they had appointed their first female captain. Inger Klein-Olsen became master of the *Victoria* while Sarah Breton assumed command of the *Artemis*. In July 2015, Celebrity Cruises would be the next to open its top position on the bridge to a woman with its announcement that thirty-seven-year-old Kate McCue would become captain of the *Summit*. History was clearly being made with the appointment of McCue as she became the cruise industry's youngest and first American woman captain.

And yet there are tough choices to be made by women who chose to make a career at sea. As one junior assistant purser explains, 'Even if you can get past the male bastion of power and secure coveted officer status, you must also give up the idea of having a personal life. Could you see a man taking care of the children and waiting on the pier for his officer wife to return home?' And yet for centuries, women have been the ones left on shore with the children while their men went off to sea with no eyebrows raised at such a thought. The prospect of making more money on board than any comparable position at home could pay is definitely an added incentive for many. The chief housekeeper, who was in her seventh year with the same company, admits that 'I'm still studying myself,' and doubted that she would make a permanent home at sea. The assistant purser concurs. 'For women who are still searching within themselves, ship life can be frightening,' she explained. 'There is that ever present fear that life will pass them by. If one develops a relationship on board, there is always a choice to be made.' The consensus is that women cannot have it all, especially on a ship. But Captain Olsen takes a more philosophical approach: 'We are very bound in our minds and our thoughts and our actions by traditional thinking and by traditional ways of doing things … If you want something bad enough, you can always get it … It's a matter of personal preference. It's all about what you want in life. When we say we can't have it all, what do you want? Do you want it all? What 'all' means to some is different for others. It all depends on one's priorities in life.'

Like Jessop, Scobie, Sowerbutts and others before them, these women have a love/hate relationship with the sea. They are frustrated by the regimentation and restrictions of ship life, but as one admits, 'when you return home, you feel disoriented and disconnected with people on shore from whom you have grown apart and gone separate ways.' Working on board, says the twenty-five-year-old assistant purser, is like 'entering another world that outsiders don't understand' – a world, perhaps, that seafarers themselves will never quite fully comprehend.

1. The *Ile de France* under construction. (Steamship Historical Society of America Archives (www.sshsa.org) and Collection French Lines)

2. *Ile de France* butcher taking his 'charges' for an afternoon stroll on the promenade. (Collection French Lines)

3. 'Le Bowling' on the *France*. (Collection French Lines)

4. Passenger balloon contest, White Star Line. (Cunard Line Archives, courtesy of the University of Liverpool)

5. *Berengaria* passengers on a tourist outing. (Cunard Line Archives, courtesy of the University of Liverpool)

6. Illustration from *White Star Magazine*, February 1931. (Cunard Line Archives, courtesy of the University of Liverpool)

7. Window display set out in the store of Messrs Eason's, Lower O'Connell Street, Dublin (published in *White Star Magazine*, June 1933). (Cunard Line Archives, courtesy of the University of Liverpool)

8. Attractive cruising display at the Manchester store of Messrs Lewis (published in *White Star Magazine*, June 1933). (Cunard Line Archives, courtesy of the University of Liverpool)

9. Cunard White Star bellboys ready for inspection. (Cunard Line Archives, courtesy of the University of Liverpool)

10. *Ile de France* bicycling club. (Collection French Lines)

11. Stewardess on board the *Ile de France*. (Collection French Lines)

12. Promotional brochure, *Georgic's* 1937 season highlighting its cruise staff. (Cunard Line Archives, courtesy of the University of Liverpool)

13. Illustration from *Cunard Magazine*, vol. X, no. 4 (April 1923). (Cunard Line Archives, courtesy of the University of Liverpool)

14. Poster advertising *Compagnie Messageries Maritimes* voyages to Japan and the Far East by Sandy Hook, *c.* 1920. (Collection French Lines)

15. The *Ile de France* with its catapulted aeroplane, *c.* 1928. (Collection French Lines)

16. Poster advertising French Lines with view of the *Normandie* in New York harbor by Albert Sebille. (Collection French Lines)

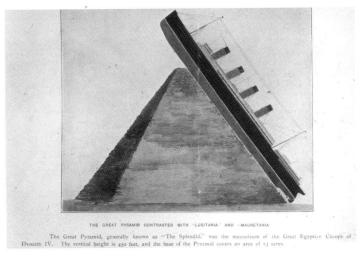

THE GREAT PYRAMID CONTRASTED WITH "LUSITANIA" AND "MAURETANIA"

The Great Pyramid, generally known as "The Splendid," was the mausoleum of the Great Egyptian Cheops of Dynasty IV. The vertical height is 450 feet, and the base of the Pyramid covers an area of 13 acres.

17. Caricature of the *Mauretania* or *Lusitania* shown resting along the side of Cheops Pyramid. (Cunard Line Archives, courtesy of the University of Liverpool)

18. Caricature of the *Queen Mary* placed in Trafalgar Square with smaller insert of former 1850s steamer RMS *Persia*. (Cunard Line Archives, courtesy of the University of Liverpool)

19. The lounge of the *Lusitania*. (Cunard Line Archives, courtesy of the University of Liverpool)

20. The first class smoking room of the *Paris*. (Steamship Historical Society of America Archives (www.sshsa.org) and Collection French Lines)

21. The *Berengaria* shown leaving New York harbor. (Steamship Historical Society of America Archives (www.sshsa.org))

Opposite above: 22. Launch of the *Britannic 2*, August 1929. (Cunard Line Archives, courtesy of the University of Liverpool)

Opposite below: 23. Exterior view of the *Normandie*. (Collection French Lines)

24. Artistic rendering of the first class dining room of the *Normandie*.
(Steamship Historical Society of America Archives (www.sshsa.org))

Chapter Five

Projecting an Image: The Allure of Transatlantic Travel

If Tourist Third Cabin passengers were to replace steerage class immigrants as the main source of company profits, steamship lines would need to find ways of attracting the new breed of mass traveler. Not only would it be necessary to redesign the ocean liners to accommodate this group, but new approaches to advertising were required. Publicity in written and pictorial media was intended to entice people with a sense of cosmopolitan style and adventure and suggest good times and unique experiences on the other side of the Atlantic Ocean, with an interval of boisterous high living during the crossing.

Frivolity and leisure, however, were not the sole attractions evoked in the images projected on to the public arena. As Cunard-White Star and TRANSAT attempted to sell their product to nationals, they also raised themes and issues at the center of social, economic, political and cultural concern and commissioned artists to create visually gripping works that would arouse among the mass audience a fascination with ocean liners and all the modern allure attached to them. Such artists tantalized the potential audience with a stylistic flair carrying with it hints of the modernity already evident in the age. As they perceived in steamship travel the shades of modern life highlighting their surrounding world, they sought to convey that observation in their attempt to awaken a desire to travel.

Despite the striking novelties of engineering and technology behind the ships' great size and speed, sea travel was still highlighted by a sense of tradition and heritage. Companies wanted to attract clients with suggestions of that maritime past. As the fascination with modern forms and rhythms grew, it was a great challenge to balance tradition and the modern, but advertising used both elements to lure potential passengers through external suggestion. Whatever the reality of frequent conflicts between traditional and modern forces, they have also at unique moments reinforced each other in an unsteady alliance.

Modern advertising uses enticing words and images to create an aura around commodities. Such a process rests on a prevalent popular acceptance of capitalism as an economic system tied to particular methods of conducting business. Ads not only evoke fantasy and imagination but as one historian has stressed 'a certain vision of the good life'.[322] Advertisers, in fact, understand the psychological gratification of dreams and fantasies as a primal force in people, which they manipulate to their advantage even in harsh economic times because:

The aim of mass publicity is to make the dream world as uniform as possible in order to entice as many people as possible ... fantasies [need to be reduced] to their lowest common denominator. This is why the idea of wealth is of such importance in the symbiosis of commerce and dream. Desire for wealth is infinitely malleable. People have diverse ideas about how they would indulge themselves if they were rich, but their daydreams depend on the basic fantasy of possession of great wealth. With wealth other dreams can come true ... Environments of mass consumption are places where consumers can indulge temporarily in the fantasy of wealth.[323]

One can certainly see such processes at work in the structure and decorative design of department stores seen by Michael Miller as lying at the heart of the bourgeois world.[324] When they emerged during the last half of the nineteenth century, the 'grands magasins' not only offered a greater variety of goods to people, but also aroused demand and created acquisitional fantasies among the humbler classes. This phenomenon is clearly seen in Charles Chaplin's magisterial film of 1936, *Modern Times*, especially in the scene depicting a night spent in a department store by a 'gamin' and tramp who is temporarily employed as a night watchman. The pair had already scoffingly imagined lives of domestic bliss conceived along middle class lines. During the course of the night, they indulge this dream by wearing various items of clothing, basking in a huge, plush bed, and whiling away the time roller skating. As the situation could only be temporary fulfillment of a fantasy, the scene takes on both a comic and a poignantly sad aspect. Yet it provides succinct commentary on the ways in which consumer goods and luxurious settings work upon the mentality of people in arousing unconscious desires.

Perhaps it is too Freudian to view advertising as means of offering people the chance of fulfilling ardent dreams. It may be more a matter of advertisers using new revolutionary means of communication to seduce consumers. Eventually such means take on a life of their own. Such is the perspective of Warren Susman in his portrayal of Bruce Barton, a 1920s pioneer in advertising. As Susman wrote,

> What Bruce Barton possessed was an insight into human nature, especially into the character of the American middle class in a period of transformation. He had a special sensitivity to its fears and hopes, yearnings and ideals ... Bruce Barton understood the power of communication in an era when new techniques of communication were remaking the social order.[325]

Susman's view is of a world of clashing cultures against which were set the consumer revolutions and the publicity possibilities of modern communications. As steamship companies sought to drum up business, they relied on posters and publicity brochures to rouse desires, stir fantasies, even instill dreams of national greatness among different levels of potential passengers.

While addressing much of their publicity to American customers across the Atlantic, Cunard-White Star and French Line also sought to attract compatriots in Britain and France with persuasive themes and images. Their publicists surrounded company liners with symbols and metaphors suggesting power and a historical heritage that connected the present to the past. Expectations were hard to satisfy for those unable to afford First Class passage and who bitterly resented their economic lot. In their public attempts at persuasion, the companies sought to overcome class divisions by emphasizing the features common to liners as they presented passengers with majestic images of the national liners and urged a patriotic response from future passengers to America who would feel pride and delight in power at the sight of the 'floating palaces'. In an age when nationalism affected the military, sports, art and other realms, all classes were to be unified in their pride of steamships, which were, at all costs, to surpass those of rival countries – even those not considered hostile. If the grinding and deadly character of the First World War dampened some of that nationalistic fervor, one could still witness its appearance everywhere during the '20s and '30s.

Posters commissioned by Cunard-White Star and French Line offer visions of ocean liners in keeping with industrial notions of monumentality. Poster advertisement had been in use for some time and during the latter part of the nineteenth century was becoming more artistic in character. Company placards of the late nineteenth century had often been dominated by large script conveying such utilitarian information as schedules and fares with pictorial images of ships or destinations restricted to mere outline form or in miniature – if visible at all. Nevertheless, as posters for dance halls, cigarettes, liquor, chocolates, and other 'products' expanded their visual field, transport companies began including increasingly appealing and colorful images. Railway companies, for instance, made the exotic nature of an alluring destination the central focus, with images of a train and connecting ship mere sideshow. Most captivating to the eye were evocations of such sites as the Eiffel Tower, Tower Bridge, the Alps and the beautiful blue of the Mediterranean along the Côte d'Azur, which not only dominated the central area of the poster but also frequently filled the margins. There were countless other striking examples. Clear, strong colors gave posters an especially vivid character, and their usefulness in attracting potential clients was increasingly obvious throughout the interwar years. As was later noted in Fodor's *1938 in Europe*, 'for all but really experienced ocean travelers the voyage often begins with the contemplation of posters, examination of photographs and the perusal of booklets by the score.'[326] Though photography would become most significant in circulating images, the dominant assumption regarding posters was they were most appealing to audiences when painted or hand-drawn. Henry Adams described the view of a steamship's funnels in Boston harbor during his youth in 1851 (using the third person to represent himself):

He watched with vague unrest from the Quincy hills the smoke of the Cunard steamers stretching in a long line to the horizon, and disappearing every other Saturday or whatever the day might be, as though the steamers were offering to take him away, which was precisely what they were doing.[327]

Adams' words approach the effect desired by Cunard poster artists, whose dabbed-on paint and swirling brushstrokes simulated the effects of actual smoke. Certainly the attendant wanderlust was welcomed.

During this time, poster art took root against the larger background of an avant-garde revolution reflected in the continuing influence of Impressionism, Neo-Impressionism, Art Nouveau, Symbolism, Fauvism, Cubism, Futurism, Surrealism, and Art Deco. At times, the two worlds of poster art and avant-garde painting interconnected, revealing symbiosis between the poster and the surrounding social and cultural environment.

Poster artists increasingly sought more aesthetic sophistication as they turned to modern form and even inspired Toulouse-Lautrec and Théophile Steinlen to mimic the poster form in certain paintings intended for display in art galleries. The ultimate result would be heightening of the poster as a serious aesthetic object. Many modern works (like Andy Warhol's Campbell Soup Cans) present baffling, ambiguous images of mundane objects with no apparent purpose beyond teasing viewers. Cubist collage works by Picasso and Braque, with their signs and fragments of posters displayed another point of contact between the monumental and commercial worlds. Italo Calvino's words in *t zero* echo this particular avant-garde concern, describing the emergence of civilization as:

A collection of signs, articulated sounds, ideograms, morphemes, numbers, punched cards, magnetic tapes, tattoos, a system of communication that includes social relations, kinship, institutions, merchandise, advertising posters, napalm bombs, namely everything that is language, in the broad sense.[328]

Signs and symbols are external social expressions revealing particular forms of human activity and are used by advertisers to arouse wants and appetites, including the urge for travel. People make decisions and decipher life according to the words and images surrounding them, and in the shady area between the corporate and popular worlds, advertising plays a large area in provoking desires for escape and travel.

On the other hand, posters also served many overtly practical purposes – among them the publicizing of political causes by artists who had emerged from a background of political engagement and subversion. For instance, Steinlen had previously contributed politically oriented works that attacked the capitalist and statist order to anarchist publications, which he later scorned as '*pages comiques*' when he opted to go in a different direction.[329] During the 1920s, artists propagandized Russian Bolshevism in a variety of styles in exhibiting a similar weariness with political art. National governments during the First World War also used posters with their catchy and gripping devices to stir up popular support for the war effort. Politics had certainly found a place for poster art, but especially strong publicity strategies to reach the public were found in corporations resorting to styles and motifs well suited to absorb people's attention. Aside from their character as publicity items, posters varied in appearance as particular artifices, angles and colors were chosen by the artist to connect to the corporate purpose. Artists, in fact, were increasingly urged to be individually creative in marketing the 'goods'.

Poster art was never quite up to date with the styles found in the latest artistic movements. A time lag was obvious. Even today the styles of previous Italian or French film directors are parodied in TV ads for fashion, perfume and banks – well after the time of their greatest period of achievement. When cubism, fauvism, expressionism and futurism were in vogue among avant-garde circles of the 1910s and 1920s, steamship poster artists relied on realism and some impressionistic flourishes for maritime scenes. By and large, poster artists still aspired to convey maritime atmosphere and the sense of heritage to which the new large steamships were connected. In time, growing familiarity with avant-garde styles resulted in a reorientation of ocean liner advertising guided by the conviction that an audience was best swayed by modern styles of lettering, experimental colors, and novel angles and styles. Nevertheless, the sailing to that view was not smooth and took time and much internal debate about proper methods.

The noted maritime painter and Cunard poster artist, Walter Thomas, added his voice to the debate on the method preferred for depicting ships. Thomas emphasized the need for aspiring artists to use a pre-conceived composition with a specific perspective of the ship in view and the various points of interest drawn in pencil – color added later. Figuring very prominently are the sky and body of water, with the sky painted first and the water later in correspondingly darker tints.[330] Only then should the artist add color to the vessel. Maritime artists, above all, needed to spend much time at the docks and to practice sketching river craft. Not only did artists need to have a good knowledge of nature, but they had to learn about the technical details of ships such as the curve of the hull and the position of the funnels. Thomas wrote that although the *Mauretania* and the *Aquitania* were similar in having four funnels, they had different lines. As he stated, 'just as a man has his portrait, and is painted by the portrait painter, so much the marine painter aims at painting the portrait of his ship.'[331] Attention to the particular nuances was all important.

Thomas's artistic method of the 1920s (focused on realistic renderings of light and color), was hardly in keeping with avant-garde calls for inventiveness. Thomas did take up impressionist renderings of light and color. But by that time, impressionism was dated and his work still seemed bound to a conventional understanding of reality that he could not question since he saw his mission as a maritime artist centrally shaped by his talent and experience with the sea.

If not at the center of avant-garde debate, maritime poster art nonetheless reflected the excitement sweeping through the artistic world. Artistic style was now a great concern, even when used to depict utilitarian machines. Visual images no longer included only 'acceptable' scenes. The interplay between stylistic concerns and the external world suggested that the range of artistic subjects had widened considerably as the definition of what constituted art had changed with the times. For example, some, like Le Corbusier, detected aesthetic possibilities in modern machinery itself as art and technology converged. At the same time, certain concentrated views of 'real' objects offered new avenues for abstraction. As maritime poster artists depicted ocean liners of unprecedented volume and speed, they departed from strict realism and kept little to Thomas's demand for large patches of sky and water. The allure and wonder of transatlantic travel in the machine age around them compelled artists to search for images adequate to the job of representation. Some were content to stay within the traditional scope of their 'craft' and to restrict their work to the suggestion of basic utilitarian facts. Others, reflecting both their renewed status as artists and larger social currents, continued to expand their aesthetic ambitions and to develop styles and imagery that may have ultimately surprised them. It was further true that the artists of Cunard and TRANSAT used contrasting styles as they responded to different visions of the future. British and French artists worked in different environments and within distinct national traditions; the avant-garde revolution began in France and shaped the character of commercial art there, which would be more successful if it tapped into modern forms.

Odin Rosenvinge's posters for Cunarders during the 1920s, although diverging in some respects, were in the tradition endorsed by Thomas. Like other publicity artists, he began his career in a technical mode. Rosenvinge was born in Newcastle-on-Tyne in 1888 into a seafaring family, his father a chandler for a Danish ship. This background shaped the son's interest both in seafaring and painting. Until the First World

War, Rosenvinge worked for a printing firm in Leeds and for Turner & Dunnett in Liverpool. Though he lived most of his life in Cheshire, during the interwar years he created posters for Cunard in Liverpool and Southampton that brought him some fame and membership in the Royal Society of the Arts in Birmingham.[332] Nothing stands in more opposition to the independent sphere of avant-garde artists than Rosenvinge's dependent position on Cunard that resembles the artisanal and corporate status of medieval artists who worked collectively in the making of Gothic cathedrals. His posters helped Cunard establish a definite iconographic image of its ocean liners immediately recognized by the popular audience. It was almost reflex to say 'Cunard' when observing the tall red funnels ringed in black lines and lined three or four deep.

As he moved from simple views of docked or approaching ships to others with alternative perspectives, Rosenvinge took liberties with the constraints of realism so urged by Thomas. While stressing the essential details of the ships' structure and colors, Rosenvinge began to alter a scene's perspective. In one famous poster, for instance, he placed the *Berengaria*, the *Mauretania* and the *Aquitania* alongside each other at sea, within precarious range of a collision, and obviously part of a situation that would be any navigator's ultimate nightmare especially after the *Titanic* catastrophe. Maritime reality was obviously being pushed aside in favor of an indelible impression of majestic beauty, massive size and power found in ocean liners.

In other works, Rosenvinge verged on abstraction as he intensified the tint and color of the sky and overhanging clouds, the ship's profile competing with great swirls of blue, red, or yellow paint. It is tempting to think of certain lithographic works of Edward Munch. A sunrise or sunset with such tones was only conceivable in one's wildest imagination, but such views of steamship travel were clearly inviting. One poster of a four-funneled liner by Kenneth Shoesmith (who later would create canvases for areas of the *Queen Mary*) showed it either entering or leaving New York harbor against a uniformly complete pink sky and seeming to float in the air with an abstract novelty that during the interwar years appealed to growing numbers of transatlantic travelers. Walter Thomas himself departed from his exhortations in new experimental works.

It was clear that the sweeping lines, towering funnels and overall massive size of the liners (reinforced by the minuscule tugboats attaching themselves to the hulls) in themselves conveyed a beautiful and unforgettable image to the viewer. Maritime posters were very appealing and assumed an important commercial position within steamship company policy. Their gripping quality was due both to the aesthetic quality of the works and their connection to modern currents. No matter the relative lag in style, steamship posters displayed an undeniable modernism – both in style and in content. The changing position of women, for instance, was evident in scenes found on menu covers and posters. Flappers were shown wearing new styles of clothing and smoking cigarettes. One woman on the promenade holds binoculars (a device traditionally associated with men and a military purpose) as she gazes at another liner in a Cunard poster by an anonymous artist. Elsewhere, posters were designed to lure female recruits for domestic 'labor service' in Canada in 'Cunard's Call to Women' campaign.

French Line posters most reflected the modernity of the time with artistic styles that were up-to-date, if not always avant-garde. TRANSAT affiches in the past had conveyed much of the flamboyant and festive atmosphere of the 'banquet years' with vibrant colors, waving flags, swirling seas and proud hulls connected to the mythic air of departure and arrival and exuding euphoric expectation. Later Europeans would cast these times, the years before the First World War, as 'the banquet years'. Despite the many disturbing features of the late nineteenth century – alcoholism, prostitution, absinthe, opium and anti-Semitism, to name a few – a nostalgic yearning in succeeding generations transformed it emotionally into an era of festivity and leisure. Maritime posters confirmed this perception in celebratory scenes of travel with steamships in the background. When contrasted to later posters that emphasized the monumentality of the new steamships, the scale of liners seems at a human level. Human celebration is at the center of our attention.

Georges Taboureau, popularly known as 'Sandy Hook', developed an instinct for maritime imagery during the war when he directed camouflage operations for submarines and conducted aerial observation of enemy submarines. Expanding his designing interests in 1917, Taboureau became a maritime painter and over the years worked as a poster artist for shipping firms like Penhoët, CMM, TRANSAT and Chargeurs Reunis.[333] As Messageries Maritimes' ships cruised to the Levant or the Far East, Taboureau's posters for the line focused on the exotic realities of these distant regions – such as Geisha girls in Japan looking out from a pagoda to an arriving ship. One poster shows a ship destined for Egypt superimposed against the large, imposing statuesque face of a pharaoh – perhaps Ramses II. Other scenes depict modern Europeans at leisure gazing from a shore or the deck of a ship at another CMM ship in a modern impressionistic, symbolist style and with large doses of Japonisme in the flat space, blankets of colors and unique angles of vision. (See Figure 14.) Above all, the posters reflect the leisured perspective of elites whiling away the time, not pressed to search for work but looking ahead to the relaxation of a cruise. This time, after all, saw the advent of the idea of pleasure cruising as people boarded ships with the mere intention of reaching one holiday spot after another by sea. Not surprisingly and in line with pre-war posters, ads downplayed the scale and modernity of the ship, focusing instead on the joys of confronting foreign culture.

TRANSAT ads resumed the celebratory tone after the war, but with an increasingly modernistic accent stressing the spell of 'wanderlust'. Artists began depicting ships from unusual angles and perspectives and employed bright, metallic colors associated with the industrial age. Albert Sebille, for one, portrayed the pier at Le Havre from a near ground-level perspective as a locomotive unloads passengers ready to embark either the *Paris* or the *Ile de France*. The ships themselves are shown only in partial views, as in a photograph, which adds to the sense of their monumental size and scale and the excitement and chaos connected with embarkation. One can imagine the waves of expectation sweeping through passengers' minds anticipating the transatlantic voyage to New York (going from 'covered pier to covered pier' as company brochures boasted). Adding a surreal quality to the scene is the overhanging yellow sky, which complements the metallic sheen of the train.

With art and technology both playing critical roles in the design of ocean liners, the modernism of such French Line posters was clearly a reflection of visible mechanical products designed with the utmost concern for artistic statement and commercial purpose. Poster artists hired by the steamship lines, in fact, portrayed the increased mechanization and electrification evident throughout the western world and effected a public fascination with the modern. Although brewing for some time, by the 1920s the results of this process invaded everyday life in dramatic fashion. The public response was diverse. Some embraced the possibilities with great fervor as part of a wave of excitement over the possibilities of technology for improving communications and transportation and making life more comfortable. Italian Futurist artists like Marinetti, Boccioni and Balla were enthusiastic about the impact of electricity and motorized vehicles, and transfixed by the great speed and dynamic energy of machines. Most specifically, they dreamt of a frenzied race to the future that would leave behind all traces of the past and even result in the destruction of all museums devoted to that tradition.

Such movements struck millenarian and apocalyptic chords tuned to a utopic, future, expressed in manifestos and works of art, which from today's vantage point can be criticized for excessive zealousness and a quasi-fascist mentality. Futurists called for sudden, shocking, revolutionary change – the abrupt break of disconnection as opposed to the gradual change and progress emphasized by the Enlightenment. As the possibilities for ocean liners grew in scope, such fervor for machinery and technology was partially embraced by the steamship companies themselves, which nonetheless sought to exploit such forces for commercial purposes, not for social revolution, placing the profit motive not surprisingly above any artistic or political considerations.

Poster artists conveyed peoples' marvel at the novel size and beauty of the liners. Passengers reacting to the *Mauretania*'s initial voyages in 1907 and 1908 were fixated most on the speed, lavish interiors and awe-inspiring exterior that made the ship an obvious example of modern technological prowess. Also drawing immediate notice was 'the extensive use of electricity [which] on these Cunard express turbine steamers provides a striking contrast between these vessels and the liners of a few years ago, a contrast as marked as is the difference in size and speed.' The *Campania*, inaugurated in 1904 and credited with providing passengers with the first maritime newspaper, was seen as a 'triumph of electrical science'. Most responsible for such developments in maritime communications was 'wireless telegraphy [the Marconi], an electric marvel which puts passengers au courant with the latest news even when a thousand miles from land.' This phenomenon culminated with the appearance in cabins of telephones, which by the '30s were virtual symbols of the changing times as were radio broadcasts transmitting static-laden voices and music from afar. By the time the *Queen Mary* set sail, the presence of telephones and radio had displaced electricity in its power to awe:

> Perhaps the single feature of the Queen Mary which most impresses a passenger with her extreme modernity is the fact that he can pick up the telephone on the bedside table of his stateroom and talk with friends in New York, London, Paris ... or any other part of the civilized world. To achieve this, the low-wave transmitters and receiving equipment of the Queen Mary has been made more powerful than any previous ship ... designed to overcome all but the most exceptional electrical disturbances ... Regular radio programs from American and European stations will be picked up and distributed through 38 loudspeakers into 8 separately controlled groups ... so that throughout the ship passengers may choose from a variety of the best features on the air.[334]

The world was at one's fingertips as passengers were able to keep up with business, political and military developments in a world that was changing by bounds and sometimes with reckless abandon. This global communication network on board furthered the sense of completeness to the liners.

Previous appause had been given to the *Mauretania*'s electric dishwashers, electric boot-cleaners and clocks 'synchronized and regulated to the smallest fraction of a second by electric connection with the master clock.' If that wasn't enough, there were also electric egg-boilers, electric dough-mixers for 2,500 lbs of flour per day, and electric bread-slicing machines facilitating the work of chefs. Such modern kitchens cleaned dishes in the numbers necessary to please so many passengers. By the time the *Queen Mary* was sailing, technological change was even wider in scale. For one, kitchens were

Electrified to an amazing extent ... electricity furnishes the motive power for the 'Mechanical Molly', an automatic maid-of-all-work that can wash, rinse, polish, and sterilize thousands of dishes in an hour without smashing even the most delicate china. Electricity also operates machines to slice bacon and bread, to toast bread, to make coffee, to burnish the silver, to measure the tea, to mix the dough, to break the ice, to cut butter ... to divide the dough into rolls, to grind coffee.[335]

As the second *Mauretania* was coming off the rafters in the late thirties, refrigeration made it possible to store large quantities of foods that would rot or cause disease.[336] If Chaplin mocked the hopes for 'feeding machines' in *Modern Times*, passengers and staff on board ships were, in fact, delighted by mechanization of the food industry as seen on the liners.

Further signs of the revolutionary changes in maritime life were seen in the shift from coal to petroleum fuel that was more efficient and allowed better propulsion for increased speed and fire alarm and sprinkler systems that made liners more likely to avoid catastrophic fire.[337] Complementing the introduction of the revolutionary communication devices noted above, and reinforcing the views of liners as expressions of modernity, were film showings. If their quality was not very high and disgruntled people with their silent format, films still seemed a novelty at sea. By the late twenties and early thirties, the sound era had arrived. 'Talkies' came into vogue and created an instant sensation on the *Aquitania* and other ships.[338] With all of its ties to tradition, the *Mary* was portrayed as presaging the future not only by its size and speed but also in having an air-conditioned dining room and 'talkies'. While it was still a long way from the later miracles of Cinemascope, Vistavision, and Dolby sound, the introduction of films on board the liners created a sensation and highlighted their revolutionary culture even further.

Microphones and loud speakers added to the assortment of sensual attractions as magnified sound complemented a glitter of electrical lights. These devices that more sinister figures like Mussolini had used for mass propaganda allowed public figures on board to achieve greater projection and enhanced communication. At the same time, improvements in lighting made the *Mary* a model of modernism as special control systems coordinated illumination and color effects with the sound system to enliven the atmosphere within the ballroom and Verandah Grill. In such a way, 'the lighting is directly and automatically affected by the pitch of the notes played or sung. For example, a high note will immediately produce color lighting of utmost brilliance.'[339] It would not take long before the notion of a unified room environment became a familiar reality in recent night clubs and discotheques.

For all of the undeniably modern nature of the *Queen Mary*, Cunard went to great lengths to highlight its traditional manor house character. Wood veneers were used to create a homey, comfortable environment still tied to the past. Cunard pointed to a 'manifold British tradition', explaining:

It is this which tempers London's gayety by a racial flair for correctness ... which adds to the pleasures of today, by the contrast of age-old custom ... which only makes modern luxury warm and inviting, by the intuitive deftness of the true British servant.[340]

Summing up, 'the British tradition distinguishes Cunard/White Star'. Publicity writers were clearly trying to balance the modern features of the massive liner with maritime heritage, which the British felt they best represented. A souvenir brochure for the *Mary* not only pointed to the ship's 'vast air conditioned' main lounge but also its 'size, speed, dignity – all ... qualities ... immediately suggested by her massive hull, clear cut cruiser stern and three shapely funnels.' Called 'Britain's masterpiece,' 'the greatest achievement in the History of British ship building,' and 'the sublimation of nearly a century's experience of the needs of the North Atlantic service,' the *Mary* was deemed a success because 'the finest brains in the country have contributed to her creation.'[341]

Technical expertise and engineering know-how were important to the Mary's creation, but revered emotional considerations loomed large as well as the British devotion to native maritime tradition evoked ancestral, pre-modern forces and references to 'race', 'tradition', or 'custom'. Ultimately, the balance between the ultra-modern and the traditional gave voice to nationalistic and imperialistic sentiments and even provincial loyalties to town or county. Bates received a letter in 1937 from Maude Royden, the sister of his predecessor, Sir Thomas Royden, requesting that scenes of British dominions and colonies made by Jane Jackson be considered for the decoration of the new liners. As she said:

> A series of such panoramas illustrating the life and interests of our Dominions and Colonies would be of great value; and … others similarly illustrating places touched by Cunard liners when on pleasure cruises would have their advertisement value also.

Jackson herself wrote of the further appeal of holiday scenes in places like the Alps and Scotland, stating that images of 'surf bathing in Australia would have unmistakable echoes of the empire.[342] It is no surprise to hear sentimental evocations of the Empire as challenges to it were mounting. With the Empire breaking apart during the late forties and fifties, such imperialistic sentiments were connected to Cunard's essential role in connecting the mother nation to the colonies. A company report wrote of Cunard that it was 'a grand team and a glance shown on the attached map of the World will give an idea of how widely the members of our Team are distributed ashore and of how far our staffs afloat carry our flags on the Seas.'[343] Such language, even during a time of slowdown in passenger ship service, echoed the mentality that had shaped Cunard's earlier development.

Similar inclinations were found in French Line and CMM. Sandy Hook's posters, in particular, expressed French pride in the empire and the line's links to remote areas of the globe. TRANSAT Bulletins during the 1930s began publicizing automobile travel through the French colonies in North Africa where one could stay at company-connected hotels built in the 'oriental' manner. Among other things,

> The Roman ruins of three countries remain as majestic testimonies to Latin Africa so passionately rediscovered. Still, today Islam gives an enchanting poetry to this Berber area. Its faith created the mosques, adorned in arabesques, with green tiled patios, veiling women in the process, but giving a deep charm to the towns, cities, kasbahs, and oases. Without spoiling anything of Islamic Africa, France has carefully and passionately cultivated a new plant with striking fruit. This juxtaposition of splendor and grandeur and a marvelous decor is the seduction of our North Africa.[344]

TRANSAT's hotels in such lands served travelers whose only way of getting around was by car and delighted to find such 'oases' of hospitality and sources of leisure scattered along their auto route. As they retraced the colonial path, they also witnessed the company's nature as a 'French connection' to international empire and assumed renewed notions of superiority.

Cunard-White Star and French Line both sought to balance the modernistic and traditionalistic worlds in the publicity they distributed. Nevertheless, Cunard's attitudes reveal a greater reluctance to immerse the company in avant-garde modernism.

As a result, posters of the *Mary* highlighting the ship's modern features would also focus on congenial, smiling faces of people (mostly, it seems, American tourists) who were relaxed and informal in dress and demeanor, awaiting the promise of good times during the transatlantic crossing but enjoying the exuberant festivity flourishing on the deck during departure. Posters by Bruce Jarvis reveal the outline of the great liner against a mostly red background interlaced with brown lines, reminding one of the legendary wood veneers found inside. Even the angle from which the ship is shown is undramatic, not intended to overawe the viewer – contrasted to French Line posters. Taking in a view of a Cunard ship, one is to think of a process and experience extending back to the era of the Spanish Armada. Jarvis made a replica of this poster for the *Queen Elizabeth* as the anticipated date for its maiden voyage in 1939 approached, revealing the motif itself as a part of the Cunard heritage.

A notable exception was a 1936 poster by C. H. Calder with the persuasive words 'See the *Queen Mary* Southampton Docks' juxtaposed upon the ship's bow, which in this image towers above the viewer's position and a diverse group of curiosity seekers that includes a dog. Its unmistakable metallic sheen, the white area by the bridge protruding in a geometric manner and the receding funnels releasing blue-hued smoke all convey a strong modernism and connect us to the euphoria over technology found in many artistic circles. Rather than a floating, wood-paneled manor, the *Mary* is unabashedly depicted here as a product of the industrial age.

Nevertheless, the general image of the liner projected by Cunard-White Star was deliberately contrasted to the poster perspectives of German, Italian and French ships. Posters of these companies depicted their liners in vibrant colors and from unique, often jarring, perspectives projecting to the observing would-be passenger a true sense of industrial awesomeness.

TRANSAT further and dramatically stressed the connection of ocean liners with modernity through verbal publicity boasting about technological novelties in its ships, aspiring to dazzle the public in the process. For instance, the airplane (dramatized by Lindbergh's landing at Le Bourget) haunted French consciousness. As transatlantic air travel now seemed on the verge of becoming a feasible reality, French Line equipped its *Ile de France* with a small plane launched by catapult, in what appears like an absurd imitation of ancient Roman military tactics (See Figure 15). Yet the catapulted plane took off when New York was within reach to deliver the mail sooner. Any daring passenger willing to pay extra could also fly on board and take advantage of the early arrival – an added plus for the business traveler. Publicity revolving around this service was meant to reach the public imagination and immerse it in the spirit of the modernity whose mythic appeal was furthered. At the same time, use of the plane to quicken the mail delivery appealed to those in business impressed with the need for efficiency as measured in units of time. This particular point was most driven home with the awareness of transatlantic speed records represented in the Blue Riband, sought by all new steamships but ironically eluding the *Ile de France*, whose engines were not up to that challenge – perhaps a reason for bringing in the aviation gimmick.[345]

During an age when aviation and taller buildings were creating much excitement, maritime posters began to feature aerial views of ocean liners in New York harbor. Italian Lines during the late twenties, for one, began issuing posters of the Blue Riband holder, *Rex*, beneath the Statue of Liberty. Artistic ingenuity gives 'Lady Liberty' the appearance of saluting the liner in the fascist mode – as 'Il Duce' would have done. Such perspectives reflected both the possible vantage points available from the ever-increasing high skyscrapers dotting Manhattan and the rarely experienced views offered to pilots of planes flying into New York from the

Ile de France. It is striking that in a time of relative peace, Italian Line artists connected their enthusiasm for the *Rex* to New York City's dynamic skyline even while most obviously paying homage to Mussolini's fascist creed.

Excitement about the transatlantic scene during the thirties could be sensed in Albert Sébille's posters of French Line ships shown against the backdrop of the Manhattan skyline but from the perspective of greater height. Even when the aerial view obscures the ship's identity, an educated guess could be made on the basis of the striking lines, funnels and bow that they belong to the *Normandie*. Adding the essential tone to these posters was the Van Gogh-like yellow sky which Sébille used to enhance the scene in a modernistic wash of abstraction. It would be difficult to be unimpressed by the scene given the scale of the ship, the staggering view, and the striking colors. Such perspectives of ocean liners from great heights underlined the awesome spectacle connected to the achievements of modern technology. The words 'French Line' running across the scene added the final accent in what was a vivid celebration of the unique quality of modern life and especially of the dynamic experience of the company's particular brand of transatlantic steamship travel intended to evoke French nationalistic pride.

Both Cunard and TRANSAT sought to give the public a sense of the unprecedented size of their liners, which at the time were the largest movable objects in the world. In the process, they compared their ships with famous monuments and public areas from the past or present. Various pamphlets and brochures published by the two lines highlight pictorial images with juxtapositions that joined the ages in impressive, albeit absurd, suggestiveness. In the process, potential passengers were compelled to contemplate the enormous scale of the liners they might board. The *Lusitania*, for instance, is shown floating above the Thames, nearly covering the Houses of Parliament. Another image shows one of its funnels on its side but dominating the whole of Argyle Street in Glasgow.

Other pictures show the *Lusitania* or the *Mauretania* passing the peak of Cheops Pyramid in Giza when perched diagonally on one its sides.[346]

Such pictorial comparisons were perhaps absurd and comical, but they also conveyed to the audience a vivid sense of the magnitude of the liners and undoubtedly drew hushed sighs of amazement. By placing the outlines of the *Aquitania* and *Berengaria* against Copley Plaza in Boston, the United States Capitol Building, or a large department store in Winnipeg, Manitoba Cunard artists made an immediate impact. In another image, the world's tallest office building, New York's Woolworth Building, still needed nearly 130 feet before it reached the *Berengaria*'s bow. Tapping into the public's appreciation for Yankee Stadium, company drawings forecast that the longest conceivable home run hit by Babe Ruth (600 feet?) would fall a third short of the bow of the fences and caught as a harmless fly ball if the outer reaches of the liner defined the stadium's outfield. White Star Line publicized the *Olympic*'s length in the same manner. If placed upright, it not only surpassed the height of the Woolworth Building but also St Peter's dome in the Vatican, the Washington Monument, and the Pyramid of Cheops.[347]

In suggesting the *Ile de France*'s length, TRANSAT evoked visual comparisons that were remarkably similar to those found in Cunard brochures, but with examples more directly connecting with the French. While one sketch showed the liner to be twice the length of the Washington Monument, another represented it as 13 meters longer than that modern symbol of French pride – the Eiffel Tower. Furthermore, placed on an imaginary scale, the liner weighed seven and a half times as much.[348] If the publicity ideas churned out from the offices of both companies had such common features, we should not be shocked to assume that copying and imitation were also commonplace.

Publicity additionally tried to impress popular audiences through comparative notions of mass and power. A Cunard caricature showed the majestic *Mauretania* equal to the power of 780 racing cars with 100 horse power engines. Accordingly, the liner is seen chained to a mass of such cars in an unfathomable and ridiculous 'tug of war'. Images of 'Gorgo' come to mind in a similar pre-war depiction of the ship trying to back into Trafalgar Square, propellers and all, through Northumberland Avenue – a cause of congestion and gridlock if ever there was one. One can virtually hear the angry cars' horns pushed by consternated drivers. The *Mauretania*'s tight squeeze also causes the buildings on either side of the street to lean back as if attempting to avoid damage.[349] During the twenties, then, the sense of colossal size attached to ocean liners was already apparent, meriting comparison either with ancient wonders or with recent earthbound constructions. When suggesting to the public the awesome power of a liner's engines, however, the most recent creations of the mechanical age made the most powerful impression.

As the mega liners of the thirties began appearing on the horizon, new standards of comparison were found. The *Queen Mary*, for instance is seen spreading across all of Trafalgar Square and intruding on much of the nearby neighborhood. Placed upright vertically (as was the *Lusitania*), the liner's length is greater not only than the pyramid, the tops of the spires of St Patrick's Cathedral and Cologne Cathedral, the top of William Penn's head on Philadelphia City Hall, the Washington Monument, and the Eiffel Tower, but just 130 feet shorter than the tallest building in the world at the time – the Empire State Building. (How would King Kong have managed this climb? one wonders.) Another statement claimed that the 10 million rivets used in constructing the *Queen Mary* 'would make a pyramid totaling 25,000 cubic feet' if placed in a heap. Several camel riders are shown gazing at the wonder in bewilderment.[350] With Egyptology at its height, archaeological comparisons were very much in vogue.

French Line brochures evoked similar comparative images of the *Normandie*. One caricature shows the great liner afloat at sea easily carrying before its front funnel the thirteenth-century Gothic church of Sainte Chapelle, which seems but one tenth its length. The Roman arched aqueduct of Pont du Gard (found in Provence) is shown falling 43 meters short of the *Normandie*'s length while one of the paquebot's funnels holds not only a Parisian metro train, but also the platforms of the station and the pay booths. In another brochure, the *Normandie*'s length measures four city blocks and its bulk embraces both tubes of the Holland Tunnel, with some 10 million rivets, stretching 406 miles if placed end to end, necessary to hold the ship in place. Furthermore, 'imagine a ship of 83,423 gross register tons, which, if stood on end, would tower 175 feet above the tallest skyscraper in Rockefeller Center. That is the *NORMANDIE* – steady, ever dependable, possessing every scientific device known to modern day navigation.'[351] Reflected in the gigantic body of the *Normandie* were all the dramatic possibilities of the industrial age, including technological prowess and an immense scale amazing to contemplate. TRANSAT considered the ship's achievement a reflection of the maritime imaginations of Archimedes and Jules Verne, the difference being the *Normandie*'s material reality.[352] While the grandiose ocean liners of the previous decade were already awe-inspiring, the gigantic size of the *Mary* and the *Normandie* provoked other types of monumental parallels as engineering expertise and modern technology made new towers of Babel possible.

While the *Normandie*'s immense mass and impressive shape immediately achieved international renown, TRANSAT-commissioned posters magnified the extent of its appeal. If ever a liner and poster art seemed bonded it was in the case of the *Normandie*. Indeed, poster artists were captivated by the ship's monumental, larger than life aura, portraying it in a variety of ways. Jan Auvigne made the brilliant metallic sheen of the hull the sole object of his poster, a partial angle from below providing a sense of the ship's industrial character and undeniably modernistic design. Auvigne's pronounced angular vision evokes both a strange perspective and a notion of the overwhelmingly impressive power of the *Normandie*. André Wilquin presented the *Normandie* from a mostly frontal-side profile focused, however, on the bow, with a brilliant blue tonality. Striking the viewer's eye most immediately was the way in which the ship towered not only above the Statue of Liberty but the whole of the ever-increasingly vertical Manhattan skyline – a hint of how massive *Normandie* seemed to onlookers as it came into port.

The artist who gave the most lasting and famous image of the liner and was himself most defined by that image was Adolphe Mouron, otherwise known as Jean-Marie Cassandre. This artist not only engraved the *Normandie*'s modernistic character in the minds of all contemporary and future beholders but made it, at the same time, a virtual icon both of transatlantic liners and of modernist aesthetic ideals. Cassandre's image conveyed the utopian aspirations connected both to modern artistic style and technology. Ocean liners seemed the best representatives of the tide. Yet Cassandre had already achieved fame as a poster artist before he ever saw the *Normandie*.

Born in Kharkov, Russia, in 1901, Cassandre made his way to Paris where he studied at the Julian Academy and became influenced by the Cubist movement. During the twenties, he relied on unique geometrical depictions of people and objects that resembled the cut-out silhouette technique found in Picasso or Braque Cubist collages and that was not out of place in advertisements for Dubonnet. The presence of blacks in his works also worked to give his posters a Jazz Age atmosphere during a time when the new musical form was well received in Paris. At about this time, he also worked with Maurice Moyrand and Charles Loupot to cofound a public relations firm, 'Alliance Graphique'. Subsequently, he created posters in an immediately recognizable style for trains and other modes of modern transportation, relishing the chance to highlight the sheen and tonalities of the vehicles. Focused views of trains highlighted their geometric structures and extended to the signal lights found along train tracks. Their circular forms and bright orange colors penetrating the blue darkness like a lighthouse beacon could dominate a poster's composition, through abstraction and modernism.

Cassandre's posters, while expressive of avant-garde style and composition, also embraced the rhythms and values of the surrounding world. As a commercial artist, Cassandre sought to bridge the gap between avant-garde and popular art and to revive in artist-craftsmen the status they held in medieval society. His son, Henri Mouron, wrote that Cassandre felt uncomfortable with the usual distance separating artists from their audience. With all his attraction to Cubism and Walter Gropius' Bauhaus school, Cassandre called for commercial artists to: '... join ranks and form a new corporation of craftsmen ... overthrow ... the wall of pride between the fine arts and the applied arts.'[353] As seen below, Cassandre's conception of commercial artists was translated into unique works that seemed to hover between the realms of high art and popular culture, among them posters with flashes of Cubist collage. His artistic novelty and jarring composition were at odds with conventional advertising. Nevertheless, he satisfied managerial demands by unabashedly acknowledging the product and company and accepted limitations on his inspiration and creativity. Today we recognize the genius involved in the most popular art forms, but at a time when high art was discussed in the hushed tones of religious awe, his aesthetic visions were sometimes seen as compromisingly commercial.

It was inevitable that Cassandre brought his talents to steamship companies that commissioned him to create maritime posters for publicity. His style was well suited for presenting ships in a commanding manner, and his use of Cubist ideas was modified. While he departed from Cubism in restricting the number of angles and vantage points, his geometrical approach was indebted to the influences working upon him. His were not the first works to use Cubist methods in maritime art. A 1914 painting by C. R. W. Nevinson, the *Arrival*, presents an incoming transatlantic liner from a multitude of angles, adhering to the Cubist creed of multi-perspectivism and provoking the viewer to piece the scene together. Cubist collage effects are found with words like 'transatlantic' floating amidst the set. Nevinson's painting, nonetheless, is still a modified, more easily comprehended form of Cubism, and Cassandre's commercial posters, which depended on immediate accessibility, would be even more streamlined. In promoting ships, companies were not so comfortable with any further Cubist 'disassembling' of liners into 'parts'.

Cassandre's modern style of poster art was recognizable throughout his career. One poster for Holland America's *Staatendam* focused exclusively on the curved circular tube-like ventilators that reminded one of Charles Delaunay's Orphism. The striking poster of *L'Atlantique* (a large liner of Compagnie Navigation de Sud sailing to South America) emphasized the ship's massiveness, pronounced bow and geometric shape marked from the water and background in a near-Bauhaus manner of industrial abstraction. For all of his artistic flair, Cassandre's aim in creating posters was tied to a view he held of their place in modern art. As he wrote in 1926:

Painting is evolving increasingly toward individual lyricism, toward purely poetic works rather than pictorial one ... the poster on the other hand is moving towards a collective and utilitarian art. It strives to do away with the artist's personal characteristics, idiosyncrasies and any trace of his personal manner. A poster unlike a painting is not ... a work easily distinguished by its 'manner' – a unique specimen concerned to satisfy the demanding tastes of a single more or less enlightened art lover. It is meant to be a mass produced object existing in thousands of copies – like a fountainpen or automobile. Like them, it is designed to answer certain strictly material needs. It must have a commercial function.[354]

Cassandre contrasted industrial-commercial poster art to monumental painting in its not demanding the same degree of individual style. While mass-produced and intended for strictly business reasons, posters, in fact, were highly recognizable through the unique styles of the artists. Cassandre himself sought to balance his self-defined craftsman's status with a freely chosen individual style. As he himself wrote:

All my life, I have been solicited by two innate tendencies; a need for formal perfection, which has led me to pursue the work of a craftsman who knows where his duties and limits lie, and a burning thirst for lyrical expression that aspires to free itself from all constraints. Contradictory impulses – and difficult ones to reconcile in this day and age.[355]

Cassandre also acknowledged the more onerous types of limits imposed by commercial clients:

Complete freedom in the choice of the means used to solve an advertising problem – this, it seems to me, is the supreme favor you can do for a poster artist. Whereas the young painter today is reduced to slavery by the picture dealers – his benefactors, but at the same time his tyrants and task-masters – the poster artist is the slave of the prejudices

and passing fancies of the client who, by removing or adding
to his design may totally disfigure the original project.[356]

According to Cassandre, company affiliations confine artists to
popular tastes and inclinations of the day, which just happen
to grab the attention of businessmen. In some instances,
these tastes are in vogue with artistic trends, but in others,
they are archaic and outmoded, hardly in tune with modern
artists' creative aspirations. On the other hand, Cassandre also
cautioned against gallery owners and dealers able to distort a
great artist's development.

In time, poster artists became renowned for the composition,
color and themes identified with their name. Today, posters are
highly valued as works of art, sought after in auction houses
by collectors, and regularly featured in museums and gallery
exhibits. Perhaps Marcel Duchamp's dadaistic and farcical
L.H.O.O.Q., showing a moustached and goateed Mona
Lisa, has evolved into a parody of this development as we
are essentially looking at a touched-up poster. Obviously, any
work of an artist as well-known as Duchamp would acquire a
high artistic status and value. Over time, however, commercial
posters have also attracted serious artistic interest and are
scrutinized within the larger framework of modern art as part
of a current influencing important artists.

Critics and artists during the interwar years detected
novel changes in the condition of art that meshed with the
unprecedented reality of the film age. Some critics detected
what they described as a debasement of the status of art. Among
other things, they pointed to the growing numbers of duplicate
images in circulation that diminished the authority of originals
– an especially acute situation with photography. While no one
could deny the photographer's skill and preparation time, the
reality was that images were instantly snapped without the
exertion required in painting and drawing.

The cryptic critic, Walter Benjamin, acutely assessed the consequences of the new situation as he described the impact of photography and other forms of image duplication on the status of art. In his view, such a development had robbed works of art of a quality they had carried since ancient times – their aura. As he wrote in *The Work of Art in the Age of Mechanical Reproduction*: 'In principle a work of art has always been reproducible. Manmade artifacts could always be imitated by men ... Mechanical reproduction of a work of art, however, represents something new.' While nineteenth-century lithography was revolutionary in making images accessible to increasing numbers of people, the invention of photography most dramatically transformed the nature and character of art itself. As Benjamin stressed, 'for the first time in the process of pictorial reproduction, photography freed the hand of the most important functions which henceforth devolved only upon the eye looking into a lens.' Not only were greater numbers of images made available but also mechanical processes intruded into the making of art.

The result was a fading of the magical qualities of the original highlighted by 'its presence in time and space, its unique existence at the place where it happens to be.' The prestige, weight and 'authority' of the original fade since 'that which withers in the age of mechanical reproduction is the aura of the work of art.'[357] Cassandre's own reflections echo Benjamin's observations in underlining the connection between poster art and commercial function. Benjamin's Marxism imbued his insights with a rather caustic quality, while Cassandre was unabashedly open about his goal as a poster artist. Those who have viewed collections of posters in galleries, or 'shopped around' for original posters, will wonder about the veracity of these statements. Originals are starkly contrasted even to the best reproductions, and their presence still exhibit if not a 'magical' quality at least the nature of an historical artifact. Poster paper yellows and fades in acquiring its own aura, and posters are valued both as works of art representing an artist's unique style and as icons of an era to which they give evidence of a special quality.

No one ocean liner poster is more familiar as a reproduction than Cassandre's superb *Normandie*, which serves as a virtual icon of the great ship's modernist design and confirms the historical moment both of the ship and of poster art. If one thought back to earlier poster images and mused on their 'archaic' old-world qualities, the contrast was striking. Cassandre's image of the *Normandie* was not only in harmony with modernist and mechanical ideals, but seemed to beckon to the future. His direct frontal view of the surging bow and front smoke stack in metallic colors brought to mind the views of architects like Le Corbusier who described ocean liners as the most concrete examples of modernistic design. The image was so simple and impressive that it gained overnight familiarity among both the maritime and artistic crowd. It also became a symbol of French Line (along with the cursive script) as an international commercial presence. As logos and trademarks of corporations in a variety of enterprises became increasingly familiar to consumers, Cunard-White Star and French Line made their presence known through their signatures on posters and brochures and, in the process, became household names. Along the way, the itineraries and varieties of passage offered by the lines became public news in a world highlighted more and more by marketing.

Their national origins made the two giant ocean liners of Cunard-White Star and French Line natural rivals as they sought superior size design. Perhaps central to this rivalry was the race for the Blue Riband, which both companies realized would in times of amazing technological change require crossings of under four days.[358] TRANSAT anxiety about the threat to the *Normandie*'s possession of the Blue Riband is evident in statements of relief over the failure of the *Mary* to capture the prize – at least on its maiden voyage. As was noted, 'TRANSAT cannot help but feel happy over the failure of the *Queen Mary* to take the Blue Riband on its first crossing.'[359] The following years saw the two liners capturing the prize in alternating fashion until the *Mary*'s final triumph in 1939.

Both companies kept a close watch on each other's liners with sly spying that still lacked the tension of wartime espionage, with only commercial success and bragging rights at stake. Each company was deeply conscious of the rival liner even as it was still being built. As the *Normandie* made its appearance on the transatlantic scene in 1935 and awed onlookers with its spectacular size, form and speed, Percy Bates wrote that 'next year we ourselves will have a typical *Normandie* in *Queen Mary*.'[360] Jingoistic journalists chimed in. One *Daily Telegraph* article devoted much coverage to the issues of waterline length and tonnage, taking comfort in the belief that 'subtracting the useless projections at bow and stern, we get the *Normandie*'s actual waterline length as 946 feet, against the *Queen Mary*'s approximate 990 feet. *Normandie*'s gross tonnage is claimed as 79,000. This will be easily surpassed by the *Queen Mary*.'[361] French Line expressed an equally anxious concern about the competition even as it gloated about its superior style. Company minutes reveal a great confidence that 'the *Normandie* will stand up to any comparison with the *Queen Mary* except with regard to tourist cabins. In all other areas, especially First Class, the *Normandie*'s superiority is obvious.'[362]

TRANSAT's discernible dividing line between First and Tourist Class tastes may reveal its sense of superiority regarding the ship's most luxurious quarters, but it also betrays anxiety about anticipated revenues from the more modest passengers, including those from Second Class. If TRANSAT asserted that the *Normandie* appealed to everyone, the ship's inaugural season in 1935 revealed vast differences among the three classes. The line received many complaints from Tourist and

Third Class passengers and demands for refunds. Passenger accommodations were not at all satisfactory judging from comments about vibrations and noise in the narrow cabins, absence of suitable public space, and a 'tiny and hot main lounge'. In his report to the general manager, Chief Purser Henry Villar warns that such negative publicity does not bode well for the company: 'These passengers are responsible for the negative campaign being waged against the *Normandie* in America and England. Such people fail to tell people that their bad experience was in Tourist Class and thus doubt is cast over the entire ship.' Villar urged improvements for Tourist Class and Third Class and limiting the numbers of passengers. His fear was that adverse publicity would cost the line not only Tourist Class sales but also serve to discredit other classes on the *Normandie* and other French Line ships.[363]

Villar's fears were confirmed by an experience of *Normandie*'s master, Commandant Thoreux, while on vacation in London. In his hotel, he made the acquaintance of a Mr Smith, who, unaware of Commandant Thoreux's position, offered his new friend some advice – not to sail on the *Normandie*. 'That ship is a failure,' the Englishman told him, 'everyone in London knows that life on board is impossible. The stern of the ship is so weak that the ceilings fall on your head.' He even hinted of rumors that the *Normandie* was to be retired.[364] Thoreux portrayed such exaggerations as part of a highly orchestrated English publicity campaign underway in England to tarnish the name of the *Normandie* and French Line.

Fear of the competition luring away passengers was always a preoccupation of shipping company executives. After extensive refurbishment, Henry Villar assured French Line company executives in a 1936 report that passengers had given the *Normandie* 'thumbs up' after sailing one way on Cunard Line's *Queen Mary*. Commenting on the *Normandie*'s superior cuisine, passengers felt that 'there is no comparison possible between the two ships'. With all the acclaim given to French cuisine and so much scorn heaped up on England's, such remarks would not be surprising. Another area singled out by passengers was service. Villar quotes passengers' feelings that 'the crew on board the *Queen Mary* is tired and doesn't like their ship. Not only does it show but they say it themselves.' Passengers contrasted the low morale of the Cunard Line seafarers with 'the amiability, the optimism and the desire to please of the *Normandie* crew.'[365] Captain Thoreux recalls a discussion about the merits of different ships among passengers seated at his table during one transatlantic sailing. Americans generally agreed that the *Normandie* was the best ship afloat. Even the one English woman present admitted that France had produced the more exquisite vessel: 'In my eyes the *Queen Mary* is a grand and beautiful English lady in sports attire; *Normandie* is a very pretty French woman in evening dress.'[366]

A French Line publicity brochure for 1938 boasted of the signature 'Gala Night' featuring noted celebrities traveling on board: 'You knew their names appeared on the passenger list, but scarcely hoped they might contribute to the great ship's intimate get-together.' With all the technological wonder of the liners, it was still thought important to convey to prospective passengers their genial setting. One of the characteristic features of a French Line crossing was 'an atmosphere of friendliness, spontaneous enthusiasm', which 'encourages its noted guests to enter into the spirit of such occasions.'[367] Cunard Line felt the pressure and acknowledged by 1932 that entertainment is 'a very important factor for drawing passengers together as well as for retaining their patronage for the line ...' Company executives were concerned by passenger comment cards which called their ships' officers 'aloof' and complained that not enough was done to bring passengers together. They concluded that passengers must be given more attention since 'Americans are as a nation given to much greater freedom in making friends, while there is considerable restraint as a rule in the English character, [which] may cause some of our American patrons to feel that there is a lack of geniality which is entirely misunderstood.' Captains were called upon to 'infuse a great warmth of atmosphere' on their ships so that passengers would return on their vessels instead of sailing on the 'friendly ships' of their competition.[368]

Fearing possible price wars among shipping companies, French Line strongly objected to Cunard Line's application to the North Atlantic Conference to register the *Queen Mary* as a Cabin Class ship. French Line-Board of Directors agreed that 'it will not be admissible that the tariffs for the *Normandie* are superior to those of the *Queen Mary*'.[369] Eventually, the conference voted to end the distinction between First and Cabin Class ships, thus satisfying French Line demands that the *Normandie* and *Queen Mary* have the same status.[370] One essential distinction sought by both companies, however, was that drawn between higher cabin category liners and more modest touristic ships catering to popular taste and budgets.

Nationalism no doubt was at the center of the rivalry between the two gigantic liners of the 1930s. Britain and France had been rivals for centuries, and although they had most recently been allies against Germany in the First World War, their sense of national competition remained. Feelings of culture, language and race went back to the distant past and were not forgotten. Similar currents were evident in the steamship companies of the early twentieth century as their publicity reached into pockets of feeling never entirely suppressed. While English and French liners shared the period look and expressed an affinity for the old order, their styles and characters revolved around different patterns, and by the twenties one could see the emergence of a distinct TRANSAT style that sharply contrasted with that of the cross-channel rival companies.

National economic concerns were certainly tied to the competition, especially in the aftermath of the bad times of the early thirties. On the launch of the *Mary* in September, 1934,

Bates received a letter from Balmoral Castle from the king and queen, who stated their 'hope that it [the *Mary*] may herald the beginning of an era of renewed prosperity for workers in shipyards and engineering works, whose destinies, in the difficult times through which they are passing, are so closely linked with those of the British Mercantile Marine.'[371] Bates also received a telegram of concern from that renowned writer and imperialist, Rudyard Kipling.[372]

Competition between the *Normandie* and the *Queen Mary* was to be fierce and revolved around a number of factors. The June 1936 issue of *The Shipbuilder and Marine Engine-Builder* predicted a 'titanic struggle between the two latest and greatest Queens of the seas', which would end in the official dominance of the *Mary*.[373] Perhaps *titanic* was not exactly the most appropriate word to use, considering pent-up memories of the ill-fated liner. Nevertheless, the challenge was clear. Statements in a Cunard brochure in the aftermath of the Second World War took aim at the French and in the process unleashed emotional national attitudes exacerbated by the effects of the Depression. As it pointed out, 'Napoleon called the British a nation of shopkeepers, but he might with more truth have said a nation of sailors, for since the days of Drake and Raleigh the tradition of the sea has been one of the strongest and most enduring elements in British life.'[374] Statements like this basked in the recent triumph over Hitler and over Napoleon more than 130 years earlier, but they belonged to a string of proclamations and pronouncements heard on both sides of the Channel during the preceding two decades. That such bellicosity still exists can be seen in recent French objections to the name of Waterloo Station in London where passengers from the chunnel-crossing Euro Star formerly got off, having begun their trek in Paris. Perhaps the existence of a Café Napoleon within the station lobby was an olive branch to French travelers. For its part, French Line publicists not only emphasized the *Normandie*'s technical and aesthetic features, but also its importance to the nation and the home province. As in the case of the *Ile de France*, provincial loyalties and memories of historical and mythic proportions were stirred by the name 'Normandie' carried on the great liner's bow. Monumental ships coming out of the French shipyards were reviving feeling about the national importance of the provinces. Similar pride was felt for Le Havre, the national port and a Norman city. At this time, Normandy seemed to convey French nationalism as vocally as any other factor. As one writer stated, 'it [the *Normandie*] has increased in the eyes of the world the prestige of France, which is and always will be in the forefront of progress.'[375]

Published proceedings of TRANSAT-sponsored conferences on the liner quoted President Jean Marie, one of the officials most involved in the making of the *Normandie*, discussing its technical and artistic features. Referring to the *Normandie* as the 'giant of the sea', he found a metaphor in Gargantua, the mythical French figure immortalized by the sixteenth-century writer, Rabelais. As Marie emphasized the importance of the gigantic ship in publicizing French achievements (what he called *propagande nationale*), he also paid homage to the Normans and their vital contributions to French life.[376] Not only was Le Havre a Norman city in origin, but the entire province was dotted with great Norman châteaux, and Mont St Michel was a monument to Norman greatness – a claim disputed heatedly by the Bretons to this day. There was no denying the central role of the Normans in the development of France, and the plaques on the door leading into the First Class dining room gave pictorial homage to that role. Indeed, 'if [*Normandie*] does not evoke the conquering nobility, the maritime supremacy of this immense coast, it nonetheless glorifies a magnificent province, the first on which a foreign visitor sets foot when disembarking in France.' [377] Shipboard references to the province's legacy were also found in such works as Schmied's *Le Chevalier Normand*, commemorating a soldier commanded by William the Conqueror and the plaque to Bayeux Cathedral. *Normandie*'s name would soon take on a new resonance with the D-Day landings at Omaha, Juno, Sword and Utah beaches even as the gigantic liner was prepared for the scrappers following the terrible fire that consumed it.

Such tendencies to honor the history of the province could find the liner itself obtaining spiritual and mystical qualities. In the preface to a book on French Line produced at the time, Andre Maurois wrote:

> *Normandie* [is] the greatest ocean liner in the world. Ships embody the characteristics, and even the spiritual and the physical strength of the soil from which they spring. *Normandie* is not only the largest and fastest ship in the world; she is also a true reflection of the soul of France, to which illustrious artists, scientists, engineers, technicians in all the crafts and professions have contributed. *Normandie* is the ship of the future, perfectly realized in the present.[378]

Maurois clearly envisioned the *Normandie* as the embodiment of past French spiritual and cultural greatness, which he saw as a 'unique combination of poetry and order, grace and gayety'.[379] Yet, he saw no contradiction in also pointing to the liner's futuristic character found in its speed, massive size, and artistic design – a view expressed also by the playwright, Jean Giraudoux, when he wrote, 'Of all national characteristics of décor, none marked a French liner so indelibly as the grand staircases leading to her [the *Normandie*'s] various salons and dining rooms ... the *Normandie* was the floating embodiment of the will and the soul of France.'[380]

It has been a common paradox to find twentieth-century cultures linking spiritual sustenance from the past to pride in technological achievement. Although tradition and modernity seemed to clash in early twentieth-century Germany, the Nazis bypassed the problem by combining archaic symbolism with dazzling technology, exhibiting a related form of modernism.[381] In a completely different vein, French nationalism and Norman feelings were enhanced by the *Normandie* which bridged past, present and future and more innocuously when compared to the German and Italian examples.

Company rhetoric about the *Normandie*'s national importance could nevertheless veer in more questionable directions. French Line, for instance, described the ship as 'the synthesis of French genius, carrying the essential qualities of the race – elegance, clarity, and proportion.'[382] A parallel is found in Cunard-White Star's boast regarding the *Mary* that 'the British tradition is manifold. It is this which tempers London's gaiety by a racial flair for correctness … which adds to the pleasures of today, by the contrast of age-old custom … which makes modern luxury warm and inviting, by the intuitive deftness of the true British servant.'[383] A company brochure reprinted comments by King George V saying of the *Queen Mary*:

> Her passengers know the confidence that generations of seamen inspire. Even more they know the serenity and solid comfort, the instinct for correctness and unobstrusive service, which have always been part of the tradition. Those who serve aboard the Queen Mary share the same racial heritage with the officers on the bridge … They complete that impression of stateliness which Britain's artists and architects have so splendidly achieved in her.[384]

Another booklet on the liner's First (Cabin) Class accommodations, again calling the *Mary* 'Britain's masterpiece,' stated 'British tradition is inexorable … a code of principles founded in the hard-learned lore of the race and made clear and definite in the 96 years of Cunard-White Star.'[385] Such references in ocean liner parlance are striking during an era when ethnicity was attached to chauvinistic calls for greater cohesion among 'master races' and the exclusion of minorities. Race, in fact, was commonly discussed throughout the West and used by companies with national orientations to reach broad audiences. Both TRANSAT and Cunard-White Star found appeals to racial and ethnic feeling to be irresistible in promoting their highly sophisticated modern liners and provoking a response from their domestic populations prone to think in nationalistic, and, at times, jingoistic and racial terms. Much modern style conflicts with tradition and archaic current. Italian futurists, even threatening to destroy museum collections, dismissed that past. Yet for those accepting the foundation of nation and race as preliminaries for the future, the embrace both of technology and tradition was not a necessary oxymoron.

Most striking, however, was the use of 'cathedral' in descriptions both of the *Normandie* and the *Queen Mary*. Given the religious, spiritual and medieval connotation of the word and the secular, pleasure-oriented and modern nature of the two gigantic steamships, no word could seem more incongruous. If the chapels found on both liners represented important spiritual spaces, it was impossible to think of their character in medieval terms. The *Normandie*'s, which was the first found at sea, was created in a striking modern style design and confined by the reality of the larger secular setting of the huge ship.

When Emmanuel Bourcier described the *Normandie* as a 'cathedral', he thought of a structure so massive and with so many different areas that only the cooperative work of a diverse group of expert artisans could achieve its construction. [386] 'Cathedral' alone could express the impression made by such an unprecedented modern structure. Just as stonecutters, sculptors, stained glass window masters, and countless other medieval artisans had collectively built the medieval cathedrals, so in like manner had their modern counterparts constructed the *Normandie*. Medieval churches benefit from the total accumulating effect of the various works of art added to them – a feature also evident in the *Normandie*.[387] As one writer put it, 'it seems to compare to the age old cathedrals that with their vast spaces stand as eternal symbols of faith and hope. What better example could French genius give to our troubled world?'[388]

There were perhaps other parallels to be found with Gothic cathedrals, which especially evoked pride among townspeople and a sense of splendid beauty that contrasted strongly with the harshness of the outside world. During a time of economic slowdown, when the terrible costs of the First World War were still felt and further dangers seemed in the air, the construction of enormous transatlantic steamships served as a temporary reprieve. As one walked along the pier to which such liners were tied or into the vast spaces within, the effect was overwhelming. At times, all classes could share in that sense of ebullience – as long as they did not go on board! British feelings about the medieval character of the *Queen Mary* could resemble those of the French toward the *Normandie*. H. M. Tomlinson, for instance, wrote of the *Mary*: 'she lifts as buoyantly as the ascent of Chartres', suggesting a pictorial parallel between the verticality of cathedrals and the soaring bows of the liners. Tomlinson also wrote,

By the work of the hammers that built her the *Queen Mary* is an auspicious ship. The men who made her are proud of her, though they would never admit it, being Clydesiders, unless challenged; and more than that, the contrast for the liner had the effect of filling the cupboards of Clydebank again, where despondent shipwrights, not understanding all the implications of a depression, had begun to suppose their ancient and famous skills were no longer needed till they were told to lay her keel plates. The building of the ship brought welfare to a city. So her builders are not only proud of her, but are grateful to her. Something comparable to the release of body and spirit, the lightness of heart and duty, which once lifted the cathedrals, went to her creation ... Her terrific power is guided by the skilled fingers of craftsmen to whom engines have the sensitiveness of delicate things.[389]

Tomlinson sees the work going in to the *Mary*'s creation emanating from riveters and others who hummed and sang proudly, body and spirit in unison, as they carried out their industrial work with a renewed sense of medieval artisanship.

The *Mary*'s economic importance in lifting the workers' position during the Depression was all too apparent. Yet Tomlinson did not mention the working class tension intrinsic to industrial British society as labor unions confronted management with demands for higher wages, improved conditions of work and shorter hours. Cunard-White Star's hope was that the bad economic conditions and the great importance of the great new liner would convince British workers to set aside their everyday gripes with management. Nationalistic themes and consideration of the 'general good' were raised to divert workers from their needs – a role fulfilled in the past by imperialism. Overriding class considerations would be the pride felt by all Britons as the *Mary* was built – similar to that felt collectively by medieval townspeople as they witnessed the soaring presence of their cathedral's nave. Such a modernized medieval work process was to result in unity and transcendence.

Despite its own medieval reference points, the *Normandie*'s undeniable modernity also represented another French tradition – the Enlightenment. With popular consciousness still under the impressions made by the 1925 and 1937 Expositions, the progressive achievement of modern culture and technology seemed summarized in the *Normandie*. As was reiterated, the liner 'contributed to enlarging to the eyes of the world the prestige of France, which is and always has been, at the forefront of progress' (à l'avant garde du progrès).[390] One reviewer, noting its *luxe babylonien* deemed it one of the Beaux Arts.[391]

The liner's famous huge scale and image as a floating city soon drew a more global metaphor. Jean Claude Roger-Marx saw *paquebots* as

> floating cities where everything is so arranged that passengers believe they are still home, live among the same certainties, the same birds, the same flowers, in a place where all their wishes are granted. *Normandie* has an incomparable force. Never has anyone achieved such a beautiful dream or parachuted into such a live abstraction …[392]

Something of the pastoral quality of eighteenth-century France comes through in this view of progress. Entire universes seemed encompassed in the expanse of an ocean liner, and life in its infinite varieties most complex, twentieth-century character thrived in the reflecting pools that were the transatlantic ocean liners. Part of that complexity involved the social chasm among the different classes of passengers. Floating cities offered luxurious comfort and stunning decor to the upper classes who had already relished the cool settings of Art Deco back home, but ordinary, utilitarian accommodations for Third Class passengers. The vast spaces on both the *Normandie* and the *Queen Mary* offered the countless possibilities, positive and negative, connected to the modern world, and the labyrinthine passages leading from one world to another brought the social sectors uncomfortably close together for the duration of a trip, even if barriers divided them.

Adding spice and enchantment to the experience above all, however, was the sensation of movement and speed connected to the ships. With all the wonderful evocations of comparative scale offered in the above sketches, the fact was that the ocean liners were most astonishing in their movement. It was beyond belief that such large objects, on a scale with the Giza pyramids or the largest buildings of the day, and riveted together as industrial products, could move. Not only could they move, but they could cross the ocean in ever-faster speeds in the process, breaking records and granting their companies the Blue Riband prize, Hales Trophy. After all, that same writer for *Revue de Paris* who focused on *luxe baylonien* also stated that the passengers on the *Normandie*'s inaugural crossing were equally preoccupied with the conquest of the speed. As part of a century filled with unprecedented forms of transport, the increased size and speed of ocean liners seemed to confirm the amazing effects of the Einsteinian universe as mass and speed became bonded on an awesome scale.

During a time when the *Bremen*, *Europa* and *Rex* were running ever faster at speeds of over 28 knots and making it across the Atlantic in four days (more or less), expectations for the new massive liners were high. Both Cunard-White Star and TRANSAT were very keen on the competition for the Blue Riband and determined to see their ship hold it. The two companies kept an eye on the other's future mega-liner coming into form on St Nazaire and Clydebank, being perhaps most conscious of the factor of speed. They also placed greater weight on different facets of their technological achievements. French Line emphasized the electrical nature of the *Normandie*'s engines while Cunard focused upon higher horse power in the *Queen Mary*'s traditional steam engines. The eagerness of French Line to capture the Blue Riband is betrayed in the celebrations prepared well in advance and commencing as the *Normandie* approached New York harbor, its crew confident that the ship had achieved the feat on the maiden voyage. With so many celebrities and so much festivity already ensuring the liner's first voyage's legendary status, the added bonus of the Blue Riband was icing on the cake. After the *Queen Mary* claimed the Blue Riband, Cunard officials privately wondered about the folly of driving TRANSAT to pursue the prize. Could the French obsession to outrace their British rival and achieve speed records cause reckless and dangerous behavior at sea? From their superior position and the prize in their possession, they mused about the possibilities.

With memories of the *Titanic* disaster still strong, forebodings of catastrophe were still common as in an article by a Canadian theosophist named Robert A. Hughes, which Bates received clipped to a letter warning about bad astrological omens for the *Queen Mary*'s initial crossings.[393] As Bates noted, it was impossible to prevent the printing of such articles and subsequent public panic. Something about revolutionary forms of transportation evoked such fear. One could only hope that public enthusiasm would outweigh the anxiety.

With growing fears of war amid Hitler's policies, the statue of 'Peace' placed at one end of the First (Cabin) Class dining room on the *Normandie* struck a rather poignant note. Featuring a modernistic twist on the interior of the Parthenon, this room was seen as a temple to dining culture and high living with some writers expanding the metaphor to characterize the *Normandie* as a maritime equivalent to the Parthenon.[394] A statue of Peace presiding in majesty in place of Pallas Athena gave the parallel even greater veracity. The historical context, however, didn't entirely suit the presence of Peace. Athena would have emitted a warlike stand. This statue represented the revulsion with war, encouraged pacifism and seemingly countered the nationalist rivalries at work in the race for the Blue Riband. Given the nature of the Nazi regime, however, one could wonder whether the lines distinguishing pacifism and appeasement were now too blurred.

For all of the confidence in modern industry at the time, the question of where that technology would lead also was the cause of much apprehension. Not only was war a constant source of fear, but as ever faster vehicles (most symbolized by the airplane) threatened to eclipse the ocean liners, company worry grew about the viability of profit margins and a consistent audience. Concern of this nature caused a shift in publicity campaigns to emphasize travel as an activity filled with comfort and large chunks of leisure time and not a rushed, speed-driven experience. As some would say, 'getting there is half the fun'. Others wondered about the wisdom of making palatial settings out of ships, suggesting that liners were not so much palaces or museums, as hotels. An audience for such 'floating palaces' certainly existed, but a new desire for streamlining ocean liners through the use of lighter and cheaper materials and less reliance on opulent decor was evident. After the Second World War, when aviation became a truly insurmountable challenge to the liners, steamship company concern for cutting costs intensified. Interwar era images of the great liners as symbols of the marriage between new technology and modern aesthetics now became downplayed in the wake of the vast publicity given to the airplane. During the twenties and thirties, modern art movements like futurism and constructivism could connect to the wonders of modern industrial projects like the liners. With those artistic schools now part of the past and the new challenges looming on the horizon, ocean liners themselves suddenly appeared as relics and maritime travel would soon center on cruising. Poster artists themselves represented the change.

Chapter Six

The Controversies of Design: Modernism and Traditional Style on the Liners

In the years after the 1912 *Titanic* disaster, the veteran former navigator and now turned great novelist, Joseph Conrad, writing about the inquiry into the tragedy, included pithy commentary not only about the structure of increasingly huge ocean liners but also about the place of decorative accoutrements within their hulls. It was apparent, in fact, that Conrad had continued to be haunted by the sea – a fact well-known to admirers of stories like *The Secret Sharer*. In criticizing the size of ships, Conrad wrote, 'if that luckless ship [*Titanic*] had been a couple of hundred feet shorter, she would have probably gone clear of the danger. But then, perhaps, she could not have had a swimming bath and a French café. That of course, is a serious consideration.'[395] Conrad saw his remarks as 'doing a sarcasm', and obviously so in referring to experts who envisioned future liners as having the ability to bump into icebergs head on and suffer minimal damage. With undercurrents of bitter humor he discussed this 'progressive' kind of seamanship, noting,

> The proper handling of an unsinkable ship, you see, will demand that she should be made to hit the iceberg very accurately with her nose, because should you perchance

scrape the bluff of the bow instead, she may, without ceasing to be as unsinkable as before, find her way to the bottom. I congratulate the future Transatlantic passengers on the new and vigorous sensations in store for them. They shall go bounding across from iceberg to iceberg at twenty-five knots with precision and safety, and a 'cheerful bumpy sound' … It will be a teeth-loosening, exhilarating experience. The decorations will be Louis-Quinze, of course, and the café shall remain open all night. But what about the priceless Sèvres porcelain and the Venetian glass provided for the service of Transatlantic passengers? Well, I am afraid all that will have to be replaced by silver goblets and plates. Nasty, common, cheap silver. But those who will go to sea must be prepared to put up with a certain amount of hardship.[396]

Excessively sarcastic or not, Conrad was not only dismissing far-fetched ideas about the unsinkable nature of future ships but also casting much doubt on the wisdom of placing costly, fragile and very movable *objets d'art* like vases in the public rooms. His remarks about the *Titanic* catastrophe cast doubt on the creation of floating hotels and palaces by steamship companies. From Conrad's perspective, these monstrous creations were the result of upper-class pretentions centered on precious works of art and antiques set within ornate, plush salons. Steamship lines revealed themselves captive to such concerns for ornamental grandeur, meanwhile not paying heed enough to considerations of navigational safety – the only concern for a mariner like Conrad. As a novelist and psychological observer of human nature cast in imperialist settings, Conrad may have been brilliantly innovative and daring, but as a navigator he placed functional considerations far above decorative ones and emphasized caution and safety first and foremost in the design of ocean liners.

Related views emanating at roughly the same time from different motivations also entered the discussion. As avant-garde artists and architects fervently carried out a variety of aesthetic revolutions, the view of one like Le Corbusier was that decoration and ornamentation were completely unnecessary for ocean liners. Their point was that industrial products already exhibited a pure and perfect aesthetic tied to the machine age. All imposed historical decoration was like icing on the cake – only without the taste. Le Corbusier (originally named Janneau) had praised the behemoth ships of his time made possible by 'the anonymous engineers, the grease-covered mechanics in the forge, [who] conceived and constructed those fearsome things, the ocean liners.' As he saw it, 'the ocean liner is the first step in the realization of a world organized according to the new spirit.'[397] Le Corbusier's later wish to demolish many of the old streets and structures of Paris and replace them with high-rises and crossing highways would be another aspect of his 'new spirit', converting the ancient city along the way into a Los Angeles or Houston. As technology set the tone of twentieth-century life economically, so it would shape its aesthetics. While agreeing with Conrad's dismissal of decoration, Le Corbusier very much advocated the construction of gigantic ships made possible by industrial technology and was in touch with the revolutionary changes visible in the world of architecture.

No other art was more reflective of the sweeping possibilities idealistic dreamers attributed to technology than architecture. Two remarkable structures of the later nineteenth century haunted artistic sensitivities about the dawning century's utopian potential. One involved the steel cables used in the creation of the East-River-spanning Brooklyn Bridge. Another remarkable structure was the Eiffel Tower, built in Paris to commemorate the 100th anniversary of the French Revolution as part of the Exhibition of 1889.

What made the Brooklyn Bridge and the Eiffel Tower stand out as unique architectural marvels were their undeniable statements of modernity, even as the former fulfilled a true utilitarian function and the latter seemed to serve none at all – except for the restaurant placed on its pedestal to provide diners with an astonishing view of the city as they partook of their foie gras and vintage champagnes. The powerful direct functionalism of the bridge and the tower's overtly naked expression of the engineering processes at work in its making attracted widespread attention. Avant-garde artists saw both as modern structures serving as symbolic beacons to those searching for aesthetic revolt and modern expression. Some critics like Michel Serres have seen the Eiffel Tower as 'devoid of meaning' or felt that it '[exists] solely for the purpose of being there' with an apparent function only to stand within the Exposition before it emerged as a symbol of Paris.[398]

Even traditionally minded critics thus felt that buildings should always reveal a function. The reality was, however, that the tower's mere presence symbolized all of the excitement felt about the modern age – steel girders, abstract design, sheer relishing of engineering know-how, confidence in modern materials, and the radio signals sent from its apex. Despite the hostility that traditionalists expressed toward it, the tower emerged as a herald of what was to come in the next century. While its Gothic arches exuded a medieval character, the Brooklyn Bridge, also impressed visionaries as a massive, monumental span over the East River, with a spectacular perspective of the bay leading to the Atlantic, and standing as a statement of modern cultural ideals. What Roland Barthes wrote more recently of the Eiffel Tower could also apply to the bridge if a restaurant and shops were opened on it (in our day, when the model of the shopping mall seems to invade every public space conceivable, no longer a far-fetched idea):

The Tower can live on itself: one can dream there, eat there, observe there, understand there, marvel there, shop there; as

211

on an ocean liner (another mythic object that sets children dreaming), one can feel oneself cut off from the world and yet the owner of a world.[399]

Barthes' point, established earlier, is that the tower served less to function in a utilitarian manner, than to inspire dreamers and visionaries. With its unprecedented height, the Eiffel Tower transcended the confines of reason in reaching the public's imagination and yet did so by displaying only its structural features according to Mies Van den Rohe's dictum 'less is more.' Barthes' acceptance of ocean liners within the range of modern architectural marvels reveals the degree to which their mere presence conveyed such an impression. Not surprisingly, ship designers felt pressure to embrace the modernist architectural creed, with French Line's *Paris*, built during the First World War, an initial inspiration. It was during the interwar years, however, that ocean liners were designed to be more streamlined and contemporary – especially their interiors that previously had contrasted with the metallic exterior highlighted by industrial funnels and ventilators.

For visionaries like Le Corbusier, ocean liners were gigantic machines whose hulls and lines proclaimed sufficient artistic statements without need of decorative details as found on skyscrapers topped by Greek temples or Gothic spires that dominated metropolitan skylines. Prior to the First World War, Futurism and other artistic movements influenced by Cubism had stressed the need for artists to accept the aesthetics of the machine age and cast aside standards derived from long-extinct civilizations. A momentary artistic protest against the forces at work in the bloodbath sweeping through Europe from 1914 to 1918 was led by the Dadaists, who despised traditional cultural forms and pursued a cultural war upon them. Unlike Dadaism, Futurism itself emerged before the war and its artists looked forward to it finding in the war's destruction a symbol and harbinger of the new century. Futurists, in fact, glorified war, justifying the sweeping away of the past instigated by the cataclysm and admired the dazzling speed and power of modern weapons as perfect embodiments of the new century's aesthetics. Boccioni, Carlo Carrà, Luigi Russolo, Giacomo Balla, and Gino Severini in *Manifesto of the Futurist Painters*, published in 1910, vigorously tied their call for modern style to the rhythm of machines, proclaiming:

> We rebel against that spineless worshipping of old canvases, old statues and old bric-a-brac, against everything which is filthy and worm-ridden and corroded by time ... Comrades, we tell you now that the triumphant progress of science makes profound changes in humanity inevitable, changes which are hacking an abyss between those docile slaves of past tradition and us free moderns, who are confident in the radiant splendor of our future. (In contrast, these futurists described their awe at the creative power found in the miraculous devices of the modern age living art draws its life from the surrounding environment). Our forebears drew their artistic inspiration from a religious atmosphere which fed their souls; in the same way we must breathe in the tangible miracles of contemporary life – the iron network of speedy communications which envelops the earth, the transatlantic liners, the dreadnoughts, those marvelous flights which furrow our skies, the profound courage of our submarine navigators and the spasmodic struggle to conquer the unknown.[400]

While failing to distinguish between machines furthering military ends such as war and others attached to nonviolent purposes, Futurists' enthusiasm for technology extended to the great ocean liners that shared the spotlight with airplanes under their visionary umbrella. Whatever the degree of their naïveté or reckless self-abandonment to the worship of war and fascist conquest, the Futurists' ideas of change in apocalyptic language reflected a mentality still seeing in science and technology both progress and aesthetic possibilities. As evident in Le Corbusier's above statements, the language and sentiment from such a movement spilled into other areas.

Nevertheless, the early twentieth century artistic world was not marked by a progressive, stylistically consistent movement toward abstraction – especially in areas where artistic and social taste met. When it came to the design of public buildings such as hotels or ocean liners, architects had to pay attention to the preferences of a mixed audience. While many could very well favor the streamlined look of the machine age, others felt at home in traditional styles and could not be antagonized. In putting together strategies of design for ships after 1900, Cunard, White Star and TRANSAT perceived a dual audience in terms of stylistic preferences – albeit to a different degree and accent. Perhaps ornament was necessary to balance the highly futuristic and streamlined exteriors of ocean liners that with their great size and speed were already the very essence of modernity. Le Corbusier's euphoric vision, in fact, could provoke reaction against the sterility and anonymity of industrially dominated design as seen in the sets of the film, *Metropolis*. Decorative detail provided relief from the domineering presence of the machine – a factor needing consideration if a happy clientele was to be guaranteed. Conrad's scorn for Sèvres porcelain and chinoiserie was not the best barometer for gauging the proclivities of maritime audiences. Anti-modern attitudes had been seen as early as the early nineteenth century in J. W. M. Turner's painting *The Fate of the Temeraire*, which contrasts a sordid, monotonous tug boat against the majestic sailing vessel being towed to the dismantling dock. But the situation was further complicated by the diverse audiences needing to be addressed. First Class passengers could either insist on traditional decor or the more modern styles becoming increasingly fashionable among those 'who knew'.

The companies were reluctant to leap into a futuristic whirlpool. A Cunard brochure for the *Aquitania*, for instance, portrayed the liner as an English country home explaining that

> English country houses are the true homes of old and distinguished families, truly 'country' houses, splendid monuments of the earlier periods of architecture and decoration softened and made lovely by reverent use. The *Aquitania* is like an English country house. Its great rooms are perfect replicas of the fine salons and handsome apartments that one finds in the best of English manor halls ... The ship breathes an air of elegance that is very gratifying to the type of people who are her passengers.[401]

The class orientation of English society is evident here in the descriptions offered by the publicity department of Cunard, which was very conscious of the ultra-luxurious 'period' look popularized by its national rival, White Star, in the *Titanic*, *Britannic* and *Olympic*. Despite the modernism intrinsic to an ocean liner, its interior was to reflect tradition and the realities of the class system, cushioning the travel of the upper classes and providing them with their delightful visual associations like wood paneling and sculpted figures, and that certain salon setting.

Technological advance was not to be ignored, but a luxurious interior was essential. Passengers could depend on the speed and efficiency of the *Aquitania*'s engines while relishing parlors and dining rooms immersed in the palace look. This liner was remarkable 'for her speed and regularity in service. She is a triumph of scientific shipbuilding and the furnishing of her beautiful period apartments and suites has been widely admired on both sides of the Atlantic,' as noted in one brochure.[402] Although so much paneling would later be viewed as an obstacle to speed, within the framework of maritime culture, the contradiction did not then seem so obvious.

Public spaces in the *Aquitania* reflected this concern as one could ascertain in the names given to particular rooms. There were the Pompeian Swimming Bath, the Palladian Lounge, the Louis XVI Restaurant, and the Elizabethan Grill Room. The reference to the Venetian architect, Palladio, was itself an acknowledgment of the historicist focus, as seen also in the shadows of Christopher Wren's architectural forms which also hung over the *Aquitania*.[403]

The look of the country club, and the essential style preferred by those traveling in this 'club' was 'period'(See Figure 19). If modernists thought period to be archaic, its adherents thought differently, and Cunard was explicit in explaining its inspiration.

> Historical and period styles, both French and English, have inspired some of the most successful rooms, notably the smoke room of the *Aquitania* ... in the case of 'period' rooms, a considerable amount of research into old documents, or among the antique dealers, is necessary to find good models of the correct date, but which are not hackneyed or spoilt by cheap repetition. These will be carefully reproduced, and other types designed in the same spirit as the old pieces.[404]

One can understand why modernists would see such inclinations as bordering on the concerns of the museum curator. Nevertheless, with White Star's trio grandly representing the style, Cunard was eager to display it as well in the *Aquitania*, *Mauretania* and *Berengaria* – the latter seized from Germany and formerly named *Imperator*. After the war, White Star sought to reinterpret its intentions stating, that it:

> Has held an unsurpassed reputation for comfort. This term is perhaps preferable to 'luxury', for the reason that while White Star Liners are as luxuriously equipped as any others, 'comfort' is the basic essential, and hence there is no excess

of ornateness in decoration, superfluity of ornamentation, or straining after mere grandeur, factors which may appeal to the eye, but which, if carried too far, militate against the keynote of that desirable ease and cosiness which impart the home-like atmosphere to a ship ...[405]

Was this an insinuation that Cunard design was gaudy? White Star, the former apotheosis of luxury, now defined certain trends of leisure travel scornfully as 'mere grandeur'. Luxury sailing did not have to be equated with the period look of the country home, but only to be in tune with the twenties' desire for comfort. Continued Cunard-White Star competition could have yielded interesting contrasts of luxury ships, but the companies' merger in the wake of the Depression ended that possibility as Cunard came out the stronger of the two.

Arthur Davis of the Mewès and Davis Ritz Hotels team of architects delineated the problem before ship designers as he advocated the 'period' look. Addressing the Royal Institute of British Architects, Davis perceived the choice to be, 'whether liners should be decorated similarly to a house or hotel, or whether the fact that they are afloat should compel their decorations into shapes and patterns expressive of the construction of ships.'[406] As the decision about the design of British liners during the thirties was debated, the choices were obvious. While modernism was clearly on the ascendancy elsewhere, the essential British inclination was for 'period'. Davis echoed an opinion by the American designer, Benjamin Morris, that 'the opinions of some ladies of taste and discrimination should be available when the question of general color schemes and details which are essential to the artistic atmosphere of the various rooms comes up for consideration.'[407] Maritime architects' archaic approach to design and the view of women's roles revealed here showed that tradition still carried weight.

Across the channel, French Line had already emphasized a similar approach with its celebrated *France*, built before the war. Known as the 'floating Versailles' the *France* was introduced in the following manner by a company brochure:

> The ship that bears the country's name across the Atlantic isn't just a boat ... The *France* is an institution – a creation of steel and wood and brass that has somehow managed to develop a soul, a personality, that continues to attract just those people with whom one would find it interesting to pass several days at sea ... Today she has become an oil burner ... But no ultra-modern influence has been permitted to tamper with the suave gaiety of her Louis XIV mood. New cabins have been added, but they conform to tradition. She is still as French as her name.[408]

Passengers were informed of the technological improvements on the *France* put into place during the war when it functioned as a hospital ship. But the emphasis on its soul and personality also underlines snobbery as evident in the following lines:

> Providentially, there's something about the *France* that effectually discourages the traveler who estimates beauty in terms of gold leaf. Those companionable little groups of chairs will seldom be found to harbor the tourist in need of a Baedeker or the presuming person of doubtful antecedents.[409]

Such statements are curious coming from a line that was embracing the new Tourist Third Cabin passengers, modest in background and eager to learn about travel destinations with a Baedeker. One can sense the great discomfort of the upper classes when faced with the masses of new tourists whose dollars, pounds sterling, or francs were necessary for the lines' financial solvency following the devastating costs imposed by the war. No doubt, the company was pursuing a two- or three-track approach to publicity as corresponded to the various classes of passengers. Written in English, such statements must also have come as an affront to American travelers – the majority of passengers in Tourist Third Cabin or Third Class cabin space at the time. It is not surprising that the cover of the brochure adorns the 'fleur-de-lis', symbol of royalty and antithesis to the world made possible by the French Revolution – including the reality of middle class upward mobility. During the latter half of the nineteenth century, travel itself had been transformed from an aristocratic 'grand tour' to an experience accessible to a broader middle class group that clung to its Baedekers and other travel guides. One sees in the description of the *France* as a floating château, no room for class mobility and sneering reaction to the democratization of travel – only demand for luxury, service and exclusivity. Not unique to the French were tendencies to decry their revolution as a force destructive to older aristocratic traditions. British publicists did the same. Not only were spaces in the *Aquitania* named after Louis XVI and portraits of the former royal couple hung on the walls, but brochures attacked the revolution itself:

> As might be expected, there are two beautiful engravings of the unfortunate sovereigns who did so much to foster every branch of decorative arts from the halcyon days of their accession down to dark times which immediately preceded the tragedies of 1793.

A painting by Charles Joseph Natoires, *The Triumph of Bacchus*, from 1770 was praised as

> Eminently typical of those days of jollity and merry-making which, during the first years of the reign of the scientific

monarch and his light-hearted consort, preceded the Revolution which was to prove fatal alike to sovereigns, courtiers, and artists.[410]

It was no coincidence that such important public spaces in the *Aquitania*, the *France* and other liners paid homage to Louis XVI and Marie-Antoinette and the lost world of the *ancien régime*. Passengers either still infatuated with monarchy or not in accord with the world of the French Revolution were to find comfort in such sentimental elitism. While certain ambivalent feelings about the Industrial Revolution also flourished, elite passengers were too obviously relishing its benefits to make much commotion. But nostalgia for nature still was evident.

Panel paintings in the *Aquitania* depicted ancient Roman pastoral settings closely resembling seventeenth-century French arcadian gardens. Conceptions of idyllic landscapes as places of tranquil escape had for long been visible in paintings placed in châteaux, and it would not be surprising to see similar works placed in elite public rooms of transatlantic ocean liners.[411] They could provide relief from 'mal de mer', but male passengers, huddled together in smoking rooms, gathered a social and historical sense of continuity, and women descending the grand staircase may have had royal impersonation in mind. Along the way, they would pass relief panels like the one on the *Titanic* or its exact replica on the *Olympic* with classical imagery serving as monumental endorsement of the occasion. No matter how high the expectations for fast transatlantic service and a steady ride, looming equally high for upper class passengers was the desire for interior spaces to exude traditional, aristocratic ambience.

As they made themselves from place to place, travelers felt the flux and bewilderment that was commonly experienced during the 1920s.[412] In several ways, elite passengers strongly desired an environment providing escape from the outside world, as found in the above echoes of *ancien régime* life. Dark paneling, which dominated the *Mauretania* or the *Olympic*, could remind passengers of a tranquil manor house enveloped in forests and with possible hints of medieval knighthood as British officials in India imagined they found in the club.

Notions of romantic escape could also be suggested through unique architectural settings reflecting the cultures of ancient civilizations. A craze for the ancient worlds of Greece, Mesopotamia and Egypt (affecting even fashion), in fact, had swept through the West, set in motion by the excavations of ruins by Heinrich Schliemann, Arthur Evans, Leonard Wooley, and Howard Carter. Not surprisingly, a number of ships were designed with interiors reverberating with archaeological atmosphere. During the first phase of cruising in the twenties, several CMM ships venturing into the Mediterranean were imbued with particular historical and archaeological characters. Among them the *Aramis* reflected the world of Minoan Crete made famous by Evans, with unmistakable Knossos-like inverted columns adorning its central rooms. Another ship, the *Champollion*, was more Egyptian in nature with omnipresent acknowledgment of the New Kingdom (especially Luxor and Karnak). Especially enhancing the mood (and confirming the mystery suggested by Sandy Hook's posters for CMM ships cruising the Levant) were replicas of Egyptian statues posing as columns. This reflection of orientalism and the revived imperialistic presence of European nations with mandates in the region helped stimulate the patterns of renewed travel and the public appetite for the exotic décor – like movie sets of Cecil B. DeMille, a part of late romantic sensitivity. The period look was, after all, a deliberate attempt to escape the clutches of the machine age through arranged exotic aura of time or place. Nevertheless, below the decks the engines rumbled on and the speed of the massive hulls increased.

It was becoming clear as well that postwar changes in lifestyle and the arrival of Tourist Third Cabin passengers embracing the spirit of the modern world compelled steamship companies to acknowledge the modern world in some form. The *France* and the *Paris*, built by TRANSAT before the war, had their service as passenger ships interrupted during the conflict. Having been renovated, they were ready for transatlantic service at about the same time. We have already noted the *France*'s billing as a ship for those preferring traditional decor. In contrast, the *Paris* was characterized not as a futuristic, mechanical vessel perhaps, but one reflecting contemporary or recent artistic styles founded on more modern traditions. A French Line brochure wrote:

> *Paris* – that paradox of ripe age and verdant youth! Enriched by the fruits of sacrifice yet reveling in dauntless gaiety; rooted securely in great tradition, yet living – artistic to the finger tips – in the gracious moment of NOW! Something of this French capacity for enjoyment, for the carefree laughter that makes one young again, enters into the minds and hearts of her visitors with unforgettable inspiration ... These luxurious ships of the French Line are truly arrondissements of France. Each has the atmosphere, l'esprit de corps, attentions complete and unobtrusive, the diversions and conveniences 'si Française'.[413]

Homage to the dead of the First World War is certainly evident in this celebration of a new *joie de vivre*. Another booklet publicized the availability of modern motion pictures on board as another example of the modern character of the ship described as 'a great effort of modern art' and, in fact, 'a miracle of modern art'.[414] Americans thinking of Paris as a mythic city thriving with the facets of modern life (for better or worse) on the boulevards, found their vision confirmed on this ship – especially during the time when Prohibition cut down on the ability of some to feel exuberant as they saw fit. Giving architectural shape to this view was the interior design with curving lines of wrought iron balustrades and railings and overhanging domes. In echoing the Art Nouveau style, especially popular during the pre-war world, the *Paris* was not to be confused with the baroque style of Versailles or the period look of the *France*. Rèné Lalique's modern glasswork displayed here, and later in the *Normandie*, emerged as one of the special symbols of modern style. Passengers choosing to travel on the *Paris* were seeking an atmosphere both more modern and removed from the 'stuffiness' of traditional ships. They were seeking the world of Montmartre or an imagined Paris as the city of the banquet years, excluding, of course, more notorious aspects like absinthe.

The company proudly proclaimed the *Paris* to be the 'ideal modern ocean liner' and the 'image of the French artistic renaissance', claiming it 'embodies the results of the great progress made in the past few years in marine architecture'.[415] Avoiding the familiar comfortable styles of the past, the designers of the *Paris* created an interior more in tune with the contemporary world and with its intrinsic modernity embodied in the throbbing machinery and exterior.

As the *Paris* returned to service in 1923, the artistic scene was abuzz with radically new movements. Cubism, Fauvism and Expressionism were still apparent, but Surrealism expressed new ideas about reality, dreams and the unconscious. In Weimar Germany, the Bauhaus movement affected not only the pure arts but also applied arts like architecture and furniture. Emphasizing the importance of industrial methods and materials to the arts and crafts, visionary constructivist artists in the Soviet Union paralleled the Bauhaus in towers of sculpture and stylized interiors.[416] The phrase 'international style' expressed the seemingly omnipresent modern architectural style complementing the sweep of industrial life over the planet.

Since the late nineteenth century, various critics had discussed the need for the arts and crafts to express the realities of industrial production and of modern society. Among those expressing this desire from several viewpoints were William Morris, John Ruskin and Camille Mauclair, who still agreed that the aesthetic environment of modern life was not in harmony with its character. [417] Exhibitions celebrating the wonders of modern technology publicized the possibilities for the future, but critics continued to be disgruntled. Art Nouveau, found in Paris metro stations and other places, had been the significant style of the *fin de siècle*, expressing an industrial aesthetic. By the twenties, however, it seemed dated and not up to audience expectations of modernism. Something even more radical had to be devised. So felt Bauhaus spokesmen and adherents of other schools.

In this atmosphere, the Exposition Internationale des Arts Decoratifs et Industriels Modernes was held in Paris in 1925, and the streamlined style of Art Deco came to the forefront, influencing public architecture and interior design for the next several decades. Several pavilions within the exhibition highlighted the style, which was shaped by aesthetic trends coming out of Cubism and the international style. Also evident were decorative patterns (zig-zagged and angular) influenced by sets of the Ballets Russes and by ancient Egyptian and Native American art. [418] Perhaps most catching the eye were spectacular glass and light designs that would become increasingly familiar. Almost immediately, the effects were felt elsewhere, especially in New York where skyscrapers of all kinds reflected the new style.

Steamship companies were quick to embrace Art Deco as an appropriate style for their ocean liners to be launched during the next decade. Each line, however, incorporated the new style to a different degree. During the twenties, Cunard and White Star adhered to the period look – something almost impossible to avoid since the stars of their fleets had been built or designed before the war. Even while holding the speed records and exhibiting the most massive size, British ships thus remained essentially conservative. For most of the ocean-going public, Cunard and White Star vessels represented luxury in its most traditionally familiar form – most obvious when contrasted to liners designed in Italy and Germany that were both more modern and capable of challenging for the Blue Riband.

Considering a successor and companion to the *Paris*, TRANSAT designers sought inspiration from the 1925 Exposition, and the result of this search was the *Ile de France*. While the *Paris'* interior space reflected recent styles, the *Ile de France* was actually constructed and designed as an expression of the latest concern for uniting art with industry as envisioned in the 1925 Exposition. In fact, it was to be a veritable floating exhibition space of modernism, even if watered down a bit to suit the proclivities of passengers not always willing to embrace radical modernism. Within its hull, passengers could wonder at the airier space with more sweeps, geometrical shapes and columns that were contemporary or at least non-antique in essence.

French Line described the liner as having 'the same traditional comfort familiar to travelers of the line, blended with decorative loveliness.' But it went on to note that 'even the details are modern, new, smart and French in daring novelties of color and design.'[419] The company also explained that 'staterooms on board the *Ile de France* are modern American hotel rooms. Attention has been given to the smallest details: roomy clothes closets, every toilet requisite, electric fans, bed reading lamps. Almost every cabin is an outside one with private bath and a charming alcove dressing room.'[420] French Line's emphasis on 'American' rooms are reflective here of European attitudes about America's complete immersion in modern techniques and design. For traditionalists unreconciled to the encroaching wave of modernism, the Louis XV design of the *France* was recommended as a soothing alternative if they didn't mind being typecast as stodgy conservatives. They could also satisfy their underlying nationalism.

Maritime design was obviously entering a new era, heralded by the *Ile de France*'s modern design and onboard life. Combining words like 'new', 'smart' and 'French' evoked a vision of modern interiors without excessive ornament and historical reference and shaped in streamlined, geometric and linear settings in tune with the age. Materials such as metal, glass and lacquered surfaces also highlighted spaces formerly covered in traditional dark-colored woods. Lalique's spectacular designs of electrical lighting evoked further evidence of the possibilities of aesthetic modernism. As the writer Henri Clouzot put it, 'a fine audacity was needed to apply this modern beauty.' Scorning the tastes of the previous century, he stated 'all periods, except the nineteenth century, were modern in their time.' While the styles and preferences attached to that century were in the 1920s still highly visible, the suggestion here was that they were archaic, backward-looking, and out of tune with the day's tastes. Such a unique way of endorsing contemporary trends would surely upset some onlookers but also please those who were most progressive.[421]

Some compromise would be necessary. The *Ile de France* was not to be confused with the upcoming German ships, the *Bremen* or the *Europa*, whose Bauhaus severity upset travelers with a need for some luxury and traditional decor in a setting dominated by funnels and ventilators.[422] The *Ile de France* was not a mere machine but a ship enhanced by comfortable furnishings and beautiful wall surfaces, ceilings, and, of course, columns. Still, the effect was unmistakably modern and a variety of critics have castigated the interior of the *Ile de France*. Others have attacked the ship design for not being uniform, for lacking consistency. John Maxtone-Graham, for instance, has written:

In the lounge were two score columns, classicism's last gasp. But they were devoid of traditional capitals, lacquered blood red and clustered about the walls in groups as if recoiling in alarm from a blatant geometric carpet ... It seemed less a salon than a hothouse, an impression reinforced by the coffered vaults above ... Less frantic, but monumental, was the entrance foyer. Four decks high, one ponderous arch after another, it was strongly reminiscent of the lower level of New York's Grand Central Station.

As described by Maxtone-Graham,

what emerged was a riot of Establishment Modern, an extension of the International Paris Exposition of 1925, packaged in a conventional hull and delivered to New York ... The total effect was uncomfortable and overpowering, a preview of the architectural brutality that Europeans of a subsequent decade would call Mussolini Modern.[423]

Maxtone-Graham's scorn is aimed not at the departure from traditional 'period', but the very balanced and restrained modernism sought by French Line, though he goes off on some rather personal tangents.

John Malcolm Brinnin was only slightly more receptive, writing that the *Ile de France*

possessed a warmth, a palpable sense of aristocratic reserve, a sort of laissez-faire grace that hid her touches of ugliness and mellowed the strains of the brut and the stridently moderne that were evident throughout the length of her.[424]

Bemoaning the 'great slabs of laminated wood polished to a clinical glossiness', Brinnin admitted that there was much to admire in the liner's public spaces. A definite dignity and grace (as he quoted from an unattributed source) was felt in the structure and decor of the ship. What he took aim at was the hesitant modernism that characterized the ship and gave it a conservative figure. As noted, this ship 'may be the first of ocean liners – in a succession leading to the final France of 1962 – to embrace the modern at the very moment when steamship history was becoming a romance of the past.'[425] Maxtone-Graham acknowledges the liner's fatal blow to historicism: 'Eclecticism was dead; there was almost no panel, fabric, railing or motif identifiable with an earlier age ...'[426] Adding to the modern style were the varied pleasures available on board that gave the liner an amoral character.

> The emissary of 'les temps moderne' – in decor and amenity as well as in the hedonistic postwar spirit which embraced luxe, volupté, and left the sobering profundities of calme to poets and the curators of les beaux arts and la belle époque ... [Americans saw the ship filled with] Gallic élan combining laissez-faire with café sociability and a whiff of naughtiness associated with the raunchier side of French domestic life.[427]

The *Ile de France* arrived on the scene with great fanfare, *Syren and Shipping* naming it ship of the year.[428] Americans most vocally developed a love and attachment for the ship, described as the 'rue de la Paix of the Atlantic', with alcoholic beverages practically available the moment they boarded. So far did they feel from the clutches of Prohibition politics that they imagined themselves in Europe already, even with New York harbor just a few hours behind them. The plane standing near the stern augmented the sense of the *Ile de France*'s futuristic image and TRANSAT's claim as the company of the modern. As *Syren and Shipping* wrote, 'there is no other steamer on this route so representative of latter-day tendencies as the *Ile de France*.'[429] Along these lines, French Line officials and publicists saw the *Ile de France* as a model for future designers 'for the success of the *Ile de France* is but a stage and not an end.'[430]

After the appearance of the *Ile de France*, steamship companies included patronage and sponsorship of the arts as part of their mission – a much-needed gesture, one writer said, since the 'state [was] oblivious of its former role as protector of the arts' – as when French salons dominated the artistic scene during the eighteenth and early nineteenth centuries.[431] Times had changed. Only the company could gather together an 'ensemble' of diverse artists readily dedicating themselves to so massive a project as decorating a transatlantic steamship. While criticism of the state's abandonment of artistic patronage is implicit here, the reality was that avant-garde artists struggling to express individual styles had found little support from the salon. Developments in industrial arts and crafts since the last decade of the nineteenth century in fact owed much to the avant-garde's defiance of artistic convention. Design of the *Paris* and the *Ile de France* seemed to follow up on that promise following the great splash of the 1925 Exposition, and the resulting sensation revealed popular taste as no longer a uniform current but one splintered into traditionalist and modernist fragments whose adherents were fiercely vocal.

By the late twenties, Cunard, White Star and French Line were conscious of the need to build newer, faster and larger liners that would be more competitive in the world market – especially on the New York run. With the arrival of the *Bremen* and *Europa* on the maritime scene, contrasts with the relative antiquity of the Cunard and White Star ships were striking. It was a matter of a traditional format running up against the minimalist, streamlined look of the future. The *Mauretania* was aging, having captured its last Blue Riband, and in several years the *Bremen* would become a model for the future. Though a few years younger, the *Aquitania* was also showing its years of service. White Star's old companion ship to *Titanic* and *Britannic*, *Olympic*, was ready for scrapping.[432] Ships handed over to Cunard and White Star as part of Germany's reparations payments to Britain were nearing the end of their runs – as with the *Berengaria* (formerly *Imperator*) of Cunard, and the *Majestic* (formerly *Bismarck*) of White Star (See Figure 21). An anonymous White Star report of 1920 in fact cast doubt on the value of *Imperator* and *Bismarck*. Admitting their possible threat to British dominance of transatlantic travel if allowed to remain in German hands, the report stated that they were too large and, thus, not cost effective. Cunard and White Star, it was stated, would never have ordered such ships themselves and 'we regard it as very unfortunate that circumstances should now arise which make it necessary that our Companies should have to consider acquiring them.'[433] There was no questioning their seizure as part of the compensation to Britain for ships lost during the war. In the process, the damage to Germany's maritime competitive edge would add more benefits. Nevertheless, to the writer of the report, the value of these two ships for the long run seemed dubious.

Clearly, there were challenges to pre-war propensities for grandiosity and luxury. Public discussion also revealed a growing inclination for three funnels, instead of four, found in praise for the three smoke-stacks on the *Imperator/Berengaria* and *Bismarck/Majestic*, which avoided the waste of valuable space.[434] Such considerations were raised especially to effects on a ship's. A Cunard engineer wrote in *The Commodore* of the *Aquitania* that:

> Great Britain ... must, if she intends to lure passengers from her rivals, build a vessel both stately and speedy. Her engines must be capable of driving her faster than any of her competitors, and to do this will require engines capable of developing 150,000, horse-power or even more. The probabilities are she would be over 1,000 feet long by 110 feet, built to suit Atlantic conditions ... A speed of 33 knots when fully loaded is forecast by the experts ... The faster vessels ... apparently attract the larger number of passengers.[435]

This was essentially a description of the *Queen Mary*, not a pointless exercise at prediction.

TRANSAT perceived the transatlantic scene in a similar light with executives also wondering about the implications of Nordeutscher Lloyd ships, competition from White Star's envisioned *Oceanic* project (never fulfilled), vigorous upstart ships from Italian Lines and United States Lines, and speculation about new Cunard moves.[436] Special concern was expressed about the modernity of German liners since the *Ile de France* did not have the tonnage or the speed to dominate the transatlantic area of travel as had been hoped. In addressing the entire situation, René La Bruyère wrote: 'we cannot do less than Cunard … in the realm of commerce, our nation should prove the worth of its industry.'[437] Despite its influential modern design, the *Ile de France* was regarded as a disappointment and not measuring up to future standards of massiveness and great speed. Even an article promoting the soon-to-be-realized *Normandie* stated: 'France is behind in speed and tonnage vis-a-vis its rivals on the New York run.'[438] A similar tone was found in White Star's third *Britannic*, launched in 1929 but with none of the aura of its ill-fated, but majestic, predecessor in name – built simply to take up the slack obvious in a decaying fleet (See Figure 22).

French Line explicitly expected transatlantic steamships to travel at 28 knots – a speed not achieved by the *Ile de France*. With the influx of tourists and businessmen traveling in either direction, the New York line was most lucrative to companies. To keep the traffic and profits at a steadily growing level, it was essential for companies to make ships larger and crossings faster, a combination which would spur ever larger numbers of people to travel – especially those wanting to be in Paris in less than five days after leaving New York.[439] With liners becoming so much larger and monumental in scale, state support of company efforts would be ever more crucial.[440]

The aim of revitalizing TRANSAT and Cunard was obvious in two secret projects begun in the late twenties known simply as *T6* and *534* respectively. Both projects were envisioned as solutions to the stagnating passenger ship building sector perceived in France and Britain with hopes great that each liner could help overcome the difficulties of the times as ultimately caused by the costs, losses and sacrifices of the First World War. Officials of both companies believed that German shipping reparations had not been sufficient to make amends – part of the ongoing nationalistic animus pushed by the steamship companies. Thus *T6* and *534* would enable TRANSAT and Cunard to improve their situations and, in fact, leap into the future in a revolutionary manner. *T6* was commissioned to the Atelier et Chantier of Penhoët at St Nazaire, while *534* was given to John Brown at Clydebank. They would respectively become known as the *Normandie* and the *Queen Mary*. As noted earlier, the size of the new liners would be so monumental as to merit comparison with ancient temples, cathedrals and even small cities.

Ironically, both liners would be stalled by the Depression and left in embarrassing states of half-completion, beset with relentless rust. With both companies portraying the skeletal liners as vital to national renewal, they made new calls for completion proposing permanent partnership with a new player – the state. After the initial onslaught of the Depression, Cunard and TRANSAT revived interest in their projects. In France, the mood was enhanced by the 1931 Exposition Coloniale in Paris, which publicized the importance to French colonies of a unified approach to art and industry. French artists like Eugene Delacroix, Ingres and Henri Matisse had pointed attention well before to the arts of such territories, and renewed fascination with ancient and archaeological motifs grew – as seen on the *Aramis*. Such cultural fixations gave the 1931 Expo both a modern and traditional character as ongoing interests in industrial arts and exotic themes were attached to the bolstering of imperialism and nationalism. As two sides of the same 'coin' (the artistic decorative scene of the 1930s), they loomed large in the *Normandie*'s design (See Figure 23).

As with socialism, 'the international style' did not exclude national traditions or trends. Its artistic forms had universal rather than merely national or local appeal, but the reality was that this style was rarely present in a 'pure' form. National, ethnic and local mannerisms complemented the formula, and the tension between the international style and French variations in the *Normandie* provided evidence of a balancing act, accentuated by the contrast of the French concern for progress and deep-seated nationalistic beliefs in a special destiny for France, the thirst for power and irrational feelings of grandiosity. This dramatic and gripping situation evoked a variety of responses and was but another example of the unclear relation existing between modernism and nationalism.[441]

Once the work of converting the immense hull of *T6* into the *Normandie* began, the complex task of designing its public and private spaces was intensified by the challenge of artistic decoration. TRANSAT offered commissions for statues, murals and other artistic pieces as well as those for electrical units, wall and ceiling materials. Bathroom fixtures, kitchens, even surgical environments had to be considered carefully. Much expectation was placed on the liner designed by Vladimir Yourkevitch, an employee of Renault in Paris who had been a naval engineer in St Petersburg, which he fled after the Russian Revolution. Under the direction of such TRANSAT officials as Jean Marie, Henri Cangardel and others, Roger-Henri Expert and Richard Bouwens de Boijen were put in charge of the interior decoration. Both had already made a mark with their modernistic work in the *Paris* and *Ile de France*. Now faced with the impressive exterior of *T6*, they had to come up with an interior worthy of the surging bow, amazing lines, thick modern smoke stacks (making their appearance after the launch) and a size that would measure some 80,000 tons. This hardly miniscule aim demanded a unified style expressing the excitement of the age and historical acknowledgment and reverence for France and the province of Normandy. Such a swelling of national pride led to plans for another 80,000 plus ton paquebot honoring Brittany that was home of St Nazaire shipyards where TRANSAT liners were built.

With news circulating of the construction, interior design and furnishing of the *Normandie*, TRANSAT received countless requests for commissions of work. Advanced modern techniques and materials were clearly demanded for conveniences and items of comfort increasingly found ashore like telephones, cinema, air conditioning and novel forms of electrical lighting and now desired on ocean liners. Aluminum, a scorned metal in our day, was viewed as 'progressive' and appropriate for practical uses and design considerations. Certainly, even the period ships of Cunard, White Star and TRANSAT like the *Mauretania*, *Titanic* and the *France* displayed unmistakable modern features made possible by industrialization. Still, the massive displays of wood and traditional style hid the mechanical reality behind the surface, a compromise seen even on the *Ile de France* with its modernistic refraction of streamlined traditional motifs. The *Normandie* would be modern to an extent not seen before in French and British ships, and modern conveniences on board would reveal the most state-of-the-art inventions available at the time.

Its interior design would reflect the overall modern nature of the *Normandie* and avoid the omnipresent tension between their design and the reality of the mechanical age. Bouwens and Expert demanded that most furnishings and art on board the *Normandie* express the modern world's streamlined aesthetic. In some cases, 'period' furniture was allowed. Samples of work, however, that did not seem to complement the overall design were politely, but firmly, rejected. Such was the case when M. Broudarge Joailler requested the commission for the carpeting of the Grand Salon that was to include ancien régime furniture.

As Bouwens and Expert wrote to the Director General of TRANSAT after visiting Broudarge's shop, 'this room [the Grand Salon] is rather modern in execution but its decor is 17th century ... the dimensions, the design and color of the carpet do not, however, harmonize with the decoration.'[442] The Grand Salon's ancien régime furniture simply did not mesh with Broudarge's design.

Unemployment forced many artisans to seek commissions for work on this monumental ship. 'La Miroiterie Moderne', in offering to create glass and window work on the liner, emphasized that its glass was found in certain cathedrals. Sagot, a glassmaker from the historic Norman town of Bayeux, requested the commission for windows with religious and civil scenes – perhaps intended for the liner's chapel.[443]

Foreign firms also expressed interest in contributing to the interior design of this French ship. Waring & Gillow, the British firm later contributing to the design of the *Queen Mary*'s interior, formally expressed its desire to provide furnishings. Since its artisans had also created chairs and sofas for the *Ile de France*'s First Class smoking room, it is clear that foreign artisans were not precluded from work for such nationally focused ships.[444] Nationalism had its own limits in an international age and companies, whether French or foreign, that obtained commissions proudly displayed their success by placing ads in prominent books and magazines, as did French Aluminium.[445] Further padding archival files are requests for work in parquet flooring, ceramics, *serrureie*, iron work, and other departments.[446] Maison Jules Leynaert, a Dunkirk firm involved in *rayons meubles*, emphasized the high unemployment rate found there.[447] Despite the reality of such social problems, TRANSAT was not moved and instead emphasized the need for all areas of the ship, even the chapel and the smoking room, to exhibit modern style. In seeking work or exhibition space on the *Normandie*, artists and craftsmen did not hesitate to obtain outside help. Such was the case of Jacques Leudet, who wanted to display his watercolors on board the ship in an attempt to gain publicity and was supported by Paul Reynaud, member of the Chamber of Deputies and later prime minister at the time of the fall of France in 1940. Reynaud's support was fruitless as company managers would not consent to using lounge space to exhibit canvases or statues not directly a part of the ship's design.[448] TRANSAT also received letters from artists like Jean Dupas and Jean Dunand and accepted their bids, giving in to explicit demands for monetary compensation, work conditions and individual freedom in deciding on style and choice of subject.[449]

With all its different nuances (as in the Grand Salon), the *Normandie* presented an astonishingly modern statement perhaps not in the same uncompromising manner of rival ships like the *Bremen* or *Europa*, but certainly on a more monumental note. Its large public spaces, especially the First Class dining room, were reflective of the artistic trends of the day as no other ship could have been. The unifying note, as with the *Ile de France,* was Art Deco, a style by then known to larger audiences because of their familiarity with Hollywood sets for the Astaire-Rogers films and others.

In addition to its modernist high art character, Art Deco was intended to infuse modern styles into everyday settings. As with Art Nouveau, the movement saw possibilities for transforming urban environments and popular taste as banks, post offices, apartment buildings, hotels and other structures were constructed and decorated with motifs and stylistic flourishes increasingly connected to the movement. Unlike Cubist or Expressionist works, Art Deco was not created at all for exhibition purposes but to immerse people in modern style, which they were to view as the ultimate form of sophistication. New York's Chrysler Building was probably the most famous such edifice, both because of its status at the time as the world's tallest skyscraper and for its unique artistic touches, such as modernized gargoyles overlooking the streets from the dizzying heights of the structure's apex. As with the Bauhaus, Art Deco was most defined by furnishings and architectural details. It was also a broadening movement since, as one critic has written, 'Both Art Nouveau and Art Deco brought the formalist innovations achieved in the high arts of painting, sculpture, and architecture to the wider realm of popular consumer demand and advanced taste, and in the process helped to mold the distinct achievements of independent avant-garde movements into a dominant period style.'[450] If period styles were connected to particular historical times and moods, Art Deco could be seen as an evocation of the 1930s. Thomas Crow has described Art Deco as an artistic force that eased tensions within capitalist society:

> The Cubist vision of sensory flux and isolation in the city became in Art Deco a portable vocabulary for a whole modern 'look' in fashion and design. Cubism's geometricization of organic form ... were a principal means by which modernist architecture and interior design were transformed into a refined and precious high style. Advertised as such, now through the powerful medium of film costume and set decoration, the Art-Deco stamp was put on the whole range of Twenties and Depression-era commodities: office buildings, fabric, home appliances, furniture, crockery.[451]

In occupying an intermediary position between high modern art and popular taste, Art Deco thus circulated attitudes and accents from one realm into the other. Crow also notes that 'Culture under conditions of developed capitalism displays both moments of negation and an ultimately overwhelming tendency toward accommodation. Modernism hovers in the tension between these two opposed movements. And the avant-garde, the bearer of modernism, has been successful when it has found for itself a social location where this tension is visible and can be acted upon.'[452]

Art Deco can now be viewed as a period movement, although

one could begin to apply this *ad absurdum* and extend it to the Akhnaton era of New Kingdom Egypt. The style was more immediately embraced by high society than were the purely avant-garde movements of the nineteenth and twentieth centuries. Art Deco could even provide the sets for the upper class style of living as defined by the Rainbow Room in Rockefeller Center and other establishments. Its accommodating character is striking. As the steamship companies catered to First Class passengers as well as Tourist Third Cabin, they tended to promote a style that defined sophistication and status in the new modern manner. As the war had changed western society forever, it was necessary to update notions of luxury and interior design to match the times.

Every stretch of the *Normandie*, including its cabins, reflected the infatuation with Art Deco. Dark, rich woods were replaced by lighter-colored materials to create an airier, lighter ambience. With traditional decor increasingly giving way to directly linear and curved space, the eye encountered few obstacles as it swept down a salon or dining hall. The effect was both streamlined and striking and Lalique's spectacular electric columnar lighting fixtures set the mood and contemporary aura. Modernity had arrived on board both to enhance the comfort and convenience of passengers and to provide novel forms of aesthetic delight in interior space.

The First (Cabin) Class *salle à manger* was the *pièce de résistance* of the *Normandie* (See Figure 24). Its great length was enhanced by a combination of Art Deco elements (what the TRANSAT official, Dal Piaz called the 'Transat style'). Along the sides, the glass lighting fixtures of Lalique, referred to as the '*poète de verre*', served as columns, giving impressions of an electrified Athenian Parthenon afloat at sea.[453] The ceiling's coffers, another source of electrical light, reinforced the effect of antiquity even further. Placed at the same relative position at the far end of the hall, the statue to Paix recalled Phidias' monumental sculpture of Pallas Athena. If any public space within the *Normandie* could epitomize the trend toward monumentality, glorification of the modern, and the high lifestyle of the upper classes, it was the *salle à manger* with its near-religious ambience. Consecrated here, however, was Château Lafitte-Rothschild, Dom Perignon, foie gras, caviar, chateaubriand, and all the other delicacies attached to the luxurious high living of First Class passengers. Finding confirmation and near perfection in the *Normandie* was the proclivity to reconceive luxury within contemporary forms, already evident in the *Paris* and the *Ile de France*, which added modern edges to elites' lifestyles.

As Bouvens and Expert emphasized in letters and memos, all artistic works, pieces of furniture, lighting fixtures, carpeting and other articles were to have a unified presence on the *Normandie*. No space or object was to interfere with the overall design. As Bouvens wrote of a certain painting of Charles Walhain that he had rejected:

> We can appreciate the artist's talent. But such a work hasn't a place either in the main reception area or any other. It also seems to me that the work ... should be in the same spirit as the decor of the grand areas.[454]

Numerous stylistic and iconographic motifs found in Art Deco were the chief inspirations for TRANSAT's distinct maritime art and the *Normandie*'s design. At the same time, they reflected subjects that were greatly important to French nationalism and Norman pride. Walking through the *Normandie*, in fact, one would have been struck by the large bronze doors leading to the First Class *salle à manger* created by Raymond Subes. Circular medallions commemorating the historic towns of Normandy were affixed to the door and displayed the chief highlights of the city – whether religious, civic, or commercial in nature. Included on the doors were Le Havre, Cherbourg, (the ports of departure of the great French paquebots), Lisieux, Saint-Lô,

Rouen and Caen, all of which held great religious and social significance to Normandy. In Le Halle Superieur, symbolic representations of Normandy's maritime legacy were evident in bas reliefs by artists like Georges Saupique. One could recall Norman expertise on the high seas – a reality well before France became a nation. William the Conqueror's massing of ships on the shores of the English Channel as he embarked on his successful invasion of England in 1066 was the most famous instance of this history. Carrying the Norseman theme even further, Saupiques' sculptural relief accorded the Vikings themselves an important place with homage to Odin and other Viking deities.[455] Related images were also found on TRANSAT publicity brochures.[456] Perhaps the appropriate conclusion to draw was that the barbaric energy of the Norsemen had contributed to the increasingly advanced art of navigation that Normandy furthered so greatly. Granted, the statue of Paix did not exactly mesh with the violence that drove those Viking expeditions.

Art Deco was not only another modern crystallization of twentieth-century forms. Despite its obviously modern character, Art Deco absorbed themes and styles connected to the past – including those of antiquity. The relief panels of Jean Dunand and Jean Dupas gave resonance to this combined use of modern and ancient. Their gold lacquered finish and presentation were modern. Yet their portrayal of African scenes in reed-covered settings suggested ancient Egyptian art with frontal presentations of the chest and profile views of the head.

As noted earlier, fascination with archaeology had already shaped the interior design of CMM (Confédération Messageries Maritimes) ships like the *Aramis*. At the same time, increasingly abstract, symbolist and expressionistic artistic trends complemented the new interest in pre-Renaissance art. Dunand and Dupas thus reflected contemporary aesthetic developments, and, in this instance, their work meshed perfectly with the modern tone of the *Normandie*, whose modernity was rounded at the edges by older forms and subjects. At times, such reliefs seemed more reflective of the ancient world. In other works like Dupas' Poseidon, the metallic sheen and contours of the subjects were nearly Leger-like in representing the mechanical rhythms of the twentieth century even in a mythological framework. As has been said of the *Normandie*:

> The dominant impression given by pictures of the interior is one of lavish decorative luxury, with notions of modernity given a flamboyant setting designed for conspicuous consumption. The lighting and furniture represented the development of a conservative Art Deco idiom, but although simple shapes, the decoration often reverted to natural forms ... Some of Dunand's 133 feet of gold lacquer and 92 square feet of colored incensed lacquer decoration were moderately stylized, but both Dunand and Dupas consistently rejected images of modernity in favour of those of tradition. Gone were suggestions of speed, mechanization and abstraction; they were replaced by exotic but traditional maritime scenes.[457]

Art Deco's fashionable smartness was intended to further the high living of the opulent by conveying impressions of modern style without the enigmatic, challenging and thorny images of the avant-garde. If elites had been in the forefront of those sponsoring modern artists, many within their ranks desired tamer art. Egyptianesque works thrown into the modern linear spaces of the *Normandie* only reinforced this feeling, which was one reason for celebrities to feel at home on what was called the 'Ritz-sur-mer'.[458] As one French Line brochure stated, 'A liner is neither a museum nor a palace: it is both a means of transport and a hotel ... Art then must serve to divert and charm people ... Its decorative art should allude to the fantasies of the present than to absolute forms of beauty.' Roger-Marx also felt that as a product of the industrial age, a liner's artwork had to be seen in a different light and could not be as avant-garde as that to which gallery owners were accustomed.[459]

With all the accents added to give the *Normandie* a familiar human aura and offset the dominance of the machine, the liner was still overwhelmingly modern in character. Built on such an enormous, monumental scale and able to travel at great speed, the 'paquebot' seemed an ultimate symbol of the merging of science, technology and modernism. It was far removed from the château model of the *France*; its comfort and luxuries were accessible to the masses of Third Class passengers but at the same time satisfied First Class passengers that they were going in modern style. As Roger-Marx said of the *Normandie*, 'it is not a copy or aggrandizement of the past: it is something new ... it is the ship of tomorrow.'[460] Later, observers would come to view it as one of the great signs and symbols of civilized progress.[461]

The style of the *Normandie* was reflected also in the new Gare Maritime in Le Havre, which was planned to display a unified TRANSAT style evident along the pier and on the ship. Further evidence of this form was found at the 1937 Paris Exposition International, where a miniature model of the *Normandie*'s dining room was on display. Even in this artificial environment visitors could admire the design of the room and obtain a sense of what it might be like to inhabit the liner. As is evident, design of French Line ships directly connected the two expositions of 1925 and 1937, with 1931 as a transition. In the Exposition of 1937, the company managed the restaurant of the Palais de la Marine Marchande, situated on the Quai d'Orsay between the Pont de la Concorde and the Pont Alexandre III. French Line's publicity magazine boasted that the restaurant A Bord de Normandie gave visitors a taste of 'the elegant, charming atmosphere on board both our transatlantic and cruise liners.'[462] Not surprisingly, the French pavilion at the New York World's

Fair of 1939 would be focused, once again, on the *Normandie*. Events leading to the Second World War gradually closed in irreversibly on the great liner, but it remained a symbol of French achievement rivaling the Eiffel Tower, Versailles and Chartres Cathedral up to the outbreak of the war.[463]

In Britain, the *Queen Mary* was envisioned as a challenge to the *Normandie* – in terms of tonnage, speed and artistic design. Cunard placed great hopes in Hull 534, but the economic crisis of the time compelled it to seek massive state assistance and to merge with its domestic rival – White Star Line. Only under such a condition would the British government grant the type of support that would enable the company to rescue 534 from rust and complete it as the *Queen Mary*.

The *Mary* was to rival the *Normandie* in representing the new era of ocean liners. As seen already, the liner was publicized as having all the modern technology, materials and comforts considered essential to success. Air conditioning, for instance, was advertised as key to avoiding complaints from perspiring passengers about the pitfalls and horrors experienced during the *Mauretania*'s summer cruises in the Caribbean (not the wisest of itineraries). As discussed earlier, the presence of communications devices were promoted since 'the ultimate symbol of modernity is the telephone beside the bed ready to order a midnight supper from the never-closed kitchen or to call up a friend for cocktails, or to bridge the wide Atlantic to your own home or office.'[464] Such a view certainly looks ahead to our day of mobile phones, the internet and ipads, all expected to operate on today's ships though frowning passengers reflect how often the reception fails.

Under the direction of Percy Bates, Cunard planned the liner on an unprecedented scale in terms of speed and tonnage. Like TRANSAT, it was motivated by fears of competition to come from Germany, Italy and the United States. With news leaking out about the building of the *Normandie* on an epic scale, the decision was made to create a liner that would incorporate not only all the technological prerequisites for modern comfort, but also the artistic and decorative currents reflective of twentieth-century life. TRANSAT and Cunard sought to leave behind former conceptions of grandeur and style and to present a more sophisticated, updated and streamlined example of luxury. The *Queen Mary* was Cunard's answer to the *Normandie*.

Nevertheless, the *Mary* was not to be a mere duplicate of the *Normandie*. The British had always operated at a cultural distance from Continental models and were suspicious of French, German, or Italian influences. The *Mary*'s creation would be marked by formative English cultural influences, suspicion of trends from its cross-channel neighbors, and partial adherence to some of the features that highlighted previous Cunard and White Star liners. Yet the *Queen Mary* was a product of its age with enough resemblance to the *Normandie* to make comparisons inevitable.

The American architect Benjamin Morris was selected to head the *Queen Mary*'s interior design. In turn, he chose to work closely with Arthur Davis who had utilized the hotel-palace style to design the *Aquitania* and other liners of the pre-war years. Morris himself was accustomed to working with artists and decorators who experimented with new forms. The result of this collaboration would be an unwieldy combination of new and old, defined as 'stately'.

The selection of Davis speaks volumes about the demand by English travelers for traditional decor. Certain constraints still confined Cunard-White Star even as it constructed a liner with a modern character. Questions of modernity focused on technological, not artistic, concerns, as seen in the references to the telephone. Even in defining modernism and offering views of the avant-garde, the company revealed an entrenched conservativism.

Ultra-modernity, however, does not imply what might be

called ultra-modernism aboard the Queen Mary. In the B-deck staterooms, as throughout the ship, the best work of the younger school of British artists will be appreciated ... but the instinct of their race, the tradition which they share with the Line itself, has kept them from exaggeration. Passengers will find much to marvel at ... but nothing to mar the sense of serene comfort.[465]

Modernism, then is to be kept within limits avoiding exaggeration, and not marring comfort, which again is given a racial twist. Describing the smoking room and shopping center, the publicity writers continued:

You will know how much this spirit means. The serenity you feel is akin to that of an ancient English inn ... the stewards might be old retainers of a lordly manor-house in which you are the honored guest. Despite the modernity of the setting, the latest ingenious provisions for your comfort, you sense that all this has been going on for a very long time, perfected from generation to generation ... as indeed it has within this same Line. Progress ... must never be permitted to alter the feeling of being at home, of sharing the warm hospitality that has always been Britain's own.[466]

An overwhelming cover of wood veneer found in most of its prominent spaces gave the *Queen Mary* an almost immediately recognizable decor. Seemingly infinite varieties of veneer grain patterns and color tones served as substitute murals as wood took on a life of its own. One particular area of veneer even resembled the figure of a person or a gargoyle, making the need for a portrait there altogether superfluous. Perhaps, when compared to the woods on the *Mauretania*, the overall effect was lighter and airier. Nevertheless, the connection to earlier currents of Cunard and White Star design was clear with wood setting the dominant note in First Class, Tourist and Third Class areas and enhancing the sense of English maritime tradition – only this time within a vaster and more monumental interior space.[467]

Even within this traditional context, however, transformations were apparent. Public spaces and cabins were highlighted by the Art Deco style in streamlined linearity and curvature as well and in modern materials like aluminum. Metallic sheens reflected the same reality of the machine age found on the *Normandie* or in New York City skyscrapers. Walking through the central shopping area of the *Mary* could cause one to think of the main lobby of a modern office building where, before taking the elevator to the desired floor, people first stopped to buy a newspaper or cigarettes. Columns and lighting fixtures in the First Class dining room bore the same unmistakable Art Deco stamp. Covering the wall at one end, the transatlantic map by MacDonald Gill, with its silhouetted continents and contemporary clock, transmitted the modern age's dazzling nature as a crystal model of the *Mary* moved across the ocean to represent the ship's changing position. While various shades of wood softened the tone, the use of silver, bronze and other metals reflecting the electrical illumination projected modernistic echoes in a manner not too far removed from the dining room on the *Normandie*.[468]

Further hints of modernism were also found in Doris Zinkeisen's mural in the Verandah Grill. Her portrayal of circus and street performers has the air of a Henri Rousseau work or at least a derivative, naïve canvas, with a playfulness contrasting to the solemnity of typical maritime art, and a social character more popular in scope.[469] This Chaplinesque air challenged the expectations of passengers desiring murals like those on the *Aquitania*. Also commissioned to paint canvases for certain private areas of the ship were artists of the Bloomsbury circle like Vanessa Bell. As Bell was the sister of Virginia Woolf and Bloomsbury renowned for its unique cultural and intellectual character, Cunard-White Star was clear in its partial acceptance of modernism. Nevertheless, as evident in some of the above quotations, company managers also were very eager to impress the stamp of tradition on the decor. Kenneth Shoesmith, for instance, painted the 'Madonna of the Atlantic' as part of the décor in the chapel. While still undeniably linked to the ship's larger design, its gold background with a few modern flourishes looked back to a revered, iconic, religious tradition connected to the British fad for 'medieval modernism'.[470]

As the directors went about considering and even hiring certain artists, the limits of their tolerance for the modern came into focus. Benjamin Morris himself had to intervene in some matters. Stephen Bone, son of the well-known medieval modernist, Muirhead Bone, was turned down for any consideration for the library's decoration after Morris described preliminary sketches as crude. This view had circulated among managers like Bates and Lord Essendon, who found the younger Bone's paintings too unbalanced in color and form and clashing with the restful atmosphere necessary for the room. Despite adamant protests from Bone's father, the paintings were rejected. Essendon then urged Bates to send personal letters to all prospective artists and craftsmen, 'emphasizing the fact that they are engaged in the greatest marine work in history, and appealing to them for the sake of the prestige of the British Mercantile Marine to put their whole heart and soul into the work, and to cooperate in every way in making the ship a success.'[471] This appeal could be interpreted either as an endorsement of traditional art radical modernism, but Bone's fate and the stress on 'marine work' revealed the directors' mindset.

Most controversial, however, was the case of the Bloomsbury Circle artist, Duncan Grant, who had been gaining some renown as a modern painter. Because of Grant's reputation, the bitterness and rancor over his selection would embarrass Cunard-White Star in the public world and would not disappear for several years

– even returning as the 1939 New York World's Fair approached. The turmoil from the controversy would provoke other well-known artists, critics and art historians to tackle the company head-on. Morris himself recommended Grant, convincing him to create two paintings for the main lounge, for a payment of £300 each and to consider designing some of the carpeting.

Grant and Bell met frequently as they confronted the Cunard-White Star management regarding the terms of their contract. Leach sent Grant the contract compelling him to agree to such points as

> Materials which I am to furnish are to be the best and most enduring of their respective kinds and my work is to be done with my best care and attentions to conform with the importance and dignity of the setting and the nature of the surrounding work … If desired by the Company's Architects I will submit preliminary studies which shall be discussed with the object of securing a mutually satisfactory procedure … I agree to work in a spirit of helpful cooperation with the Company's representatives.[472]

As the paintings came more into view, Cunard managers became increasingly critical. Debate about the worth of the panels to company intentions intensified, and Leach was asked to communicate to the artist the company's concern:

> My directors have been reviewing the present situation concerning the Company's commitments with painters of the *Queen Mary* and I have been instructed to modify and cancel these agreements, as may be necessary, to bring them into line with a definite policy. It is felt that too high a proportion of the murals would appeal only to a limited coterie interested in the development of modern painting

248

and, that this condition must be changed to provide these
pictures with wide general appeal.[473]

Furthermore, he felt that Grant's figures were out of scale. Leach
was reflecting Cunard's suspicion and scorn of avant-garde
modernism, which did not complement the social character
and country club setting desired by the line. Grant's prospective
work, in particular, while not striking us as modernistic as
many works of the day, was not seen as fitting in with the
overall decor of the main lounge, which was conceived along
traditional lines. Elite passengers, whiling away their time in
undisturbed composure, might, it was thought, have it jarred
by unfamiliar forms of art. Their reactions, of course, would
be incomprehensible to passengers in the non-luxurious areas
of the liner.

Grant, responding to Leach, not surprisingly, expressed
consternation. He pointed to support from Morris who 'never
mentioned the possibility of interference by any other persons.'
In another letter, he suggested that the company chairman was
breaking an already existing contract made with ship architects,
and justified his expectation of full payment according to the
contract's stipulations.[474] Grant not only defended artistic
freedom, but also his right to the proper monetary compensation
for his work, which had an unquestionable financial value. Like
other artists of his day, Grant was fully aware of a market value
attached to works of contemporary art, a lesson Picasso taught
so successfully. Art was not only a pure sphere but a commodity.
Artists accordingly were to be considered not only geniuses but
also career-minded people.

Cunard's response was not encouraging. Leach received a
memo from the secretary's office urging him to see 'Mr Grant
and explaining to him that the paintings are not considered to
be in harmony with their surroundings, and it has been decided
not to have them.'[475] Bates' office approved Grant's request for

immediate payment – but only on a partial basis. One can surmise that the true tenor and nature of managerial opinion was rather more animated behind the scenes. Lord Essendon, for instance, congratulated Bates on his decision to reject the Grants, saying, 'I am tremendously relieved at your decision about the pictures in the Lounge. I think that that they were simply appalling.' Essendon went on to recommend instead that a full length painting of *Queen Mary* fill the space, a change which would assuage Cunard concerns for the harmony of the room.[476] Bates himself revealed his strong dislike for Grant's work by writing 'I told you so' to Major Hardinge who backed the artist.[477] Grant's fellow Bloomsbury associate and director of paintings at the National Gallery, Kenneth Clark, later wrote that Bates' wife, who especially disliked the panels, had said, 'we must have little deer, you know, gazelles'.[478] Since Clark initially recommended Grant for the job, he became especially upset.

In pressing for full payment, Grant used language that also revealed other important considerations for artists, writing, 'I take it that you are not proposing to do this great damage to my reputation and to my fully justified expectations without some offer of substantial compensation.'[479] With all the press coverage generated by the *Queen Mary*'s decoration, Grant feared severe damage to his career. A project of this magnitude by a giant like Cunard placed well-known artists in the harsh glare of publicity and exposed them to unprecedented risks.

Grant further requested the return of his canvases, but Cunard refused to do so for the time being, and a new tug of war commenced. In the process another instance of the condition of art as a commodity became evident. Cunard's motivation at this time, however, was also to prevent any possible damage to its reputation from Grant's exhibition of such highly publicized works elsewhere. Realizing that it may not have acted in the Grant case with the most artistically progressive manner, Cunard feared embarrassment coming from public perception of it as an unsophisticated company not up to the aesthetic astuteness of, for instance, French Line. Further reminders of that controversy would only fuel memories. After rejecting Grant's canvases, the company was not, therefore, prepared simply to return them and utter a relieved tone of 'good riddance'. Instead, Cunard hoped to achieve a huge 'sweeping of things under the rug' and avoid embarrassment by maintaining their possession.

Morris himself expressed an ambiguous position. Writing to John Brocklebank, Morris talked about the need for more regular inspections of 'the artist's work while in progress of completion, which gives the opportunity of constructive criticism.'[480] Given the degree of antipathy to Grant's panels among Cunard board members, it is doubtful that any truly constructive criticism would have been offered or any genuine accommodation between the artist and the line reached. Artists seldom accept interference in their work. The well-known dispute over Diego Rivera's frescoes in Rockefeller Center during the 1930s was one famous dispute. Grant also strongly defended his artistic decisions, though they were not affected by any strongly left wing political inclinations as was Rivera when he included Bolshevik tributes in his work. Morris was anxious about the controversy and wrote a conciliatory letter to Grant stating that he was

> Greatly distressed to hear ... that your panels for the Main Lounge had been rejected ... Having the highest personal regard for your talent and cognizant of your reputation, I was happy to suggest your name for one of the most important rooms on the Ship, and it is a matter of deep regret to me that the Committee has been unable to accept your paintings. Not having seen anything but the earliest sketches, you will realize that it is impossible for me to comment upon their character, but judging from the improvisations which I have already received, I am not able to be optimistic about a reversal of the decision.[481]

Morris' effectiveness was hurt by his being in New York while the key decisions were being made in Liverpool, but it also seems clear that he never had complete control over artistic decisions as Grant had been led to believe. The Cunard inner circle did.

Despite Cunard's efforts to restrict the damage, the controversy's range soon reached into the legal, journalistic and greater artistic worlds. In fact, its flames threatened to fan an artistic conflagration. Further negotiations were necessary before either side could find satisfaction. Nevertheless, the line braced itself for legal action taken by Grant's lawyers, Field, Roscoe and Company. Cunard's lawyers, Hill, Dickinson and Co., expressed confidence that Grant's claims had no foundation and that the company would prevail in court. Of more concern was the adverse publicity beginning to permeate the English art world. A variety of articles critical of Cunard's decision appeared in papers like the *Daily Express*, the *Evening Standard*, and *News Chronicle*, suggesting that Cunard-White Star was backward in its view of modern art.

Cunard managers were mindful of protest against its decision. An internal and anonymous memo sent to Lord Essendon explained 'that there is a good deal of indignation in London about it [the Grant controversy], and prominent people in the Art World are setting upon a protest.'[482] Bates subsequently received a collective letter of protest from Grant's supportive friends in the larger art world (including the prominent Clark, Clive Bell, Samuel Courtauld, Augustus John and John Maynard Keynes – his lover). A company official noted that Clark's address was at the head of the letter.[483] The petitioners protested Cunard's last-minute rejection of Grant's panels – a fact that they felt embarrassed him and undermined his status as an artist. There was also praise for Grant as,

There can be few men in England today whose work is more widely and sincerely admired. No one denies his charm and

power as a painter of landscape and still life, but ... his real
gift is for decoration ... and a commission by Duncan Grant
on a scale worthy of his talents would be a most important
event for English art. Such an important opportunity seemed
to have been provided by the decoration of the Queen Mary,
and in the opinion of those of us who have seen them,
the panels which he executed on your behalf are the most
important and successful examples of his work ... We hope
that the names appended to this letter will convince you that
our protest does not come from a small clique or faction, but
from lovers of art representing almost every state of opinion.
In the interest of justice and of English art we ask you to
reconsider your decision.[484]

The depth of passion regarding this controversy can be gauged by
the reference to justice. Perhaps this should not surprise readers
too much since the near religious adoration of 'art for art's sake'
is common to the aesthetic scene. Also striking is the insecure
stress on 'English art', particularly when one considers Clark's
praise of the *Normandie* as the greatest ship ever built – based
in part on its decorative art.[485] Clark clearly wrote most of the
language in the petition, and the feeling that a great opportunity
to raise the level of English art had been lost was connected to a
sense of rivalry with the French – whose accomplishment with the
Normandie he already praised. Such national consciousness was
echoed by Clark's own feeling expressed in his autobiography
that 'Duncan was the only living English painter who could hold
a candle to the French.'[486] As Clark was Scottish, his concern for
British art reveals a new level of national pride, heightened even
further by Samuel Cunard's Scottish origins and the existence of
the John Brown shipyards near Glasgow. Nationalism, even in a
more restrained form, was evident even in the world of art and
ship decoration. Bell, who was going through a row over work
for the *Mary*, wrote in a personal letter of Keynes's attempts to

persuade his friend, Bates, to reconsider the company's decision – to no avail.[487]

Such back and forth legal proceedings went on with Bates asserting Cunard's position that it had kept to the terms of Grant's contract. Fall-out from the press articles, however, caused the line considerable concern. Bates was warned by a business associate (a dealer of wheat who shipped his grain on Cunard ships) not to snub the advice of prominent people in the art world, causing Bates to admit that public proclamation only worsened the situation.[488] Lord Essendon, meanwhile, urged Cunard to excuse its rejection of Grant by pointing to the need for a portrait honoring Queen Mary in the lounge – something that would both acknowledge the company's important relationship with Buckingham Palace and state assistance and convince the public.

Grant's attorneys argued that Cunard-White Star Line's publicity campaigns and advertising in the press had caused the artist undue damage and emphasized that the decision was 'in the highest degree injurious to Mr Duncan Grant's reputation as an artist' since the *Queen Mary* was 'a work of national importance' known to all. They demanded both full repayment and return of the panels.[489]

All of the wrangling eventually led to Cunard's agreeing to full repayment for Grant's work, but not for any injuries to his reputation. Grant was also to exhibit the same panels only after receiving Cunard's permission and, in fact, 'to use the paintings only in such manner and on such occasions as the Company should approve with a penalty stipulated at a fixed sum for default.'[490] Although this wording reflected more accurately the opinions of the lawyers and not the reservations of Cunard-White Star, a consensus was reached. In the interim, the panels were to be turned over to the Tate Gallery for safekeeping, fulfilling apparently Cunard's hopes for avoiding future exhibits where references to the *Queen Mary* would spread further

adverse publicity.[491] The company's claim to own the paintings was made exactly because it wanted to ensure that their display would not reignite the controversy through press coverage.

These expectations were tested in 1939 as preparations for the New York World's Fair began. Clark helped organize part of the British Pavilion and, in planning to display the Grant panels as part of the exhibit, sought Cunard-White Star's permission, which was promptly denied. Despite the British Council's backing for Grant, the line was still concerned that displaying the panels in such a public arena near its own exhibit would revive controversial memories and cause embarrassment.[492] Reassurance from the British Council that mention or reference to the *Queen Mary* would be avoided did not reassure Cunard-White Star, which responded,

> There is no doubt that the Press and those in art circles generally would recognize the paintings as the work commissioned for the Queen Mary, and we can foresee the possibility of a revival in the Press or elsewhere of the controversy as to the rejection of the pictures for our ship. We feel, therefore, that it would be undesirable on our part to do anything which would re-awaken these old controversies.[493]

The view of New York as a modernism-wise city dominated artistic perceptions, and Cunard-White Star was very sensitive to any fall-out from a public forum that would have it deemed a company behind the times, especially as it prepared for the launch of its next liner – the *Queen Elizabeth*.

Although surpassing the *Mary* in tonnage, the *Elizabeth*'s cost was to be less – especially in regard to the decoration. Flourishes of Art Deco as found on the *Mary* were to be more restrained and overall design much plainer. Wood again dominated the interior of the ship with the familiar aim of providing hints of manor life. There were resemblances with the *Mary* on this score, but the effect was far less cosmopolitan.

Some lingering bad feeling from the time of the *Mary*'s construction also erupted. For one, nationalistic concerns came to the forefront. Since Morris was American, among the conservative British views of the *Mary* was one holding that it was more American than British in inspiration, even if sharing characteristics with the *Normandie* as a 1930s transatlantic liner. Company officials accepted the *Queen Mary*'s dual American and British inspiration as a part of the long Cunard maritime tradition connecting the two worlds.[494] Yet letters among political figures revealed great reservations about the wisdom of choosing Morris for the new liner. MP Alfred C. Bossom wrote to Neville Chamberlain (then Chancellor of the Exchequer):

> As you may know ... Morris, an American naval architect had charge of the interior fitting of the *Queen Mary*, and as there are very great number of equally competent architects here in this country who are by no means overworked, do you not think it would be desirable to see that in this second ship a Britisher has this work under control?...[Morris'] connection with the work of the *Queen Mary* has led to a very considerable amount of feeling among our people here.[495]

Unemployment and the public's resentment of foreign competition was causing MP's to pressure Cunard to hire British architects and designers – who in no way were as economically vulnerable as were riveters and dock-workers. The Cunard general manager wrote to Bates

> Would it not be better for us to select the British man we are to have before Morris comes into the picture? When we started the Queen Mary it was purely a Cunard ship and we were entitled to employ whom we liked. This second

one is perhaps more definitely a British ship ... therefore it
behooves us not to bring in at too early a date any American
or other non-British influence.[496]

Rarely was British nationalism in maritime questions more
noticeable.

Morris himself expressed his willingness to collaborate with
a British architect, although he expressed his dislike of J. E.
Whipp of Mewes and Davis. Much debate flourished among
Cunard managers as to who should be the collaborating
decorator of Hull 552, as the future *Elizabeth* was first called.
Despite the fact that Brocklebank saw him as 'rather colorless',
Grey Wornum was chosen to work with Morris, but Whipp
was to provide an assisting role.[497] Determined to avoid some
of the problems encountered in the *Mary*'s decoration – most
notably the lingering echoes of the Duncan Grant controversy
– Cunard asserted direct control over key decorative decisions.
Such an insistence stemmed, in part, from a belief that Grant's
hiring was mishandled from the start. As Bates wrote to Sir
Hugo Cronliffe-Owen, 'I ran into much criticism when I was
obliged to take a line of my own in rejecting a work by Mr
Duncan Grant which he had executed for the *Queen Mary*.'[498]
Things would be different now as Cunard decided to play it
safe and make design more a matter of maritime tradition than
of artistic statement and Morris was now to work within a
more restricted and defined British context. While getting his
wish to work with Worum rather than J. E. Whipp, Morris
had to endure Whipp's sniping behind the scenes letters (can
we call this 'Whipping'?) attacking Morris for, among other
things, 'taking too many liberties of design'. Morris also had to
face an old issue from former days: Lord Ashield, Chairman of
London's Passenger Transport Board insisted that a portrait of
the queen be placed in a prominent area.

It was no easy matter to choose between modernistic styles

and more traditional ones. Maritime design was becoming amorphous. In the end, the *Queen Elizabeth* would not have the chance to be displayed as a liner of the '30s in the way that the *Queen Mary* or the *Normandie* had. The outbreak of the Second World War meant that the liner would find its first use as a troop carrier painted in battleship grey rather than the traditional black, white and red of Cunard tradition, though as a result it would be viewed with a more patriotic aura in the long run. This halo, however, did not prevent the *Queen Elizabeth* from acquiring tarnished status as a means of transatlantic travel as competition from the airplane increased in intensity.

It was a long way from the sailing of the *Titanic* in 1912 to the first passenger voyage of the *Queen Elizabeth* after the Second World War. Much had changed, not only in the size and speed of ships, but also with their design. As Steerage Class ended and the new space allocations for Tourist Third Cabin became apparent, decorators began to envision new avenues. While for a time during the '20s the taste for historical art and decoration, especially among First Class passengers, was still evident, the interest in modern streamlined styles grew as seen in the *Paris* and the *Ile de France*. It was not that class identity had been at the heart of the period look of the *Mauretania*, *Aquitania*, or the *France*. After all, the middle and lower classes were also awed by the plush period look and expressed reverence for it. People from all classes were still drawn to the new styles, a fact that did not prevent designers from recasting upper class exclusivity and sophistication in the context of Art Deco or the international style. That snobbishness continued to flourish on the *Normandie* is all too apparent. And for all the change, it is also remarkable just how strong the pull of tradition was in matters of decor. Even as the *Queen Mary* exhibited the modern transatlantic look, the 'ship of the wood veneers' also emanated a historical resonance, reaching all classes. Traditional ambience still exerted its influence as any works out of keeping with the anticipated aura of the liner were excluded.

If modernism and decorative traditions were polar opposites in the art world, the fact was that their application to ocean liners could never be a straightforward and simple dichotomy. Too many varieties of people, emerging from the complex social realities of the modern world, were on board to make unanimous taste a possibility. Part of modernity's paradox involves the persistence within it of the past to which many in modern society still feel kinship. Such was the case in the interwar years as well.

There clearly were designers and architects with intentions of spreading styles that uncompromisingly reflected the modern age – regardless of how remote these styles were from the tastes and mentalities of people they targeted. Sometimes, they managed to make artistic statements in a revolutionary setting. They also confronted company directors sensitive about social predispositions to certain styles and reacting to statements made in boardroom meetings or in letters about this or that painting or statue. The result would sometimes be a compromise, perhaps outraging the visionaries and seeming too undefined or conservative. Since modernist style was thought transportable to all kinds of settings, museums or private homes were not alone in displaying it. On the other hand, expectations for the palace look were still strong and were being met in grand hotels. Memories of the splendor of the earlier liners also lingered. One had to accommodate the many. Even today, in the wake of the renewed fascination with the *Titanic*, nostalgia for that style is strong. Perhaps some passengers found enough modernism in the shape and size of the liner's exterior, thinking something more traditional should await after they mounted the gangway and passed through the entrance. Perhaps. But others didn't think so. They hoped to connect the interior to the exterior in a more dramatic way. As we have seen, the results of all this dialog and effort were mixed. The one remaining fact is overall reverence for the liners' appearance from the piers. No interior could ever mar those initial impressions made by an ocean liner either as it stood by the docks or came into harbor accompanied by the necessary fleet of tugboats.

Conclusion
Liners in the Afterglow

In July 1949, radio broadcasts in New York City crackled with the excited voices of announcers welcoming the legendary *Ile de France*'s resumption of transatlantic service.
For this ship, long cherished by Americans before the war and later praised as a troop transporter, New Yorkers went all out to prepare a welcome.

John Wingate, reporting for WOR Radio on 27 July, described the scene as the legendary ship entered New York harbor at 6:00. 'A pause [was] made so photographs could get a picture of one French girl greeting another French girl, the Statue of Liberty and the *Ile de France*.' Just a few days earlier Adele Hurst on WPAT in Paterson, New Jersey anticipated the liner's return in similar terms, exclaiming,

> I see where a famous French lady has gotten herself all done over after the war and she's coming over here on a big visit, arriving the 27th of July. And I guess all the great artists and designers in France have been working on her, so she ought to make a very chic appearance, even if she isn't so young. She's a boat. I'm speaking of the famous *Ile de France*, that big transatlantic luxury liner. Before the war, you know, in

fact since the 1920s, she has been hailed as just about the most fashionable thing afloat, and now they say she is more fashionable than ever. And I'm sort of glad to hear that chef Magrin has his old job back.[499]

Several assumptions are striking in these quotes: France is sophisticated and cosmopolitan and associated with fashion and high cuisine; Americans beneath the surface yearn for 'high culture', and ships resemble women. Gloria Brent, reporting for WEAM Radio, in fact, expanded on the sexualized interior of the ship she perceived on a visit onboard two days later:

> The woman's touch is obvious on many of the new luxury liners and it is especially apparent on the *Ile de France* when she arrived in New York harbor on her post-war maiden voyage.
>
> The decoration and arrangement of the apartments, suites, and cabins first class show the result of careful planning always with a special effort to please lady travelers.[500]

Co-hosts Caroline and Allen on WICC from Bridgeport, Connecticut, discussed the niceties of French cuisine as revealed in fine details. After talking about assorted desserts, Caroline observed, 'another hint ... from the *Ile de France* chef is an easy way of making those little pancakes which are such a popular French dessert, very thin little pancakes browned in butter and then rolled up and sprinkled with powdered sugar' – an offering Allen more correctly called 'crêpes suzettes'.[501]

Others like Harry Clark on WCBS noted a different reality, describing the wartime troop transport experience of the *Ile de France* and adding that 'French Line officials say she represents the spirit of post-war France, bidding all out for ocean trade.' Henry Cassidy on NBC observed,

This is an important event for all of France for it puts this country back into competition on the North Atlantic shipping lanes. The French merchant marine, partly through the aid of the Marshall Plan, is now nearly back to its pre-war tonnage, and the *Ile de France* will bring in more dollars where they are badly needed.

More cautiously, Paul Harvey, also on NBC, concluded of the ship, 'she's not the greatest ship afloat, but it's her first trip since her post-war refurbishment; and to the Frenchman it means that his nation once more has its boots in the sea and its head in the air.' This evaluation was referring to recent ships built by Cunard-White Star, United States Line and other companies that had surpassed the expectations of the late 1920s when the *Ile de France* had been launched. It was nonetheless true that having a presence in the transatlantic passenger market was vitally important to national pride everywhere, especially for France. At an earlier time, the renowned poet, Charles Péguy, had described the region after which the liner was named as 'the most French, the most profoundly essential, authentic, and traditional province, a province by itself, an old French province ...'[502] For a people that felt such national humiliation as the French did between 1940 and 1945, the revival of a competitive place within the transatlantic market signaled a return as well to pride and glory. While the *Normandie*'s fate continued to symbolize the greater horror of the era, hopes were already being expressed that a new liner might become the ultimate yet in technological novelty and design. As the French wondered whether Charles de Gaulle would emerge as the future leader of the country, plans were being hatched for such a new superliner to forge the way into the future.

Revelry and enthusiasm did characterize the mood as older, newer and refurbished liners resumed a transatlantic passenger heritage interrupted by the war. But changes were apparent to travelers and critics alike. The maritime scene of the late 1940s was not to be confused with that of the interwar years. Contemporaries forty years of age and older held memories of the previous revival of transatlantic service after the First World War. Hopes for a similar resurgence were evident once again. The reality was, however, that by 1939 transatlantic steamship service had seen its best days. While the full potential of Cunard-White Star's *Queen Mary* and *Queen Elizabeth* was yet to be reached, and while great liners like TRANSAT's last *France* and United States Line's SS *United States* were still to come off the slipways en route to newer, more exciting dashes across the Atlantic for the Blue Riband, the Second World War proved to be more damaging to the steamship lines than the First World War had been. This blow, coupled with an ever advancing aviation industry with its newer jet-engined planes finding an increased presence on the transatlantic scene, dashed the hopes of the ocean liner companies. Officials within felt that an alternative form of crossing was necessary and feebly protested that 'getting there is half the fun'. But with the new age of jets and supersonic concords just around the corner, that argument would find deaf ears among those wanting to reach destinations as soon as possible.

Steamships made dramatically public contributions during the war years. While darker events clouded the late '30s and '40s – Blitzkrieg, extermination camps, the dropping of the atomic bombs on Hiroshima and Nagasaki – ocean liners continued to occupy a place in the political and military picture. By the end of 1938, British and French leaders had effectively handed over parts of northern Czechoslovakia to Hitler and devastating attacks on Jews were unleashed in the infamous Kristallnacht in Germany. Such was the reality of appeasement, which also revealed a maritime side. Some months later, in May 1939, Hamburg America's *St Louis* sailed from Hamburg with 937 Jewish refugees bound for Havana, Cuba. Over a month later, at that end of that journey, American officials in Havana and Miami would deny it entry into the 'melting pot', provoking cartoons of 'Lady Liberty' turning her back on those desperate people, many of whom would end up being deported to the concentration camps after being forced to disembark in Belgium.[503]

The *St Louis*'s ill-fated voyage served to dramatize the western world's clumsy and tragic response to Nazi Germany's treatment of Jews. It also brought reminders of the fact that ships had frequently been conveyors of misery. Ships in the past had often been associated with flights from persecution, although they carried another legacy as in the wooden vessels used to carry out the murderous transatlantic African slave trade. English Puritans had left behind uncertain conditions, sailing on the *Mayflower* in search of new lands offering them religious freedom. Even more recently, the ocean liners had transported immigrants to America in the terrible confines of steerage class passage. Homer's epic, *The Odyssey*, equated the maritime voyage with endless despair culminating in Odysseus' tortuous experience listening to the Sirens' voices. Mythology transformed the journey into an odyssey that represented the agony of the hero in search of his long-remembered home, Ithaca. The voyage of the *St Louis* followed a long line of sea journeys accented by melancholy, which the lapping waves of the sea intensified. But in this case, the *St Louis* represented the unprecedented conditions of the late thirties and forties felt internationally as ships lost their former aura of luxury and leisure and became attached instead to the nature of the times.

Part of the history of the war directly involved ocean liners. Italian Line lost two ships with the sinking of its *Conte di Savoia* and the former Blue Riband holder, *Rex*, by Allied bombers. German liners were tied up in harbor, left to rust away and were captured later by the Allies. If they did not go out in the same blaze of glory as the Italian liners, they still were debased in stature, their fates determined after the war's conclusion. To make up for the destruction of French Line's fleet, the former *Europa* was given over as reparations and renamed the *Liberté*, as if in denial of the notorious Vichy regime and reaffirmation of the French democratic tradition repressed by the Nazis. Not surprisingly, the *Liberté* was celebrated in various Hollywood films of the fifties, most notably in Billy Wilder's *Sabrina*. If representing a chance for TRANSAT renewal, however, this agreement only served to further the demise of Germany's passenger fleet.

For the liners of Cunard-White Star and TRANSAT, the war also proved devastating, although nowhere near the level suffered by their Italian and German counterparts. The gigantic new ships – *Normandie*, *Queen Mary* and *Queen Elizabeth* – were all readied for transformation into wartime troop carriers, capable of most quickly transporting greater numbers of troops across the Atlantic. In this case, their immense size had advantages that airplanes, with their greater speed, lacked as the numbers of military passengers needing to be moved was uppermost in the minds of military strategists. Both the *Queen Mary* and the *Queen Elizabeth* acquired a new maritime and military status most visibly represented by their battleship-grey-painted hulls. For the *Queen Elizabeth*, the war meant delay of its maiden voyage as a passenger ship. Her real inaugural voyage involved a dramatic escape from European waters and a dash across the Atlantic during the early phase of the war. 'Dash' is the right word, as both gigantic liners had 'prices on their heads', given the Nazis' well-known promise of a massive reward to the German naval commander who managed to sink one or both. The historical allusion to the sinking of the *Lusitania* was no doubt intended.

The *Normandie*'s wartime situation proved more perilous. French Line itself seemed to have lost its independence even before the defeat of 1940, although its chief officials had continued to try to maintain operations. They had sailed the *Normandie* to New York just before the outbreak of war and it stayed there for security reasons. Even before Pearl Harbor, American military authorities decided to occupy the liner – an act that re-aroused French patriotism as sailors on board sang the Marseillaise and saluted the French flag when asked to leave the ship.[504] Fortune seemed to be on the great ship's side at first, with its seemingly propitious location in secure New York harbor as the fall of France unfolded. Fortune proved fickle as American military officials impounded the *Normandie* after Pearl Harbor and planned its conversion into a troop carrier. It was to be given the symbolic name *Lafayette*, referring no doubt to the first episode of American and French alliance. As the object of the Marquis de Lafayette's engagement in the 1770s had been to help American colonists gain independence from Britain, it may be assumed that the British government was not overly amused by the choice of new name for the troopship. Still, the times did not allow for much debate on names since it had taken so long for the United States to enter the war. With Churchill having vowed to fight to the end against the German military, the expression 'let bygones be bygones' could not have been more apropos.

Cunard officials had been wondering about the *Normandie*'s future with one New York representative of the company writing to Bates in 1941, 'The *Normandie* at the pier month after month getting rusty is a rather sad sight. The facts of the French situation are still something of a mystery here.'[505] Bates, meanwhile, was hearing and feeling the effects of the explosions of German Luftwaffe bombs near his house and wondering about the future of Britain, let alone Cunard-White Star. A catastrophic fire ended the great TRANSAT liner's brief history. As the *Normandie* was being converted into the *Lafayette*, a worker's torch being applied to lighting fixtures ignited life jackets nearby. As a result, much of the interior was consumed, and in an effort to save the ship, firefighters carried out a massive, ill-considered fire hosing that caused it to capsize.

Newspaper photographs of the *Normandie* in its tragi-absurd position were emblazoned on the public consciousness for months and years. People passing along the West Side Highway near the pier were curious and tried to gain a glimpse of the scene. Some took photographs. Others had spectacular views of the capsized liner from nearby high rise buildings. In the midst of world war, the capsized *Normandie* was a reminder both of the war's broadly destructive nature and of the ironic and painful memories of peacetime travel. Observers from various background offered their perspectives of the scenes before them. Jack Barry Bamford, a Royal Navy sailor who was one of 10,000 troops on the *Queen Mary* as it headed to New York (he was eventually to go to the Falklands), talked about the scene along the piers of New York harbor:

> There in the adjoining dock I saw a sight that I will long remember, the burnt out hull of the giant Normandie – once the glory of France's merchant fleet – now prostrate and helpless and sprawling on its sides ... It was indeed a sorry spectacle truly eloquent of the foul destruction wrought by the saboteurs [rumors abounded then that the Nazis had carried out the ship's destruction] ... And as I stood on the decks of our great liner I surveyed the plight of her former rival. My reflection took me back to those days, not very long ago, when the interest of the two nations was stirred by the keen competition which existed between these two great vessels in their struggles for the Blue Riband of the North Atlantic, and I could not help but dwell on the circumstances which had brought about the fall of France and which, in like manner, were so closely linked with those that resulted in the disaster which had befallen her greatest of ships.[506]

Those suspicions of Nazi involvement in the fire turned out to be false, but they did reflect the public's hysteria and paranoia of Germany's destructive reach. No one and nothing seemed safe. Such attitudes are common in wartime, but indirectly the *Normandie*'s destruction was caused by the vicissitudes of war.

Bamford also described the transformed *Queen Mary*, 'the three-funneled liner painted grey and somber-looking in its wartime coat but still, despite this, retaining its air of majesty' and immediately recognizable by its size and sweeping lines. Seeing the *Mary* as 'the former pride of Britain's merchant fleet, he defined her as 'conscripted to the nation's effort.'[507] Suites and cabins in the privileged decks were preserved to serve Winston Churchill and other political, diplomatic and military officials on the way to allied meetings in Québec or other areas. Some of the preparations for plotting strategy to end the war were held on board. In other areas, much of the living space had been transformed to house the 6–10,000 troops with eight or more people in bunk-bed arrangements crammed into each cabin.

Bamford perceived this situation as a test for British organization and military discipline. Tickets for cabin assignments were distributed to each person to ensure that there was 'no confusion or misunderstandings.' Some breakdown in order was to be expected, Bamford believed, given his guess at the 9–10,000 people on the ship during his voyage. And when it came time for meals, that dedication to order was severely challenged and sometimes broke down as a crowd pushed toward the saloon and 'the rush to obtain meals became a mad scramble as even this sized ship was not accustomed to so many on board.' He admitted that organization could have been better. Despite this crush of people, however, Bamford complimented the quality of the food and the generosity of allotted portions:

It consisted of three good solid meals a day, but it was that infernal quavering and pushing and shoving to obtain admission into the saloon which detracted so much from the actual enjoyment of eating.

As for the interior space itself, Bamford observed of the saloon that

> stripped and shorn of its former luxury appointments it now more resembled a true-to-type service mess with its innumerable rows of long tables and benches. All that survived this mutilation were the mural decorations or the oak paneling and the impressive gilded clock alongside the huge colored map of the North Atlantic.[508]

This comment especially pertains to the altered state of First Class areas. The changes there were far more dramatic than in the tourist sections, which had always been of a non-luxurious nature.

Despite good weather, the *Mary's* heralded 'roll and pitch' was the cause for much seasickness and a constant commute between one's bunk bed and the bathroom. Had they made the Athenian Parthenon into a military camp, ancient Spartans, with their legendary contempt for luxury and art, would not have envisioned a more perfect way of replacing artistic decor with utilitarian additions. Nevertheless, while the needs of the time definitely made art and decor secondary considerations, soldiers on board the *Queen Mary* and *Queen Elizabeth* were aware of the 'majesty' of the ships' pre-military characters and of their significant art and design features. The liners' military functions in hastening the demise of Nazi Germany only added to the awe they evoked.

Though on a smaller scale than the *Queen Mary*, Cunard's four-funneler, *Aquitania*, completed in 1914, left an even richer legacy. It had also served in the First World War as a troopship, and by 1946 was bringing back prisoners of war held in Japan and areas of Southeast Asia to Western Australia, South Africa, and other parts of the Empire.

P. C. Kieppe, a native of Holland, who had joined the Royal Navy during the course of the war and was held captive by Japan, described his voyage home that began with the *Aquitania*. Like Bamford, he observed the crowded conditions:

> I was given a bunk in a twin first class cabin, with thirteen others. A large metal contraption had been built in the center of the cabin to accommodate the extra bunks.[509]

Bathrooms usually supplied salt water, with fresh water available two times per day for shaving purposes. Two meals a day were served – breakfast and one hot meal – but 'seating in lounges was non-existent, you just found a spot to park yourself on the deck.' Kieppe's comments testify to the cramped space, which would have been more of a problem on the *Aquitania* – a much smaller and less roomy liner than the *Queen Mary*.

As so many hours were left blank in such crowded conditions, diversion was much demanded. In this case, 'the main pre-occupation of the troops during the long sunny run up to South Africa was booze. Being a day ship it was astonishing to watch what some of them were up to and the nervous energy spent trying to ferret out any secret place in this great ship where alcohol might be obtained.'[510] Kieppe found his supply readily available from the Second Engineer.

W. G. Riley was a prisoner of war, who spent time in the infamous Changi prison in Malaysia where so much torture was inflicted. His journal describes the humiliation and degradation he felt at being a prisoner, the constant beatings he and others were subjected to, and the beheadings in the camp. He was liberated on 30 January 1945 and was taken to the United States on the SS *Monterey*. After taking a train from San Francisco to New York, Riley boarded the *Queen Elizabeth* for England. As he wrote,

> We boarded this floating city and were accommodated in cabins, six men to each cabin. Although space was extremely

limited, we were generally comfortable compared with the conditions of accommodation for the many thousands of American troops who followed on board during the next two days. When finally we sailed out of New York harbor, it was reported that 24,000 servicemen and women were on board the ship. The organization defies description, suffice it to say – magnificent – when one considers the implications of such a large number of persons on one ship. On a cold grey day in late March, 1945 the *Queen Elizabeth* put out into the North Atlantic and although the War was still raging in Europe and Hitler's U boats were still operating, the *Queen Elizabeth* was unescorted by any Naval vessels or air cover.[511]

As they took note of cabin conditions, the quality of food and soldiers' social habits, among other things, Bamford, Kieppe and Riley reflected a concern for leisure on board these liners, even in the difficult, crowded conditions. Time for such recollections was now available and Kieppe's account was especially detached as it was written after the war's conclusion. The *Aquitania*, *Queen Mary* and *Queen Elizabeth* also lived out the rest of their sailing days in different ways. The *Aquitania* was taken to the scrappers in 1954, and the *Queen Mary* eventually was converted into a luxury hotel, which still functions today. In the case of the *Elizabeth*, purchase by businessmen for her conversion into a floating university ended with a mysterious fire that consumed the liner in Hong Kong harbor in 1972. Other liners and crew also had unlucky fates, as already seen in the *Normandie*. Cunard's *Laconia* met a more sudden end. On 12 September 1942, it was carrying 2,700 people (including crew, British, army, navy, and RAF personnel, and 1,800 Italian prisoners of war) when it was torpedoed by a German U-boat in the Atlantic after setting out first from South Africa and then Iran. 1,649 of the people on board, including the captain, were lost. T. Walczak was aboard the ship at the time. A former

Polish solider who had been captured by Soviet forces during the Nazi-Soviet partition of Poland in 1940, Walczak joined an anti-Nazi force after the launch of Operation Barbarossa – Hitler's invasion of the Soviet Union. In the course of his anti-Nazi activities, Walczak boarded the *Laconia* sailing to Europe. His account written much later initially notes the culture on board the troop carrier. Among other events, Italian prisoners sang 'Sorrento' and staged an opera, and he comments on the Italians' hatred both of Hitler and of English food served to them. Such a tone of frivolity and detached leisure changed suddenly, and with a bang, not a whimper. Walczak was in the middle of a shower when,

> Suddenly we felt an enormous blow followed by a horrifying explosion and the ship keeled over almost immediately. Everything started to clatter across from one end to the other; the lights, though, did not go out for a while ... Then came the second explosion – the second torpedo.[512]

Walczak, completely nude, made his way to the lifeboats, but the *Laconia*'s sag and incline pushed him overboard, forcing him to swim or sink. At some distance, he heard the ship's boilers explode, and soon afterward the French battle cruiser *Gloire* found him.

The shock and jolt of the moment are evident enough in this recorded memory to remind one that despite their monumental size and awesome scale, the magnificent liners (and military vessels like the *Indianapolis* or the *Bismarck*) of the twentieth century were undeniably vulnerable to icebergs, storms and the vicissitudes of war. *Laconia*'s fate reinforces the inescapable reality of twentieth-century industrial warfare. Technology, in fact, made possible both the construction of new ships and their potential destruction, with masses of rivets and thick metal sheets torn apart with just a few shells.

We also notice the connection of ocean liners not only to European and American transportation patterns, but to the international movements of people. Walczak originally joined the Polish Army. After the partition of Poland by Nazi Germany and the Soviet Union, he was deported to a Soviet camp near Tashkent where typhus was widespread. Then after Hitler's attack on the Soviet Union, he was encouraged to join a patriotic, reorganized Polish Army nearby and traveled to Persia where he boarded the *Laconia* and found himself faced with peril off the coast of Africa. War forced people to move to unforeseen areas as a tidal wave displaces so many seashells, and the ocean liners took part in this phenomenon even as they themselves resembled those seashells. It was a strange circle that Walczak traveled to return to Poland, but also one traveled by the many victims of war during the turbulent century just ended.

Whether such accounts were recorded in diaries written at the time of the journeys or recollected later, they owe much to the nature of long ocean voyages. Something about the maritime experience encourages the revival of memories either as they are brought to the surface after some degree of suppression or revived to focus on one or more particular parts of the recent past. Sea voyages arouse such states of contemplation even as travelers are immersed in countless sensations of physical beauty and accommodate themselves to a frenzied existence on board. In peacetime conditions when vacation and pleasure make up the sole reasons for traveling by ship, the memories and thoughts are perhaps connected to romance, love and thoughts of the passing of life. Wartime evoked other types of thoughts having to do with surviving a world devastated by human ingenuity in inflicting violence and havoc on others. How one managed to endure it all seems always present in the mind of one having survived the horror. With so many soldiers and prisoners of war having very little option but to return home by ship, the possibilities for such reflection varied depending on the nature of the individual. But the vast time spent at sea gave vent to these stored thoughts awaiting revival.

Such ocean voyages did not merely testify to the reality of wartime situations. They could also represent the nature of reconciliation and relocation of people at the war's end. As the war in Western Europe neared its close and D-Day came and left, military personnel were sent from the United States to Europe in mass numbers. After VE Day, as the post-war reality was being prepared, countless other military, diplomatic, and other political officials made their way to the conquered territory. It was also the case that wartime soldiers began returning home. Their voyage home was always one of celebration. Some especially so. Many had meanwhile developed romantic relationships and married. One of the remarkable episodes of the immediate postwar years was the use of the *Queen Mary* to transport 'war brides' to the United States and Canada to assume domestic lives with their new-found husbands. America's connection to Britain was once again confirmed nearly two centuries after the Revolutionary War, in a novel form of immigration that would cause a shift in the character of the 'melting pot'.

The 'war bride' voyages of the *Queen Mary* early in 1946 were among the happier moments in the grey liner's history, although the vast crowds and masses of people seen everywhere on board negated any notion of the private space and calm for which the ship's First Class had been so renowned. However, the dread of what lay beyond – both on the seas and after disembarkation – was gone except for the most anxious of brides. The war was over and only the challenge of domestic life in a new environment lay ahead. While some people found the cultural dislocation difficult (as was also the case with immigrants), such nervous energy about a new home was seen as a blessing next to the doubtless edginess of soldiers previously en route to the war's battlefields. One could imagine the angst dominating soldiers in 1944 transported by the *Mary* to England where they prepared for the D-Day landings.

In due course, as troop space was reconverted to passenger accommodations, the transatlantic sailings resumed with Americans eager once again for inexpensive travel after a world war that left European cities and currencies ravaged. Hopes for a renewal of 'old times' seemed plausible despite the reality of the Cold War and potential nuclear annihilation. The backdrop of such political and military tension, given further dramatic expression in the witch hunts of Joseph McCarthy, was a strange one for the renewal of festivity and leisure on the ocean liners. Yet celebration and the macabre are often linked. Even with the new tension and existentialist anxiety about the world's future, a renewed exuberance for travel abroad found Americans eager to see Europe more so than ever as the European nations began to build tourist industries. The process, noted by Waugh, of travelers giving way to tourists became an increasing reality.

It would have seemed a promising time for the steamship companies. The *Queen Mary* and the *Queen Elizabeth* were back, now much-famed as heroic vessels basking in the glow of their wartime records. That majestic duo would finally begin to cross and recross the Atlantic as they were intended to do, painted in their familiar Cunard colors, and meeting each other in transit every so often. They seemed to justify the company's initial enthusiasm for the incredible visual impression two such megaliners would provide both on the high seas and portside. (In the summer of 2015, the harbor of Liverpool was centered on the presence there of the spectacular new trio of gigantic Cunarders – *Queen Mary 2*, *Queen Victoria* and the new *Queen Elizabeth* – to commemorate the 175th anniversary of Cunard's founding. Even with the transformed world of sailing, the anticipated wonder of planners of events in the earlier years can be imagined.) As the *Elizabeth* was only completed in 1939, the delay of this impression was very long, but it now seemed worth it. In fact, the ships confirmed British determination to resume the normal state of things – no matter how much the loss of India and other parts of the Empire and economic stagnation seemed to prove the contrary point. Both liners would continue the Cunard transatlantic tradition until well into the sixties and with so many passengers, First Class, Tourist and Third Class, wanting to travel, the future seemed endless.

Nonetheless, it would soon be apparent that the world had changed forever. As in the recall of the 'good old days' just after the First World War, former passengers wistfully evoked their sense of ease interrupted by the Second World War. In both cases, the rosy picture of life before wartime was a bit exaggerated, given the ongoing tension and problems of the prewar years, but the contrast to the present was strong. Because of the shock left by the war, little seemed left of the ways and manners with which people seemed to carry on their lives. The picture was affected both by the situation of the ships and by larger political and social developments. For one thing, the *Normandie* had been scrapped and its component parts dismembered and sold. Many other ships had suffered similar fates, and as with the time after the First World War, some vessels were reacquired by new companies as part of the post-war swapping intended to justify the cost and outcome of the conflict. In addition, air service had become a reality and its domination of transatlantic travel was on the horizon. Western Europe was still rebuilding and its dependence on American aid like the Marshall Plan was all too evident. Along with the loss of empires in Asia and Africa, such a reality made it difficult for Cunard-White Star and French Line to resume their old maritime positions to the same degree. The old imperial allure of these companies was now fading as the new reality saw global dominance by the two new super powers. In the coming years, even the speed records of these lines would be broken by newer ships of United States Line – a fact which represented a shift not only in the transatlantic contest, but also in the general fact of American political and military influence around the globe. Still, there were the two Queens of Cunard giving the impression that old times had returned, emitting their wartime glory. As noted above, by 1949 France was also back on the transatlantic scene in a major way with the return of the *Ile de France* and soon thereafter the *Liberté*.

For France, however, memories recalling the social divisions of the thirties, the illusion of the Maginot Line, the humiliating defeat to the Nazi Wehrmacht in 1940, and the disgraceful record of Vichy were hard to surmount. TRANSAT's fragile, helpless state after the collapse itself reflected the domestic situation. Henri Cangardel and Jean Marie had tried to keep the company going, even moving the various points of management from Le Havre to Nantes to Bordeaux as internal authority continued to collapse before the relentless Nazi Blitzkrieg. They, and the various other authorities, even tried to maintain the company after the installation of the Vichy regime and made it subject to Admiral Darlan's direction.[513]

With the capsized *Normandie* in New York harbor for three years, TRANSAT's hopes for post-war rebuilding were greatly diminished. Its greatest ship, perhaps the most magnificent liner ever, was gone, a devastating loss to the French – not only financially but also psychologically and symbolically. From the onset of the twentieth century, the French had greatly believed in the connection of progress to ever more sophisticated technology. Such faith persisted even though France had not been as completely industrialized as had Britain, the United States and Germany. The century's lessons regarding technology were shattering. As with so much else, technology had proven to be an ambiguous force that by no means ensured safety and stability. Symbolically, the fate of the *Normandie* echoed the political instability of the Fourth Republic and the troubles of the French Empire in Indochina and Algeria as well as the record of the recent past. French Line publicity efforts to link its ships to the international prestige of the country would now seem tarnished. There were other casualties with which to contend. TRANSAT had lost 338,000 tons of ships. Prospects, thus, from the point of view of the Minister of the Merchant Marine, G. Deffère, seemed dim.[514]

Nevertheless, there were also the facts of the French resistance, Charles de Gaulle's Free French forces marching under the Arc du Triomphe during the Liberation, and the hopes for the future. From 1945 to 1957, the Fourth Republic saw economic revival with Jean Monnet's Planning Commission and the movements towards the Common Market and the Treaty of Rome. French Line attempted to revive transatlantic service by appealing once again to the interwar American fascination with French culture. American soldiers who had served in France during the war upon returning also evoked desires to travel to that region in peacetime. So a mood for renewed American travel there was set in motion.

French Line's course for the immediate future was set by the resumption of service of the *Ile de France*, after its renovation and conversion from a three-funneler to a two-funneler, and *Liberté*. Formerly the modernistic German liner, *Europa*, the renamed ship symbolized France's return both to democratic status and to the high seas. As Jean Marie, so instrumental to the *Normandie* project, said at the inauguration of *Liberté*,

> It is hardly necessary to repeat the type of national necessity for France to be represented by the presence of its ocean liners in the most brilliant way possible on the North Atlantic, realizing how they serve as agents of publicity for our national genius. But it seems useless to me to recall the role they played in obtaining for the French economy considerable dollars since their construction and use stimulated so many varied branches of native industries.[515]

Hopes were high in 1950 that *Liberté* and the *Ile de France* could carry French Line into the next decade before a new superliner, the natural successor to the *Normandie*, could be built. Meanwhile, the former Bauhaus severity of the renamed *Europa* would be replaced by *Liberté's* 'gäiêté et clarité'.

Deffère connected the revitalization of French Line to national themes, emphasizing that despite 'the devastation and ruins, France is a great nation, the French a great people capable of will and courage, a people that is not only as they say in a pejorative way the most intelligent in the world, but which knows how to work and achieve.'[516] With all the positive affirmation in this statement, it doesn't take too deeply an analytical mind to detect French apprehension concerning international attitudes about their character.

In the same speech, Deffère downplayed the significance of the Blue Riband as a national goal. He admitted that in the post-war years, 'the airplane had definitely surpassed the ship in intercontinental travel: the era of ocean liners seems definitely over' as one could travel by air from Paris to New York City in just a few hours. Accordingly, he urged that the rebuilding of French Line be based on those aspects in which ship travel already surpassed transport by plane: comfort, luxury and service. Those in need of speedy travel would fly, but those with time at their disposal would opt for the comfort of a liner. Cunard raised a similar theme in its publicity in emphasizing the leisure and pleasure involved in travel by ship. While the *Ile de France* and *Liberté* both fulfilled maritime passenger needs for the present, TRANSAT looked forward to a new, more modern vessel. That liner would be the latest *France*, launched in the early sixties and the last of the great French Line ships.

Despite the optimistic airs, Deffère's reference to the plane reflected a growing apprehension among steamship company officials everywhere about the threatening competition from the aviation industry as it developed better and faster airplanes. One thinks back to the launch of an airplane from the *Ile de France* in 1927 to shorten the time to New York for mail and to accommodate hurried passengers by cutting their travel time by a few hours. Among such passengers, one could already sense a diminished need for relaxation and the more pressing pace of work.

In fact, the ship lines had by then already used planes as part of their own service. In 1919 Cunard arranged for some passengers to fly to the port where their ship awaited them. Passengers of the *Paris* were doing so as well by 1921.[517] The idea of the airplane, thus, at first, seemed an attractive complement to the ever faster vessels at sea, but the focus was on shaving a few hours off the time spent aboard ship. Rarely did officials consider the possibility that planes would become so fast that they would make ships obsolete as a means for transatlantic passenger travel. Consequently, managers of both Cunard-White Star and TRANSAT kept a close eye on the times of crossing of the *Normandie* and the *Queen Mary* during their early sailings because they wanted to lure passengers with their speed. That did not prevent TRANSAT during that same decade from helping to form Air France in its quest to remain in the forefront of transportation developments. Ironically the same obsession with speed that drove the steamship companies' desire to build larger, more efficient, and faster ships would prove their undoing as nothing they constructed could ever approach the speed of planes. Nevertheless, TRANSAT hoped that both forms of transportation could thrive through their respective qualities that could not be recreated.

By the mid-1950s, the threat was real. Allusions to the problem were already made by a French Line official even as the company launched a new ship. Cunard reports in 1957 underlined the gravity of the threat, with one particular report focused on the reduced fares of planes: 'air roundtrip [is] half as expensive as ship except at tourist rate.' Even the enticements of shipboard life and the savings of four days of hotel and food costs did not make the line competitive. Cunard's strategy was to pressure the British government to force air fares higher, seeming especially annoyed by the practice of government subsidies to the airlines that made for lower-priced tickets.[518] TRANSAT, for its part, focused on providing a complement to air travel. The sketch for the future was vague, but hopes were that travelers could use several different means to reach destinations, depending on where they were going, the purpose of their trip, and how much time they had on their hands.[519]

It was a losing battle. The planes kept getting faster and gradually governments throughout Europe reduced their subsidies to the ship lines. By the early 1970s, many famous national lines had disappeared. French Line itself followed suit in 1974 by dramatically ceasing operation of the *France* – despite the impassioned protests of its crew and Le Havrians that culminated in a strike. Cunard continued to sail with its new *Queen Elizabeth 2* launched in 1968, and intended to function both as a transatlantic liner and cruise ship. Like all maritime passenger companies, Cunard was forced to go in the direction of cruise ships – as inaugurated in the late 1940s with its famous 'green goddess', the *Caronia* – and was purchased by Carnival Cruise Line, one of the giant companies responsible for redirecting maritime audiences to cruise ships.

The recent resurgence of interest in transatlantic ocean liners, intensified no doubt by the public fascination with the *Titanic* as dramatized in the 1997 film by that name, marks a true reversal in the relationship of Cunard with filmmakers. When in 1956 the BBC asked for assistance in a television production on the *Titanic* disaster, Cunard revealed great reluctance to provide it. Among the BBC's requests was an interview with a Cunard employee who had been 'quayside' when the *Titanic* sailed from Southampton. After much internal discussion, the employee turned down the interview request, much to the relief of Cunard officials, who were also worried about the filming of Walter Lord's book, *A Night to Remember*. As they put it, 'were it not for such books the whole matter would remain undisturbed as past history.'[520]

Cunard had wanted the memory of the *Titanic* (a White Star ship but with a legacy absorbed by Cunard after the 1934 merger) to be put to rest as sales were never exactly enhanced by speculation on maritime disasters. As noted above, the company was accustomed to receiving among its piles of mail, letters from theosophists who in 1934 talked about 'bad omens' for the *Queen Mary*.[521] Obviously if such irrational forms of feeling and behavior got out of hand, panic could ensue and, with it, a drop in passenger tickets sold. The sinking of the Italian liner *Andrea Doria* in 1956 did not help matters. After the release of the film in 1997, Cunard publicized itself again as 'Cunard-White Star', showing that it no longer minded the associations with *Titanic* and, in fact, was willing to exploit them.

James Cameron's *Titanic* attracted scores of filmgoers at a moment when transatlantic sailing had virtually become a relic. It also came, however, after the discovery by Robert Ballard in 1985 of the famous ship's remains. The ensuing fascination with the liner's class-bound luxury seems especially to have come from the newly prosperous groups who profited from the business boom of the '90s.

From that point, interest in revival of pre-1940s decor soared, which caused Cunard to begin work on the successor to the *QE2*, the *Queen Mary 2*. Newer cruise ships, some of them between 90,000 to 140,000 tons, include areas with a Belle Epoque look. In one case, wood paneling from *Titanic*'s sister ship, *Olympic*, has been used to decorate the walls of a 'special' dining room. Some ships include smoking rooms – harking back to the old aristocratic setting of the liners – despite anti-tobacco feeling. Of course, while seeking to relive some of the moments of the 'ancient' past of ocean liner travel, passengers retreat to their cabin to watch a DVD (perhaps *Titanic* or the anti-tobacco film, *The Insider*) or go to the computer center to surf the web. It is a mix of antique and ultra-modern that imbues the character of ships today, and so it would inevitably be.

Though airplanes will forever dominate world travel in terms of carrying passengers to their place of destination, the new interest in ships indicates that travelers desire something more than speed when they go on vacation. They insist upon certain types of moments and leisured languor unique to large ships. For that reason alone, the demand for ships will remain. And the ship sails on.

Notes

Preface

1 It is also true, however, as we shall see, that during the twenties and thirties, cruising first emerged in this sense.

2 Already, in fact, smoking rooms have appeared in many of the expensive cruise ships that began sailing during the last three years.

3 Some word on the various names of these companies is necessary. Until 1934, Cunard Line was known exclusively by this name. After that year, it became Cunard-White Star Line as it merged with its greatest British rival, White Star Line. Compagnie Générale Transatlantique (CGT) was the official name of the French steamship company called also TRANSAT or French Line. Our use of names depends on the time at which the company finds reference.

Chapter One

4 Henry Adams, *The Education of Henry Adams* (Boston: Houghton Mifflin, 1918) p. 319.

5 For a classic discussion of this phenomenon, see Johann Huizinga's *The Waning of the Middle Ages* (New York: Doubleday, 1924).

6 Marthe Barbance, *Histoire de la Compagnie Générale Transatlantique* (Paris: Arts et Metiers Graphiques, 1955), p. 155.

7 R. A. Fletcher, *Traveling Palaces (Luxury in Passenger Steamships)* (London: Sir Isaac Pitman and Sons, Ltd, 1913), pp. 18, 20–32. Inman was responsible for a number of innovations in the interior design of modern steamships, i.e. placing passenger cabins forward of the engines to lessen the vibrations and noise, introducing the idea of small tables with revolving chairs in the dining room for saloon (First Class) passengers, and providing electric bells in every cabin.

8 Ibid, p. 275.

9 Ibid.

10 Robert Louis Stevenson, *The Amateur Emigrant*, cited in John Maxtone-Graham, *The Only Way to Cross* (New York: Collier, Macmillan, 1978) p. 155.

11 A new interesting account of eugenics as connected to questions of race and Social Darwinism is found in J. W. Burrow, *The Crisis of Reason: European Thought 1848–1914* (New Haven, Yale University Press, 2000).

12 John Malcolm Brinin, *The Sway of the Grand Saloon* (London: Arlington Books, 1971) p. 431.

13 Terry Coleman, *The Liners: A History of the North Atlantic Crossing* (Middlesex, England: Penguin Books, 1976) p. 123. See also, *Immigration and Naturalization Services* statistics.

14 SHSA, Brochure Files, White Star Line, 'The New Russia'.

15 UL, Cunard, D42/PR4/21, *Memorabilia – Aquitania*.

16 UL, Cunard, D42/PR5, *White Star Magazine*, 'Third Class Holiday Tours (Large Movements of Teachers and Students Between America and Europe)', Vol. XIV, No. 5 (May 1925).

17 CGM, CGT, J/75 – *Paris*, Publications, *Voyage aux Etats Units des Anciens Combattants Français* (21 Juillet–18 Août 1933).

Chapter Two

18 Pierre-Henri Marin, *Les paquebots ambassadeurs des mers* (Paris: Gallimard, 1989) p. 79.

19 Coleman, *The Liners*, p. 126.

20 SHSA, Brochure File, '*Normandie*, Tourist Class Deck Plans' (*c.* 1935).

21 'Middle Class Americans Come Over (Welcoming the Largest Number of 'Tourist Third' Who Have Ever Crossed in One Vessel)' *The Evening Standard* (13 July 1931).

22 August Mencken, ed., *First Class Passenger* (New York: Alfred A. Knopf, 1938) p. xvii.

23 Paul Fussell, *Abroad* (Oxford: Oxford University Press, 1980) p. 59.

24 Ibid, pp. 3–5.

25 Ibid, p. 9.

26 Ibid, p. 51.

27 Alec Waugh, quoted in Fussell, *Abroad* (1980) p. 71.

28 Ernest Hemingway, quoted in Fussell, *Abroad* (1980) p. 72.

29 UL, Cunard, D42/PR3/9/14f, *Cunard Business News*, No. 6 (16 February 1920).

30 UL, Cunard, D42/PR3/9/14g, *Cunard Business News*, No. 7 (16 March 1920); D42/PR3/9/14j, *Cunard Business News*, No. 9 (18 June 1920).

31 UL, Cunard, D42/PR3/9/14e, *Cunard Business News*, No. 5 (18 November 1919). Great Britain was the first country to establish a Women's Army Auxiliary Corps in 1917. By the war's end, the WAACs numbered 40,000 women, 8,500 of whom were sent abroad. Margaret Higgonet, Jane Jenson, Margaret Collins Weitz, Sonya Michel, eds., *Behind the Lines: Gender and the Two World Wars* (New Haven: Yale University Press, 1987).

32 UL, Cunard, D42/PR5 – *Cunard Line Magazine*, Vol. XII, No. 3 (March 1924).

33 UL, Cunard, D42/C2/242, Chairman Correspondence (16 and 19 March 1930), Maurice Caillard, Esq to Thomas Royden; Royden to Caillard.

34 UL, Cunard, D42/PR3/9/6, *The Daily Telegraph* (19 March 1924).

35 UL, Cunard, D42/PR6, *White Star Magazine* (June 1930).

36 UL, Cunard, D42/PR3/9/11A, *Aquitania* (*c.* 1931).

37 Evelyn Waugh, *When the Going Was Good* (London: Little, Brown & Co., 1934) p. 17.

38 IWM, 89/6/1, EFMS2, Edith Sowerbutts, *Memoirs of a Merchant Seaman, No. 1108113*, p. 88.

39 The first maritime newsletter printed on a French Line ship was in 1905 on *La Provence*. According to French Line management, *L'Atlantique* was both the first contact between France and her visitors and liaison between ship's officers and the passengers. See *CGT Bulletin*, No. 508 (November–December 1953). By the early 1930s, it became more of a monthly magazine that carried feature articles on fashion, culture and the arts.

40 CGM, CGT, Côte 1997 .004 5402 and 5437, *L'Atlantique* (1922, 1927).

41 Cited in Coleman, *The Liners*, p. 118.

42 Captain E. G. Diggle, *The Romance of a Modern Liner* (1930; reprint, Northamptonshire, England: Patrick Stephens, 1989) p. 142.

43 Roydon Freeman, *Sea Travel – The Serious Side and the Humorous Side* (London: St Catherine Press, 1930) p. 26.

44 UL, Cunard, D42/PR5, *Cunard Magazine*, Vol. 5, No. 2 (August 1920).

45 UL, Cunard, D42/PR5, *Cunard Magazine*, Vol. 2, No. 3 (March 1919).

46 *De Grasse* was the first post-war 'one cabin' or 'classless' ship to join the French Line fleet. Along with the *Rochambeau* (1911) and the *Lafayette* (1929), described as the flagship of the cabin-class fleet, the *De Grasse* was marketed as being 'dedicated to those who prefer to economize.' See also: CGM, CGT, Côte .1997 .004 .5423, *L'Atlantique* (1925). See also: Commandant Pierre Thoreux, *J'ai Commandé 'Normandie'* (Paris: Presses de la Cité, 1963) p. 94.

47 SHSA, Brochure file, White Star Line, 'Famous Cabin Liners to Europe', n.d.

48 CGM, CGT, J-12, *Normandie* Presse (1932–38), *Nautical Gazette*, 25 May 1935.

49 UL, Cunard, D42/PR6, *White Star Magazine* (September 1928).

50 NMM, Cunard publicity brochure, 'Tourist Class – Formerly Second Class – the Latest Phase in Atlantic Travel', *c.* 1931. Tourist Third Cabin Class was renamed 'Tourist Class' on 7 August 1931.

51 NMM, Cunard Publicity brochure, 'What Passengers Say', n.d.

52 Diggle, *The Romance of a Modern Liner*, pp. 151–52.

53 Ludwig Bemelmans, *I Love You, I Love You, I Love You* (New York: The Viking Press, 1942) pp. 10–19.

54 Freeman, *Sea Travel*, p. 22.

55 Diggle, *The Romance of a Modern Liner*, pp. 239–40.

56 R. A. Fletcher, *Traveling Palaces*, pp. 144–45, 163.

57 Sutton Vane, *Outward Bound* (New York: Boni and Liveright, 1924) pp. 29–31.

58 Roger Joubert, 'Palaces Des Oceans', *Journal d'un commissaire de bord* (Maisonneuve et Larose: n.d.) p. 87; Sowerbutts, *Memoirs of a British Seaman*, p. 128.

59 UL, Cunard, D42/B4.69, Executive Committee Minutes (30 June–31 December 1930).

60 CGM, CGT, Côte 1997 .004 5115, Rapport de Voyage – *Normandie* (14 October 1935).

61 CGM, CGT, Côte 1997 .004 5115, Rapport de Voyage – *Normandie* (14 July 1937).

62 UL, Cunard, D42/GM24/1/3, Instructions to Ship's Captains (4 April 1930).

63 UL, Cunard, D42/B4, Executive Committee Minutes, No. 70 (6 April 1932).

64 CGM, CGT, Côte 1997 .004 4979, Rapport de Voyage – *De Grasse* (1 July 1933–18 March 1934).

65 See report of Commisaire Armand de Nieuwenhove, CGM, CGT, Côte 1997 .004 .5086, Rapport de Voyage – *Lafayette* (15 May–2 June 1937).

66 UL, Cunard, D42/GM24/1/3, Instructions to Ship's Captains (26 July 1926).

67 UL, Cunard, D42/ASC/12.3, White Star Line: 'Precis of Old and Important Circular Instructions Issued Prior to 30 June 1926', Preface to Vol. 1.

68 UL, Cunard, D42/PR14, 'Cunard Steamship Company: Regulations to be Observed in the Company's Service' (October 1927).

69 NMM, MS84/172, *Souvenir of Scholars' Summer Cruise*, White Star Line – SS *Doric*.

70 UL, Cunard, D42/GM24/1/3, Instructions to Ship's Captains (19 May 1932).

71 Ibid. A memo of 18 December 1933, following the repeal of the Prohibition Law, dropped all such restrictions.

72 The Volstead Act (named after Rep. Andrew Volstead who introduced the act) was the Prohibition legislation (18th Amendment) in effect in the United States from 1920–1933.

73 CGM, CGT, Côte 1997 .004 5470, *L'Atlantique* on board the *Ile de France* (13 October 1929).

74 UL, Cunard, D42/B1/10-11, Cunard Steamship Co. Ltd – Minutes of Board Meetings (15 October 1924).

75 UL, Cunard, D42/GM24/1/3, 'Instructions to Ship's Captains' (22 February 1926).

76 Violet Jessop, *Titanic Survivor*, ed. John Maxtone-Graham (Dobbs Ferry, NY: Sheridan House, 1997) p. 190.

77 Cited in John Maxtone-Graham, *The Only Way to Cross*, p. 170.

78 Raoul de Beaudean, *Captain of the Ile* (New York: McGraw-Hill, 1960) pp. 21–22.

79 Ibid.

80 Thoreux, *J'ai Commandé 'Normandie'*, p. 145. Captains on today's cruise ships share the opinion of their predecessors and comment on the overly casual tone being set by cruise ship passengers who quickly change to flip-flops and shorts after the captain's gala dinner, roam the public decks drinking beer out of a bottle, and engage in rowdy and offensive behavior.

81 CGM, CGT, Côte 1997 .004 5423, *L'Atlantique* (1925).

82 CGM, CGT, Côte 1997 .004 5470, *L'Atlantique* (13 October 1929).

83 Diggle, *The Romance of a Modern Liner*, p. 145.

84 Freeman, *Sea Travel*, p. 87.

85 Ibid, pp. 166–170. Freeman explains the rules for quoits: 'The flat discs score the number of the circle in which they lie when all have been thrown. They must be inside the circle, clear of the chalk line. The quoit can be thrown either to fall flat or to slide to a standstill. It makes no difference if several finish on the top of one another. It is usual to play up to 21 points for game.'

86 CGM, CGT, Côte 1997 .004 5470, *L'Atlantique*, 1929–1930.

87 Diggle, *The Romance of a Modern Liner*, pp. 148–151.

88 CGM, CGT, I 170, *Gangplank* 2, No. 9 (summer 1933).

89 UL, Cunard, D42/B4.69, Executive Committee minutes (29 October 1930).

90 Freeman, *Sea Travel*, pp. 87–89.

91 'Reminiscence of a Cunard Cruise' (London: 1 September 1934), from the Peter Radmore Collection, on board the *QE2*.

92 On one voyage of the now defunct *Norway* (ex-*France*), the same behavior was observed, only in this case, men were trying out for John Travolta doubles from Saturday Night Fever and engaging in acts on NCL's private island in the Bahamas that resembled the then 'hit' television series *Survivor*.

93 Freeman, *Sea Travel*, pp. 98–99.

94 MMM, DX/1166, Rose Stott diary, 1923.

95 Coleman, *The Liners*, p. 125.

96 CGM, CGT, Côte 1997 .004 5402, *L'Atlantique*, April–December 1922.

97 Brinin, *The Sway of the Grand Saloon*, pp. 435, 472.

98 Ibid, pp. 431–32.

99 Cited in Ibid, p. 435.

100 Fussell, *Abroad*, p. 39.

101 Cited in Brinin, *The Sway of the Grand Saloon*, p. 435.

102 Cited in Ibid, pp. 491–3.

103 Joel Burdick, *Our World Tour 1922–1923* (Liverpool: Merseyside Maritime Museum, 1990) p. v–x. Cunard Line appointed American Express as its agent in 1915 and was followed shortly afterward by French Line and other major transatlantic operators. By 1915, American Express had set up a separate travel department in the United States and was organizing a wide range of escorted tours for Americans eager to travel abroad.

104 The concept of world cruising dates back to the 1890s, but these ventures were combination sea and land tours. Passengers crossed the Atlantic on one vessel, traveled across the United States by rail, and then picked up another ship to continue their journey. Cunard Line and American Express were breaking new ground in 1922 with the *Laconia* voyage.

105 Comment of Judge Gary, head of the Steel Trust, who paid $25,000 for his suite on a cruise that lasted six weeks, quoted in Humphrey Jordan, *Mauretania (Landfalls and Departures of Twenty-Five Years)* (1936; reprint, Northamptonshire: Patrick Stephens, 1988) p. 241.

106 Brinin, *The Sway of the Grand Saloon*, p. 498. Beginning in October 1929, the *Ile de France* carried a Speak-O-Phone on board. For the first time on a ship crossing the Atlantic, passengers could speak a message into the microphone which was recorded on a disc and sent home, all for a modest fee of $1.25. In this manner, passengers could communicate with both their relatives and business associates at home. See: CGM, CGT, Côte 1997 .004 .5470, *L'Atlantique* (1929–1930).

107 Charles T. Spedding, *Reminiscences of Transatlantic Travelers* (London: T. Fisher Unwin Ltd, 1926) p. 55. Spedding was purser on Cunard Line's *Aquitania*. See also MMM, DX/1246, *Franconia – World Cruise Log Book* (1927).

108 Ibid.
109 UL, Cunard, D42/PR6, *White Star Magazine* (November 1932).
110 CGM, CGT, Bulletin de la Compagnie Générale Transatlantique, No. 403, 15 November 1933.
111 UL, Cunard, D42/PR6, *White Star Magazine* (July 1931).
112 UL, Cunard, D42/PR6, Jane Gordan, 'What to Wear – Best Dressed Women on Cruises', *White Star Magazine* (May 1933). See also, *White Star Magazine* (June 1933).
113 'Make Every Costume Count', in *Vogue*, cited in Rupert Prior, *Ocean Liners, The Golden Years* (London: Tiger Books International, 1993) p. 143.
114 Emily Post, *Etiquette* (New York: Funk & Wagnalls Co., 1940) p. 716.
115 UL, Cunard, D42/PR6, *White Star Magazine* (June 1933).
116 Dave Marlowe, *Coming Sir! The Autobiography of a Waiter* (London: J. B. Lippincott Co., 1938) pp. 105–07.
117 Coleman, *The Liners*, p. 137.
118 UL, Cunard, D42/PR6, *The Daily Mail* (18 April 1933), cited in *White Star Magazine* (May 1933).
119 UL, Cunard, D42/PR6, *White Star Magazine* (May 1933).
120 CGM, CGT, I70, *Gangplank* 4, No. 2 (autumn 1937).
121 Ibid., pp. 434–35.
122 Brinin, *The Sway of the Grand Saloon*, p. 500.
123 Evelyn Waugh, 'In Defence of Pleasure Cruising', *Harper's Bazaar* (1930), cited in Ruppert Prior, *Ocean Liners*, pp. 112–14.
124 Evelyn Waugh, *When the Going Was Good*, p. 18.
125 Waugh, cited in Prior, *Ocean Liners*, p. 117.
126 UL, Cunard, D42/B4/70, Executive Committee minutes (January 1932–December 1933).
127 UL, Cunard, D42/C3/436, F. H. Samuel to Percy Bates (4 June 1937).
128 CGM, CMM, Côte 1997.002 3487, Correspondence à la Ministère de la Marine Marchande (10 February 1939).
129 MMM, 411.1SCO/PM, Dorothy Scobie, *A Stewardess Rings a Bell* (Bolton, England: Stylus Publishers, 1990) p. 11.
130 SCC, MO126, Frank Mortimer interview (18 December 1997).
131 Bemelmans, *I Love You, I Love You, I Love You*, p. 21.
132 Joubert, *Palaces Des Oceans*, p. 64.
133 CGM, CGT, Côte 1997.004 4979, Rapports de voyage, *De Grasse* (12 February–15 March 1940).
134 UL, Cunard, D42/C3/436, Robert Crail to R. S. Hudson, MP, Secretary of the Department of Overseas Trade (21 February 1939).

Chapter Three

135 Scobie, *A Stewardess Rings a Bell*, p. 13.
136 A White Star Line publicity brochure for the *Olympic* gives a full range of employment possibilities on board. Among the 'specialists' we find: 586 stewards (dining room and cabin stewards including 24 women); 144 kitchen staff (including 60 cooks, 14 butchers, 20 bakers); 87 bridge staff (including 2 captains, 5 bridge officers, 80 deck hands); 161 engine room crew (including 53 engineers, 60 boiler-room attendants, 6 electricians, 2

plumbers, 40 mechanics). Other miscellaneous staff included 3 printers, several musicians, 1 bugler, 1 gymnast, 1 swimming instructor, 1 professional squash racket player, 1 tailor, 1 chiropodist, 3 barbers, 1 ladies' hairdresser, 1 masseur, 1 manicurist, several 'Boots' (whose chief business it was to shine passengers' footwear), 3 carpenters, 1 baggage master, 1 librarian, 17 bellboys, 3 elevator men, 1 typist and shorthand writer, 2 doctors, and 8 trained nurses. See SHSA, White Star Line brochure, 'Close Ups,' n.d.

137 SHSA, CGT Brochure, 'The Soul of a Ship', n.d.

138 UL, Cunard, D42/C2/3, Thomas Royden to Lady Lettice Shepard (16 April 1923).

139 Marlowe, *Coming Sir!*, pp. 14–18.

140 SCC, MO124, Frank Severini interview.

141 MMM, 411/DEM/PM, John Dempsey, *I've Seen Them All Naked* (Oxford: Alden, 1992) p. 1.

142 Ibid, p. 2.

143 QM, 'Crew Memories', Mr Edwin Praine to archivist, QM Archives (1 December 1995).

144 SCC, MOO49, anonymous male interview (18 May 1988).

145 Sowerbutts, Memoirs of a Merchant Seaman, pp. 207–08.

146 QM, Subject Files – John O. Wann, 'Personal Experiences on the *Queen Mary*', n.d.

147 *Marlowe, Coming Sir!*, pp. 284–87.

148 Ibid, p. 69.

149 SCC, MOO44, anonymous male interview (12 February 1988).

150 SCC, MO126, Frank Mortimer interview (18 December 1997).

151 UL, Cunard, D42/PR5, 'A Floating Town' in *Cunard Magazine* 15, No. 1 (July 1925). A purser had a staff of four assistants, and depending upon the size of the ship, could be as many as eight. Other people reporting to him included travel bureau personnel, conductresses, printers, photographers, musicians, barkeepers, and baggage masters.

In addition to the regular duties that fell under the purser's responsibility, he was also the master of ceremonies for social activities on board. Cunard Line rules as late as April 1950 stated that 'the organization of suitable social activity and general entertainment of passengers is regarded as an important item of service, and the Purser shall take all reasonable steps towards the organization of such entertainment for passengers.' See NMM, 347.792 Cunard Line, 'The Cunard Steamship Co. Ltd – Regulations to be Observed in the Company's Service' (April 1950). Transatlantic steamers did not carry a separate social staff. Only on cruises do we find mention of a 'cruise staff', which generally referred to the staff brought on board by the company organizing the cruise, such as Thomas Cook, Raymond Whitcomb, or American Express.

152 Diggle, *The Romance of a Modern Liner*, p. 139.

153 This was a nickname given to the captain's steward. Bisset writes that the name originated in the days of old East-India when shipmasters engaged native Asian 'boys' as their personal attendants and garbed them in gorgeous Oriental dress, 'vying with other captains in ostentatious display'. Because Oriental dress was often of striped silk, the stewards came to be known as 'tigers'. Competition among captains in dressing

their 'tigers' in fantastic garb became so intense that shipowners decided to ban the practice. The nickname, however, stuck. See: Sir James Bisset, *Commodore* (Great Britain: Angus and Robertson, 1961) p. 210.

154 UL, Cunard, D42/GM24/1/3, Instructions to Ship's Captains (9 March 1927).

155 SHSA – White Star Line, 'Useful Hints for Stewards' (1926).

156 UL, Cunard, D42/GM16/6, Memo to the General Manager (7 June 1922).

157 CGM, CGT, Côte 1997 .004 5068, Rapport de Voyage – *Ile de France*, Commissaire Henri de Fonrocque-Mercie (8–24 March 1939); see also SHSA, 'La CGT – French Line' (1864–1939), commemorative history.

158 CGM, CGT, Côte 1997 .004 0231 – Vols Divers, Folder 71 A7, Rapport: Administrateur Générale (12 March 1938); Folder 71 A5, Note pour l'Administrateur Générale (11 May 1938).

159 UL, Cunard, D42/C2/3, Memo to Thomas Royden (14 August 1925).

160 CGM, CGT, I170, Ruth Wright, 'Guignol', in *Gangplank* 3, No. 2 (winter 1935–36). Guignol originated in Italy in the seventeenth century. Translated from Italian to French by the Briocci family over 200 years ago, they peddled their wares from village to village and used marionettes to attract a crowd. When marionettes proved troublesome to manipulate (*guignolant*, thus the name) while selling soaps and pins, the Briocci conceived the idea of manipulating figures on their hands, rigging up a portable stage, and singing and talking for their characters behind draperies. The Briocci were long forgotten before Laurent Mourguet revived Guignol in early 1800 in Lyons, which became home of the Guignol.

161 Marlowe, *Coming Sir!*, p. 39.

162 Ibid, p. 118.

163 Ibid, p. 287.

164 Sowerbutts, *Memoirs of a British Seaman*, pp. 134–35.

165 CGM, CGT, J12, Normandie Presse – 1932–38, *The Nautical Gazette* (25 May 1935).

166 CGM, CMM, Côte 1997.002 3389, Circulaire 'Bords', No. 5 (1922); CGM, CGT, Côte 1997.004 0252, CGT-Union Affairs.

167 NMM, Memoranda for the Guidance of Pursers and Stewards-In-Charge of P&O Company's Ships (1914).

168 Jo Stanley, 'The Company of Women', unpublished paper, given at CNRS conference, Calgary (June 1997) p. 5.

169 Jessop, *Titanic Survivor*, p. 65.

170 SCC, M0124, Frank Severini.

171 Freeman, *Sea Travel*, pp. 10–12.

172 Sir James Bisset, *Tramps and Ladies* (New York: Criterion Books, 1959) p. 152.

173 Jessop, *Titanic Survivor*, pp. 111–14.

174 Sowerbutts, *Memoirs of a British Seaman*, pp. 202–03.

175 Sir James Bisset, *Tramps and Ladies*, p. 152.

176 UL, Cunard, D42/PR14, 'Rules to Be Observed in the Company's Service' (March 1913); International Mercantile Marine Co., *Ship's Rules* (issued 1 July 1907; reissued 1 January 1920).

177 de Beaudean, *Captain of the Ile*, p. 22.

178 Jessop, *Titanic Survivor*, p. 70.

179 QM, 'Crew Memories', correspondence, Helen Cutler (1995).

180 SCC, M0082, Delia Callaghan interview (17 August 1990).

181 SCC, Captain William Eldin Warwick interview (28 September 1998).

182 Spedding, *Reminiscences of Transatlantic Travelers*, p. 192.

183 For a discussion of the democratisation of leisure to the middle and working classes in the interwar years, see Robert Graves and Alan Hodge, *The Long Week-End: A Social History of Great Britain, 1918–1939* (New York: W. W. Norton, 1994) pp. 214–23.

184 UL, Cunard, D42/PR5, 'Athletic and Social Clubs', *Cunard Line Magazine* 7, (9 August 1922).

185 Private collection (A. Varias and L. Coons), *Commodore* 5, No. 9 (July 1930).

186 Eugen Weber, *The Hollow Years – France in the 1930s* (New York: W. W. Norton & Co., 1994) p. 160.

187 UL, Cunard, D42/PR5, '*Aquitania* Night at Southampton', *Cunard Line Magazine* 5, No. 6 (December 1920).

188 UL, Cunard, D42/PR6, *White Star Magazine* (December 1932).

189 SCC, Captain William Eldin Warwick interview.

190 SCC, M0082, Flora Ackroyd interview (23 August 1990).

191 UL, Cunard, D42/C2/257, Superannuation Fund.

192 UL, Cunard, D42/GM7/1, Allowances to Old Employees.

193 UL, Cunard, D42/C3/437, Correspondence: Bates and Logan (1934–1935).

194 UL, Cunard, D42/C2/8, Correspondence, Mr H. Moss (25 May 1929).

195 CGM, CGT 175 – Publications – *Paris*, program for the 'Fête de Bienfaissance'; see also SHSA, 'Fête de Bienfaissance' program, *Normandie* (31 July 1937).

196 UL, Cunard, D42/B4, Executive Committee minutes, No. 69 (March 1931); No. 72 (April 1937). The NUS had negotiated a gradual restoration of the seafarer's wage in three increments: 25 per cent in 1934, 50 per cent in 1935, and the final 25 per cent in 1937. See also: *The Story of the Seamen, A Short History of the National Union of Seamen* (London: Victoria House, 1964) p. 27.

197 CGM, CGT, Côte 1997 .004 .0264, Etats Majors.

198 CGM, CGT, J166, Union Sociale Maritime, report, Le Havre (16 May 1941).

199 Fletcher, *Traveling Palaces*, p. 108.

200 UL, Cunard, D42/B12/1-2, memo to general managers (9 November 1919).

201 UL, Cunard, D42/PR3/9/14j, 'Seamen's 48 Hour Week' in *Cunard Business News*, Vol. 10 (26 July 1920).

202 UL, Cunard, D42/B12/1-2, Albert Thomas to Cuthbert Laws, general manager, the International Shipping Federation (24 September 1920).

203 UL, Cunard, D42/B12/1-2, memo from Cuthbert Laws (10 March 1922).

204 In November 1916, a National Maritime Board was formed in England, which consisted of an equal number of union and shipowners representatives and a chairman from the Ministry of Shipping. After the war, the British government withdrew its official chairman and left the two sides to manage their own affairs. Among other questions of interest

considered was a proposal for a national wage. All questions relating to differences between shipowners and seafarers, wages and conditions, and the 'manning' of vessels were brought before the board. See *The Story of the Seamen*, pp. 17–21.

205 Liverpool Public Library (Local History Collection), *Liverpool Echo* (14 May 1921); *Liverpool Daily Post* (9 May 1921).

206 Cotter's Liverpool-based union played an important role in the June 1911 seamen's strike, which came to be known as 'Bloody' or 'Red' Sunday. The union charged that the police resorted to armed brutality to break up the peaceful demonstrations of the seamen. See *The Story of the Seamen*, pp. 14–15.

207 The National Sailor's and Firemen's Union, founded in 1893 by James Havelock-Wilson, was renamed the National Union of Seamen in 1926. Wilson came from long seafaring stock. His grandfather, John Wilson, was a ship's captain and his grandmother was a skilled navigator who often sailed as chief mate to her husband. In his teens, John went to sea as an engineer's apprentice. In 1887 he helped to organize the National Amalgamated Sailors and Firemen's Union of Great Britain, which became the National Sailors' and Firemen's Union in 1893. In 1892, Wilson was elected MP for Middlesbrough. See *The Story of the Seamen*, pp. 5–23.

208 Barbance, *Histoire de la Compagnie Générale Transatlantique*, pp. 189–90; CGM, CGT, Côte 1997 .004 0245, 26C2, Rapport – Grèves de CGT.

209 Barbance, *Histoire de la Compagnie Générale Transatlantique*, p. 190.

210 CGM, CGT, Côte 1997 .004 0252, Syndicat – CGT, correspondence with CGT Chef d'Armement from the Fédération Nationale des Syndicats Maritimes (9 May 1936).

211 In January 1936, $1US = 15 FF; in July 1937, $1US = 26 FF; in July 1938, $1 = 37 FF, see Weber, p. 164. For a discussion of the controversy surrounding the 40-hour week, see Weber, pp. 154–57, and Maurice Larkin, *France Since the Popular Front: Government and People, 1936-1996* (Oxford: Clarendon Press, 1997) pp. 52–61.

212 CGM, CGT, Côte 1997 .004 5207, CGT Board of Directors minutes (July–December 1937).

213 For a discussion of the legality of the application of the law of 1877 to the 1938 proposed strike action by the unions and the Daladier–Blum exchange, see *Le Petit Havre* (30 November 1938).

214 CGM, CGT, Côte 1997 .004 0245 26C2, Grèves – 1938.

215 CGM, CGT, Côte 1997 .004 0245 26C1, Grèves – 1938.

216 The Abraham Lincoln Brigade was an American leftist organization of volunteers who fought with the Spanish Republican forces against Franco. *Journal du Havre* (3–8 December 1938); see also CGM, CGT, Côte 1997 .004 0245, Grèves – 1938.

217 CGM, CGT, Côte 1997 .004 0245 26C2, Grève de 1938 – Notice – F.N.S.M.

218 CGM, CGT, Côte 1997 .004 0252, CGT – Syndicat.

219 Douglas Frantz, 'For Cruise Ships' Workers, Much Toil, Little Protection', *New York Times* (24 December 1999).

220 Jessop, *Titanic Survivor*, p. 81.

Notes

Chapter Four

221 For exceptions to the rule, see Jo Stanley, ed., *Bold in Her Breeches –
Women Pirates Across the Ages* (London: Pandora, 1995).

222 Lorraine Coons, '"Neglected Sisters" of the Women's Movement: The
Perception and Experience of Working Mothers in the Parisian Garment
Industry, 1860–1915', *Journal of Women's History*, Vol. 5, No. 2 (Fall
1993) pp. 50–74.

223 Anna Davin, 'Imperialism and Motherhood', *History Workshop Journal*,
Vol. 5 (1978) pp. 9–65.

224 Mary Kinnear, *Daughters of Time – Women in the Western Tradition* (Ann
Arbor: The University of Michigan Press, 1982) p. 165.

225 Sandra M. Gilbert, 'Soldier's Heart: Literary Men, Literary Women and
the Great War' in *Connecting Spheres – Women in the Western World,
1500 to the Present,* eds. Marilyn J. Boxer and Jean H. Quataert (New
York: Oxford University Press, 2000) pp. 275–87. Original, longer article
appeared in *Signs: Journal of Women in Culture and Society*, Vol. 8, No. 3
(1983) pp. 422–50.

226 Bonnie G. Smith, *Changing Lives, Women in European History Since
1700* (Lexington, Ma.: D.C. Heath, 1989) p. 369. See also Claudia Koonz,
'Mothers in the Fatherland: Women in Nazi Germany' in *Becoming Visible:
Women in European History*, ed. Renate Bridenthal and Claudia Koonz
(Boston: Houghton Mifflin, 1977) p. 464. For a good general summary of
the impact of the First World War on women and their experience in the
interwar years, see Françoise Thébaud, 'The Great War and the Triumph of
Sexual Division' in *Toward a Cultural Identity in the Twentieth Century*,
Vol. 5 of *A History of Women*, ed. Georges Duby, Michelle Perrot, Françoise
Thébaud (Cambridge, MA.: Harvard University Press, 1994) pp. 21–75.

227 Theodore Zeldin, *Ambition and Love*, Vol. 1 of *France 1848–1945* (New
York: Oxford University Press, 1979) p. 350.

228 Quoted in Aileen Kraditor, 'The Two Major Types of Suffragist Argument'
in *Major Problems in American Women's History*, ed. Mary Beth Norton
(Lexington, MA.: D.C. Heath, 1989) p. 263.

229 For a discussion of the emergence of the 'new woman' in England, see
Graves and Hodge, pp. 26–39. For France, see Siân Reynolds, *France
between the Wars – Gender and Politics* (New York: Routledge, 1996)
pp. 83–108. For a comparative study between England and France see
Anne-Marie Sohn, 'Between the Wars in France and England', in *Toward a
Cultural Identity in the Twentieth Century*, Vol. 5 of *A History of Women*,
ed. Georges Duby, Michelle Perrot, Françoise Thébaud, pp. 92–119.

230 Henrik Ibsen, *A Doll's House* (New York: Modern Library, n.d.) p. 248.

231 Jo Stanley, 'Women At Sea: Four Liverpool Stewardesses in the 1930s'
(article published by author c/0 6 Nazeby Ave., Crosby, Liverpool 23 July
1987) p. 2.

232 Lorraine Coons, *'Orphans' of the Sweated Trades: Women Homeworkers
in the Parisian Garment Industry (1860-1915)* (New York: Garland
Publishing Co., 1987).

233 Violet Jessop's memoirs, in which she describes her survival of two ship
disasters, have been edited by John Maxtone-Graham.

234 Edith Sowerbutts, *Memoirs of a British Seaman*, p. 1.

235 Sowerbutts, 'Men, Women & Passengers', *Sea Breezes* (December 1988), p. 831.

236 Cunard Line and White Star Line merged to form Cunard-White Star Line in 1934.

237 Scobie, *A Stewardess Rings a Bell*, p. 5.

238 UL, Cunard, D42/C2/3, 5, Employment Enquiries.

239 UL, Cunard, D42/C2/8, Employment Enquiries.

240 MMM, DX/1050c, Cunard Line, 'Company Guidelines' (1904).

241 CGM, CGT I170, Personnel, *Normandie* – 1935; SHSA, White Star Line, Brochure file, 'Olympic Close-Ups,' n.d.

242 UL, Cunard, D42/PR12/1, Cunard-White Star Line.

243 SCC, C0058, Kathleen Smith interview (14 September 1987).

244 SHSA Brochure file, Compagnie Générale Transatlantique.

245 Fletcher, *Traveling Palaces*, p. 142.

246 MMM, 410.UNI/PM, Rachel Mulhearn, 'Room Service: Aspects of Life Aboard the Ocean Liner' (Paper presented at a Research Day School, 15 June 1996) p. 37.

247 CGM, CGT J173-8 Habillement (art. 246,247); CGM, CMM, Reglement des Bords (1904).

248 CGM, CGT I 170, Margaret Gervers Falconer, 'Why Women Choose The French Line', in *Gangplank*, 2, No. 9, (summer 1933).

249 Sowerbutts, 'Men, Women, and More Passengers', *Sea Breezes* (January 1989) p. 10.

250 French liners' starting salary for stewards in 1926 was 335 francs a month while stewardesses were paid 285 francs a month. Conversely, male and female workers on British steamers earned £8.5 ($41) in 1930. CGM, CMM – Côte.1997 002 3389, Circulaire 'Bords'; Stanley, *Women at Sea*, p. 8.

251 Freeman, *Sea Travel*, p. 9.

252 *The Story of the Seamen*, p. 26.

253 MMM,DX/1050c; UL, Cunard, D42/PR14, *Cunard Line Rule Book for Crew* (1913), rule No. 39.

254 Freeman, *Sea Travel*, p. 9.

255 Stanley, *Women at Sea*, p. 18.

256 MMM,DX/1560- 2/5&6, Anne Smith (10 and 14 January 1923). For Joel Burdick's account, see *Our World Tour*.

257 CGM, CGT, Côte.1997.004 377, Blanchisserie.

258 CGM, CGT, Côte.1997.004 5068, Rapport de voyage, *Ile de France* (8 April–4 May 1938).

259 MMM,DX/1560/2/10.

260 MMM,DX/1166, entry from diary: 6 January–18 June 1923.

261 Jessop, *Titanic Survivor*, pp. 74–75.

262 Cited in Mulhearn, 'Room Service', pp. 40–41.

263 UL, Cunard, D42/PR 14/17, *Rule Book for Crew* (October 1927).

264 CGM, CGT J173-8, Habillement.

265 Sowerbutts, *Memoirs of a British Seaman*, p. 8.

266 UL, Cunard, D42/GM7/21/2, Allocation of Purser's Staff.

Notes

267 UL, Cunard, D42/PR4/21, '*Aquitania* – Memorabilia'.

268 Sowerbutts, *Memoirs of a British Seaman*, p. 8.

269 *Franconia* cruise brochure, OLM (collection on board the *Queen Elizabeth* 2).

270 Private collection A. Varias and L. Coons, 'Introducing the Staffs – Sunshine Cruises', Cunard-White Star Line publicity brochure (*c*. 1938).

271 CGM, CGT Côte 1997 004 5115, Rapport de voyage (*Normandie*) (7 June 1937).

272 American banker J. Pierpont Morgan had an interest in creating an international shipping organization. In 1902, he acquired White Star Line (Oceanic Steam Navigation Co. Ltd was its legal and official name) from J. Bruce Ismay for a total of £10 million and formed the International Mercantile Marine Co. (Morgan Trust as it was generally called) on 4 February. The company held a dominant position in the North Atlantic trade, both passenger and cargo. It was Morgan's original intention to absorb both White Star and Cunard (which was in a less secure economic position than White Star at the time). White Star had earlier considered the possibility of acquiring Cunard but the two companies eventually decided to go their own way. The IMM acquisition provoked a major uproar in the British Parliament, so Cunard opted wisely to maintain its independence and instead appealed to the British government for assistance with its building projects which included construction of the *Lusitania* and *Mauretania*.

  By 1920, IMM owned and operated the American Line, Atlantic Transport Line, Dominion Line, Leyland Line, Red Star Line and White Star Line. This relationship with White Star lasted until 1926 when the company was transferred from IMM back to British ownership through the efforts of Lord Kylsant (Royal Mail Steam Packet Co.). Kylsant was regarded as a leading British shipowner, whose empire consisted of no fewer than fifty-seven different companies, including Harland and Wolff, Ltd, over which he gained control by 1924 and served as chairman.

273 Sowerbutts, *Men, Women & Passengers*, p. 831.

274 Ibid, p. 834.

275 UL, Cunard, D42/PR5, Walter Wood, 'The Conductress', *Cunard Magazine* (18 June–July 1926).

276 Sowerbutts, *Memoirs of a British Seaman*, p. 24.

277 Ibid, p. 26.

278 Ibid, pp. 12, 60.

279 Ibid, p. 12.

280 Ibid, p. 122.

281 SCC, C0058, Kathleen Smith interview.

282 Sowerbutts, *Memoirs of a British Seaman*, p. 130.

283 UL, Cunard, PR14/6, Instructions to Chief Steward and Purser (1929–32).

284 UL, Cunard, GM24/2/2 (18 November 1931).

285 Mulhearn, 'Room Service', p. 41.

286 SCC, M0082, Delia Callaghan interview.

287 SCC, C0058, Kathleen Smith interview.

288 Jessop, *Titanic Survivor*, p. 87.

289 Stanley, *Women at Sea*, p. 24.

290 Jessop, *Titanic Survivor*, p. 75–76.

291 Sowerbutts, *Memoirs of a British Seaman*, pp. 199–200.

292 SCC, C0058, Kathleen Smith interview.

293 CGM, CGT, Côte 1997.004 0231, Folder No. 71 A3, Affaire Talbot-Rivoal (15 June 1938).

294 Stanley, *The Company of Women*, p. 15.

295 UL, Cunard, D42/C2/3, Miss Martha Murphy, Application for Employment (May 1922).

296 MMM, 411.1SCO/PM, Scobie oral history tape (August 1990). The NUS was formed in 1926 under the leadership of J. Havelock-Wilson and absorbed the Cooks and Stewards' Union. See *The Story of the Seamen*.

297 SCC, M0082, Delia Callaghan interview.

298 CGM, CGT, Côte 1997.004 0245 26C1, *Liste des Hommes Qu'il Importe d'Eliminer de Notre Personnel*.

299 Jessop, *Titanic Survivor*, pp. 78–80.

300 UL, Cunard, D42/C2/8, Employment Inquiries (16 July 1929).

301 UL, Cunard, D42/C2/7, Employment Inquiries (19 June 1926).

302 NMM, P&O Steamship Company, 77/23–30, Stewards Registers (1920–1940).

303 CGM, CGT, Côte 1997.004 0252, CGT – Syndicat (correspondence October–December 1936).

304 Sowerbutts, *Memoirs of a British Seaman*, p. 132.

305 SCC, M0082, Della Callaghan interview.

306 Sowerbutts, *Memoirs of a British Seaman*, p. 67.

307 Jessop, *Titanic Survivor*, p. 198.

308 Stanley, *Women at Sea*, pp. 17–18.

309 MMM, DX1560/2/2, 3, 5, 9, Anne Smith correspondence (16 and 28 December 1923; 2 and 10 January 1923, and 6 March 1923).

310 MMM, DX1166, Rose Stott diary (1923).

311 Sowerbutts, *Memoirs of a British Seaman*, p. 169. For an analysis of the Great Purge trials of the 1930s which Sowerbutts indirectly observed, see Robert C. Tucker, *Stalin in Power: The Revolution From Above, 1928–41* (NY: W. W. Norton, 1990) pp. 441–503. See also Robert Conquest, *The Great Terror – A Reassessment* (NY: Oxford University Press, 1990).

312 Scobie, *A Stewardess Rings a Bell*, p. 20.

313 MMM, 411.1SCO/PM, Dorothy Scobie, oral history tape (August 1990).

314 Jessop, *Titanic Survivor*, p. 102.

315 Sowerbutts, 'Westward, Look, the Land is Bright', *Sea Breezes* (February 1989) p. 83.

316 Sowerbutts, *Memoirs of a British Seaman*, pp. 196–97.

317 SCC, C0058, Kathleen Smith interview (14 September 1987).

318 Sowerbutts, *Memoirs of a British Seaman*, pp. 214–16, and *Westward, Look, the Land is Bright*, p. 83.

319 MMM, D/SCO/10/1, from Scobie scrapbook.

320 The following are personal observations of the author, Lorraine Coons, who worked on board the ships of Holland America Line, joining the cruise staff as a youth counsellor in the summer of 1976 and later working with shore excursion staff.

321 Drummond served an apprenticeship with Blue Funnel Line and qualified as an engine room officer in 1924; she went on to have a forty-year career at sea. She was awarded the Lloyds War Medal for bravery in the Second World War but was still considered 'crackers' by young male engineers largely because she had successfully dispelled the male myth of a woman's inability to make it as an engineer. See biography by Cherry Drummond, *The Remarkable Life of Victoria Drummond – Marine Engineer* (London: Institute of Marine Engineers, printed by Burgess Science Press, 1994).

Chapter Five

322 Jackson Lears, *Fables of Abundance: A Cultural History of Advertising in America* (New York: Basic Books, 1994) p. 1.

323 Rosalind H. Williams, *Dream Worlds: Mass Consumption in Late 19th Century France* (Berkeley: University of California Press, 1982) p. 91.

324 Michael Miller, *The Bon Marché: Bourgeois Culture and the Department Store, 1869–1920* (Princeton: Princeton University Press, 1981).

325 Warren I. Susman, *Culture as History: the Transformation of American Society in the Twentieth Century* (New York: Pantheon, 1984) p. 127.

326 Eugene Fodor, ed., *1938 in Europe-the Entertaining Travel Annual* (London: Houghton Mifflin Co., 1938) p. xl.

327 Henry Adams, *The Education of Henry Adams*, p. 52.

328 Italo Calvino, *t zero* (New York: Harcourt, Brace & Co., 1967) p. 91.

329 Alexander Varias, *Paris and the Anarchists: Aesthetes and Subversives During the Fin de Siècle* (New York: St Martin's Press, 1996).

330 UL, Cunard Line, *Cunard Magazine* (June 1922).

331 Ibid.

332 MMM, DX/1061/R (the Rosenvinge file) and UL-Cunard Line, D42/C3/182-195, *Journal of PSEA-Sea Lines* (winter, 1995).

333 See Daniel Hillion, *L'Affiche S'en Mer* (Rennes, Editions Ouest: 1990).

334 UL, Cunard Line, D/42/PR12/1, undated book, *The Queen Mary – A Book of Comparisons*, and MMM, Liverpool E2/11/1, 'The Lighting and Telephone System of the RMS *Queen Mary*', *G.E.C. Journal – The General Electric Co., Ltd England* (1936).

335 SHSA, *The RMS Queen Mary: A Pictorial Souvenir of the World's Largest Floating Palace – The First Superliner to Embody the Newest Scientific Improvements to Make Ocean Travel Comfortable and Safe* (New York: Pier & Ocean Line News Co., 1936).

336 UL, Cunard, D42/PR4/11, see C. J. Clarke, 'Electricity and the Modern Liner: the Wonders of the *Mauretania*', *Pall Mall Magazine* (London: September, 1908). Also the adjoining file D42/PR4/15-15, with its copy of the *Journal of Commerce* from 29 July 1938 concerning the second *Mauretania*. Also see SHSA, *The RMS Queen Mary: A Pictorial Souvenir.*

337 MMM, DX/1082, pamphlet by A. C. Hardy, *Technical Features of R.M.S. Queen Mary*, (1936). This pamphlet includes a brief history of the change from coal to oil. Also from the same file, a pamphlet on the *Queen Mary* focuses on the fire protection systems discussed here.

338 UL, Cunard, D42/B4/70, Executive Committee Minutes (19 October and 16 November, 1932).

339 SHSA, The RMS Queen Mary: A Pictorial Souvenir.

340 UL, Cunard, D42/PR12/1, brochure, 'The *Queen Mary*: Worlds Newest and Fastest Liner' (*c.* 1934).

341 MMM, Liverpool, DX/1611, *Souvenir Brochure of the Queen Mary* (1936).

342 UL, Cunard, D42/C3/182-195, Maude Royden to Sir Percy Bates (15 June 1937); Jane Jackson to Bates (19 June 1937).

343 MMM, Liverpool, DX/1107, Cunard Report and Accounts, with statement of the Chairman, Denis Haugton Bates (1957)

344 CGM, CGT, Le Havre, 'Cirucuits Transat En Afrique du Nord', *Bulletins de la CGT-French Line* (15 October 1937).

345 The obsession with speed was instrumental in motivating TRANSAT to help found Air France.

346 UL, Cunard, D42/PR3?7/16, brochure 'The Lusitania and the Mauretania: Some Interesting Comparisons'.

347 See 'Cunard Comparisons', an undated Cunard brochure from the 1920s and Louden-Brown, The White Star Line.

348 CGM, CGT, Le Havre, CGT J/13, *Super Île de France: et Maintenant Quelques Chiffres*. The image of the liner balancing seven and a half Eiffel Towers is misleading as the ship was projected at becoming 75,000 tons (next to the 10,000 tons of the tower) but it did not in fact reach 30,000. These projections may remind one of Archimedes' ancient wish to move the earth from a far enough place and with a sufficiently long lever.

349 UL, Cunard, D42/PR3/7/16.

350 The various comparisons of the *Mary* are found in Cunard's pamphlet, *The Queen Mary: A Book of Comparisons* from UL, Cunard, D42/PR12/1. It is also no coincidence that in the most recent Cunard brochure, '2001, Grand Ocean Liners of the 21st Century', the company (now owned by Carnival Cruises conglomerate of companies) advertised it's formerly anticipated *Queen Mary 2* as 'the longest, largest, sleekest ocean liner', falling just 117 feet shorter than the Empire State Building. Although no longer the tallest building in the world, the Empire State Building seems to retain its status as the ultimate structure against which to measure the length of ships.

351 CGM, CGT, Le Havre, J/16 *Normandie* brochure.

352 Ibid.

353 Cited in Henri Mouron, *A. M. Cassandre* (New York: Rizzoli Books, 1985) p. 13.

354 Cassandre from *La Revue de l'Union de l'Affiche Française* (1926), quoted in Bevis Hillier & Stephen Escritt, *Art Deco Style* (New York: Phaidon, 1997).

355 Quoted in Mouron, *A. M. Cassandre*, p. 70.

356 Ibid, pp. 77–78.

357 Walter Benjamin, 'The Work of Art in the Age of Mechanical Reproduction', in *Illuminations: Essays and Reflections*, Hannah Arendt, ed. (New York: Schocken Books, 1936) pp. 218–221.

358 See UL, Cunard, D42/PR3/25-26, company report on the *Normandie* and *Queen Mary* Blue Riband competition.

359 Ibid, minutes (3 June 1936).

360 UL, Cunard, D42/C3/437, Percy Bates to F. A. Bates (8 April 1935).

361 UL Cunard, D42/PR 121/1, article from the *Daily Telegraph* (27 September 1934).

362 CGM, CGT, Le Havre, Carton 1997 004-5206, *Procès Verbaux du Comité* (minutes) (20 May 1936).

363 CGM, CGT, Côte 1997 .004 .5115, *Rapport de Voyage – Normandie* (26 August 1935).

364 Thoreux, *J'ai Commandé 'Normandie'*, p. 165.

365 CGM, CGT, Côte 1997 .004 .5115, *Rapport de Voyage – Normandie* (30 November 1936).

366 Thoreux, *J'ai Commandé 'Normandie'*, p. 191.

367 SHSA, brochure file, French Line, *Gala Night* (1938).

368 UL, Cunard, D42/GM24/1/3, 'Memo: Managers to Captains' (26 January 1937).

369 CGM, CGT, Côte 1997.004.5206, Comité Minutes (9 October 1935).

370 Ibid (12 February 1936).

371 UL, Cunard Line, the king and queen to Bates (27 September 1934).

372 Ibid, Rudyard Kipling to Bates (9 September 1934).

373 UL, Cunard, D42/PR12/1, *The Shipbuilder and Marine Engine-Builder* (June 1936).

374 MMM, DX/1379 1/2, *The Cunard Tradition* (1946).

375 CGM, CGT, Le Havre, J/13, CGT, *Normandie* by Moreaux.

376 CGM, CGT, Le Havre, J/16, 'La Naissance du Géant des Mers, *Normandie*', Trois Conference (Paris, 1935).

377 CGM, CGT, Le Havre, J/14m *L'Animateur des Temps Nouveaux Economique*, 7th year (28 October 1932).

378 CGM, CGT, Le Havre, J/14, *France via French Line*, preface by Andre Maurois, Paris French Line Publications, (*c*. 1935).

379 Ibid.

380 Jean Giraudoux, quoted in Melvin Maddocks, *The Great Liners* (Chicago: Time-Life Books, 1978) p. 176.

381 See Modris Eksteins, *Rites of Spring* (New York: Doubleday, 1989).

382 CGM, CGT, J/16, *Normandie* brochure.

383 UL, Cunard, D42/PR12/1, brochure, 'The British Tradition Distinguishes Cunard-White Star', in *The Queen Mary: World's Newest and Fastest Liner* (Cunard/White Star Line, *c*. 1936).

384 UL, Cunard, D42/PR121/1, Cunard/White Star reprint from *The Illustrated London News*, 'The Stateliest Ship Now in Being', by King George V.

385 MMM, Liverpool, DX/1379 1/4, *RMS Queen Mary* Plan of Cabin Class Accommodations (New York: Cunard-White Star Line, November, 1936).

386 Ibid, p. 66.

387 CGM, CGT, Le Havre, J/11, Paul Marion, 'La Question du Jour – *Normandie*', *Aurore* (29 May 1935).

388 CGM, CGT, Le Havre, J/11, 'Coutuse et Moche', *Le Petit Havre* (28 May 1935).

389 MMM, Liverpool, E2/7/1-7, H. M. Tomlinson, 'RMS *Queen Mary*: A Noble Tribute to the Imagination of Man' (Cunard-White Star publication, *c*. 1936).

390 CGM, CGT, Le Havre, J/13 Moreaux book on the *Normandie*.

391 CGM, CGT, Le Havre, J/11, *Revue de Paris*, article on the inaugural voyage.

392 CGM, CGT. Claude Roger-Marx, *'Normandie et l'Art Français: Introduction à la Visite du Paquebot'*, in brochure *Normandie*, (CGT-French Line, 29 October, 1932).

393 UL, Cunard, D42/C3/436 letter from J. S. Megson to Cunard-White Star.

394 CGM, CGT. Le Havre, J/16, Emmanuel Bourcier, *Le Plus Beau Navire du Monde – A Bord du Colosse Normandie* (Paris: Editions de l'Atlantique n.d.).

Chapter Six

395 Joseph Conrad, *Notes on Life and Letters* (Garden City, NY: Doubleday, Page and Co., 1925) p. 219.

396 Ibid, pp. 240–241.

397 *L'Esprit Nouveau* (May, 1921), as quoted in Nancy J. Troy, *Modernism and the Decorative Arts in France: Art Nouveau to Le Corbusier* (New Haven: Yale University Press, 1991) p. 208.

398 Serres quoted in Philippe Hamon, *Expositions: Literature and Architecture in Nineteenth Century France* (Berekley: University of California Press, 1992) pp. 138–139.

399 Roland Barthes, *The Eiffel Tower and Other Mythologies* (Berekeley: Univerversity of California Press, 1977).

400 Umberto Boccioni, Carlo Carrà, Luigi Russolo, Giacomo Balla, Gino Severini, 'Manifesto of the Futurist Painters included in *Umbro Apollonio*', ed., *Futurist Manifestos*, (London: Thames and Hudson, 1910) p. 25.

401 QM, Cunard brochure, 'RMS *Aquitania*' (1920s).

402 UL, Cunard, D42-PR 3/11/1-16, 18, brochure, 'RMS *Aquitania*' (undated).

403 UL, Cunard, E2/7/1-7, pamphlet, 'The 1914 Cunarder RMS *Aquitania*'. Also brochures in D42/PR4/20/3.

404 UL, Cunard, D42-PR5, 'Furnishing a Cunarder', *Cunard Magazine* 5–6, No. 3 (March 1921) p. 94.

405 UL, Cunard, D42/PR3/8-9, *Olympic*, White Star Line brochure (1921).

406 UL, Cunard, *Cunard Magazine* (April 1922).

407 UL, Cunard, D42/C3433-438, memos from Davis and Morris to Cunard managers.

408 SHSA, *The France* (Paris: CGT Publications, early 1920s).

409 Ibid.

410 UL, Cunard, E2/7/1-7, brochure on the *Aquitania*.

411 For an analysis of a particular aspect of arcadian portrayals, the reader can consult Erwin Panofsky, '*Et in Arcadia Ego: Poussin and the Elegaic Tradition*', in *Meaning in the Visual Arts* (Garden City, N.Y.: Doubleday & Company Inc., 1955) pp. 295–320.

412 See Paul Fussell, *Abroad*, especially in chapter one for more analysis of this reality.

413 SHSA, *The France* (Paris: CGT Publications, early 1920s).

414 SHSA, *Un Grand Effort d'Art Moderne: Le Paquebot Paris*, (Paris: CGT Publications, early 1920s). In fact, movies were also found on the more traditional *France*.

Notes

415 CGM, CGT I/75, brochure, 'Nouveau Paqubot *"Paris"*'.
416 See John Willett, *Art and Politics in the Weimar Period: the New Sobriety, 1917–1933* (New York: Pantheon, 1978), and Peter Gay, *Weimar Culture: the Outsider as Insider* (New York: Harper & Row, 1968).
417 Deborah L. Silverman, *Art Nouveau in Fin-de-Siecle France: Politics, Psychology, and Style* (Berkeley: University of California Press, 1989), and Rosalind H. Williams, *Dream Worlds: Mass Consumption in Late Nineteenth Century France* (Berekley: University of California Press, 1982).
418 Hillier and Escritt, *Art Deco Style*, p. 32.
419 SHSA brochure on *Ile de France*.
420 CGM, CGT, J/75, brochure 'New Giants – *SS Ile de France* and Deluxe *SS Paris* and *France*'.
421 CGM, CGT, J/28-*Ile de France* files, Henri Clouzot, 'Le Paquebot, *Ile de France*', *La Renaissance de l'Art Presente* (New York: March 1928).
422 Ibid.
423 Maxtone-Graham, *The Only Way to Cross*, pp. 243–244.
424 Brinnin, *The Sway of the Grand Saloon*, p. 465.
425 John Malcolm Brinnen and Kenneth Gaulin, *Grand Luxe: the Transatlantic Style* (New York: Henry Holt & Co., 1988) p. 109.
426 Maxtone-Graham, *The Only Way to Cross*, p. 243.
427 Brinnen and Gaulin, *Grand Luxe*, p. 109.
428 'Ship of the Year', *The Syren and Shipping* (4 January 1928).
429 Ibid.
430 Clouzot, 'Le Paquebot *Ile de France*'.
431 Ibid.
432 Coleman, *The Liners*, p. 139.
433 UL, Cunard, D42/C2/257, anonymous report from Oceanic House, London, to Sir Joseph Maclay, Bart, Ministry of Shipping, St James's Park (*c.* 1920).
434 Article in the *Evening Times of Glasgow* (11 March 1925).
435 'The Mechanical Age', in *The Commodore*, Official Organ of the RMS *Aquitania* Social and Athletic Association (July 1930, private collection).
436 CGM, CGT, *Proces Verbaux du Comite* (minutes) (29 October 1929).
437 Rene La Bruyere, 'Le Normandie-Ex. 'T6', *Revue Politique et Parlementaire* (Paris, 10 December 1932). See also the brochure by Emmanuel Bourcier, 'Le Plus Beau Navire du Monde – A Bord du Colosse *Normandie*' *Editions de l'Atlantique* (Paris, undated), in which highly nationalistic phobias of Germany, the United States, the United Kingdom and Italy are expressed.
438 CGM, CGT, J/9 article 'Pourquoi at-on construit le 'T6' aussi grand?' in brochure 'Super *Ile de France* et Maintenant Quelques Chiffres'. This undated article explains also that among the *France, Paris,* and *Ile de France,* TRANSAT could only claim 100,000 tons as against 265,000 tons for the British, and 185,000 tons for the German ships.
439 See CGM, CGT, J/9, letter from the Ministre des Travaux Publicque to Cangardel (3 June 1929). This letter expresses the need for 'T6-*Normandie*' to surpass *Ile de France* in size.
440 See CGM, CGT, Carton 1997 004-5206, Proces Verbaux du Comite (minutes), (29 October 1929).

441 See Eksteins.
442 CGM, CGT, J/3, folder 9, letter from Bouwens to Directeur General, Maurice Tillier, TRANSAT.
443 CGM, CGT, J/4, folder 5, letters of November 1934.
444 CGM, CGT, J/3 folder 1, letter from Waring and Gillow to TRANSAT Ingenieur en Chef, Romano (6 April 1934), and Romano to Waring and Gillow (10 April 1934).
445 See *Normandie*, (June 1935), edite par *L'Agence Latine Section Maritime Paris*, Impremerie de Montmartre, directeur, Rene Moreux.
446 See, for instance, CGM, CGT, J/3, folder 1, letter from Maison Emile Fender-Aine regarding the great renown of its parquets (17 December 1934).
447 See CGM, CGT, J/3, folder 1, letter from Maision Jules Leynaert.
448 See CGM, CGT, J/3, folder 9, letter from Paul Reynaud to Olivier and subsequent reply (29 March 1935).
449 See CGM-CGT, letters of Dupas and Dunand.
450 Bernard Smith, *Modernism's History: A Study in Twentieth Century Art and Ideas* (New Haven: Yale University Press, 1998) p. 177. Smith has also written that 'modern formalesque art can be seen as a period style not as a sequence of avant-garde movements.'
451 Thomas Crow, *Modern Art in the Common Culture* (New Haven: Yale University Press, 1996) pp. 35–36.
452 Ibid, p. 37.
453 CGM, CGT, J/14 & J/16, Claude Roger-Marx, *Normandie*, CGT, 1935 (?), and Emmanuel Bourcier, *Le Plus Beau Navire du Monde' A bord de Colosse 'Normandie'* (Paris, undated).
454 CGM, CGT, unprocessed carton, Bouvens to Directeur General of TRANSAT (16 May 1934).
455 CGM, CGT, J/14, Roger-Marx, *Normandie*.
456 SHSA brochure.
457 Hillier & Escritt, *Art Deco Style*, p. 119.
458 CGM, CGT, J/11. See special issue of *Vu* focused on the *Normandie* (19 June 1935).
459 CGM, CGT, J/16 Roger-Marx, '*Normandie* et l'Art Francais' in brochure '*Normandie* CGT' (n.d.) p. 12.
460 Ibid.
461 See *Ship to Shore* (spring 1985).
462 CGM, CGT *Bulletin*, No. 446 (15 June 1937).
463 CGM, CGT, I/170, *Gangplank* (winter 1938/9).
464 MMM, Liverpool, DX/1379, brochure, '*RMS Queen Mary*, Plan of Cabin Class Accommodations, Cunard-White Star Line, New York' (November 1936), and DX/1611, souvenir brochure of the *Queen Mary* (1936).
465 Ibid.
466 Ibid.
467 UL, Cunard, D42/PR12/1. Undated brochure by H. T. W. Bousfield, *RMS Queen Mary – the Ship of Beautiful Woods*.
468 James Steele, *Queen Mary* (New York: Phaidon, 1995) p. 140.
469 Ibid, p. 87.

Notes

470 Michael T. Aoler, *The Avant-Garde in Interwar England: Medieval Modernism and the London Underground* (New York: Oxford University Press, 1999) p. 108.

471 UL, Cunard Line, D42/C3/427-432, letters from Morris to H. J. Flewitt Cunard/White Star Secretary (23 September 1935), and from Essendon to Bates (12 December 1935).

472 UL, Cunard, D42/C3/430, contract sent by Leach to Grant (6 July 1935).

473 UL, Cunard, D42/C3/430, letter Leach to Grant (26 September 1935).

474 UL, Cunard, D42/C3/430, letters Grant to Leach (23 September and 1 October 1935).

475 UL, Cunard, D42/C3/430, memo from secretary's office to Leach (8 February 1936).

476 UL, Cunard, D42/C3/430, Lord Essendon to Bates (2 February 1936).

477 UL, Cunard, D42/C3/430, Bates to Major Hardinge, CVO Buckingham Palace.

478 Kenneth Clark, *Another Part of the Wood: A Self-Portrait* (New York: Harper & Row, 1974) p. 248.

479 UL, Cunard, D42/C3/430, Grant to Bates (12 February 1936).

480 UL, Cunard, D42/C3/430, Morris to Brocekelbank (20 February 1936).

481 UL, Cunard, D42/C3/430, Morris to Grant (24 February 1936).

482 UL, Cunard, D42/C3/430, anonymous memo to Essendon (2 February 1936).

483 UL, Cunard, D42/C3/430, collective petition to Bates (26 February 1936).

484 Ibid.

485 Clark's praise of the *Normandie* is noted by Maxtone-Graham.

486 Clark, *Another Part of the Wood*, p. 247.

487 Vanessa Bell to Julian Bell (24 September 1935), found in *Selected Letters of Vanessa Bell*, ed. Regina Marler (Wakefield, Rhode Island: Moyer Bell, 1998) pp. 397–99.

488 UL, Cunard, D42/C3/430, letter from Earl Crawford & Balcares to Bates (26 February 1936), and Bates' reply (29 February 1936).

489 UL, Cunard, D42/C3/430, Field, Roscoe and Co. to Bates (3 March 1936).

490 UL, Cunard, D42/C3/430, Hill, Dickinson and Co. to Cunard (21 March 1936).

491 UL, Cunard, D42/C3/430, Cunard to Roscoe, Field and Co. (4 April 1936).

492 UL, Cunard, Liverpool, D42/C3/430, S. J. Lister of Cunard to Essendon (19 January 1939).

493 UL, Cunard, D42/C3/430, Robert Crail of Cunard to Grant (2 February 1939), Lords Daily & Lloyd to Cunard (3 March 1939), and Lister to Lionel Phillips of the British Council (6 March 1939).

494 UL, Cunard, D42/C3/190B2, Bates to Sir Richard V. N. Hopkins of the Exchequer Office.

495 UL, Cunard, D42/C3/190B2, Alfred C. Bossom, MP, Maidstone to Neville Chamberlain (*c.* 1936).

496 UL-Cunard, D42/C3/190 B2, Cunard General Manager to Bates (23 July 1936).

497 UL, Cunard, D/42/C3/190B2, Brockelbank to Bates (16 October 1936), and company minutes of Shipbuilding Committee (20 October 1936).

498 UL, Cunard, D42/C3/182-195, letter Bates to Cronliffe-Owen (6 July 1938).

Conclusion

499 CGM.CGT, J/32 *Ile de France* folder.
500 Ibid.
501 Ibid.
502 Ibid.
503 Gordon Thomas & Max Morgan-Witts, *Voyage of the Damned* (Loughborough: Dalton Watson Fine Books, 1974).
504 CGM, CGT, J/197, pamphlet/essay 'Les grandes heures de la Transat'.
505 UL, Cunard, D42/C3/436, Black to Bates, 1–3–41.
506 IWM, London, 96/22/1, Jack Barry Bamford, *Diary of Five Weeks in New York en Route to the Falklands in 1942*, p. 19.
507 Ibid.
508 Ibid, pp. 7–8.
509 IWM, London, 96/6/1, Lt Cmdr P. C. Kieppe, RNN.
510 Ibid.
511 IWM, London, 86/87/1, W. G. Riley account.
512 IWM, London, 97/6/1, T. Walczak account from *Polish Daily* (1979).
513 Charles Offrey, *Cette grande dame que fut la Transat* (Le Touvet: Editions Maarcel-Didier Vrac, 1994) pp. 53–54.
514 CGM, CGT, J/17.
515 Ibid.
516 Ibid.
517 UL-Cunard Line, PR 3/9/4, Cunard business meeting minutes (16 July 1919); CGM, CGT, I/75, CGT Publicity.
518 MMM, Liverpool, DX/1107, 'Cunard Report and Accounts, 1957 with a Statement of the Chairman, Col Denis Haughton Bates'.
519 CGM, CGT, J/152, Air Transport files, 'Note: La Compagnie Generale Transatlantique et le Transport Aerien en Mediterranée' (September, 1951).
520 UL-Cunard, D42/PR3/23/18-22, various memos and letters on *Titanic*.
521 UL-Cunard, D42/C3/436, letter from the Canadian Theosophical Society to Cunard and various Cunard internal memos, and a clip of an article by Robet A. Hughes in the *Canadian Theosophical Society* (11 January 1934).

Bibliography

PRIMARY SOURCES

Archives

AN:	Archives Nationales pamphlets, ephemera of CGT (French Line/TRANSAT)
BF:	Bibliothèque Forney maritime posters
CGM,CGT:	Compagnie Générale Maritime - Compagnie Générale Transatlantique French Line/ TRANSAT) Archives company files; voyage reports; crew files; brochures; catalogs; photographs; deck plans; posters
CGM, CMM:	Compagnie Générale Maritime - Compagnie Messageries Maritimes Archives company files; voyage reports; crew files; brochures; catalogs; photographs; deck plans; posters
IWM:	Imperial War Museum (London) Archives soldiers'correspondence; stewardess maritime manuscript
MMM:	Merseyside Maritime Museum Archives oral histories; brochures; catalogs; deck plans
NMM:	National Maritime Museum (Greenwich) Archives P&O Line company files
QM:	Queen Mary Archives (Long Beach, CA) oral histories; subject files
SCC:	Southampton City Council - 'Oral History Archive' oral histories with former Cunard Cunard-White Star crew and officers

SHSA: Steamship Historical Society of America Archives
                         (University of Baltimore)
                         photographs; brochures; deck plans

UL, Cunard: University of Liverpool - Cunard, White Star,
                         Cunard-White Star Archives
                         company files; voyage reports; crew files;
                         brochures; catalogs;
                         photographs; deck plans

Books

Adams, Henry, *The Education of Henry Adams* (Boston: Houghton Mifflin Co., 1918)

Angus, Cmdr. W. Mack, USN, *Rivalry on the Atlantic* (New York: Lee Furman, Inc., 1939)

Babcock, F. Lawrence, *Spanning the Atlantic* (New York: Alfred A. Knopf, 1931)

de Beaudean, Raoul, *Captain of the Ile* (New York: McGraw Hill Co., 1960)

Bemelmans, Ludwig, *I Love You, I Love You, I Love You* (New York: Viking Press, 1942)

Benstead, C.R., *Atlantic Ferry*, (Whittaker & Co., 1936)

Birt, Raymond and D.S. Watt, *The Queen Elizabeth* (London: Winchester Publications Ltd., 1947)

Bisset, Sir James, *Commodore* (England: Angus and Robertson, 1961)

_____ *Tramps and Ladies* (New York: Criterion Books, 1959)

Bowen, F.C., *A Century of Atlantic Travel* (London: Sampson Low, 1933)

Burdick, Joel, *Our World Tour 1922–1923* (Liverpool: Merseyside Maritime Museum, 1990)

Cangardel, Henri, *De Colbert à Normandie* (Paris: Nouvelles Editiones Latines, 1957)

Conrad, Joseph, *Notes on Life and Letters* (New York: Doubleday, Page and Co., 1925)

Dempsey, John, *I've Seen Them All Naked* (Oxford, U.K.: Alden Press, 1990)

Diggle, Captain E.G., *The Romance of a Modern Liner* (England: Patrick Stephens Ltd., 1989) [first published in 1930].

Fletcher, R.A., *Traveling Palaces (Luxury in Passenger Steamships)* (London: Sir Isaac Pitman and Sons, 1913)

Fodor, Eugene, ed., *1936...On the Continent* (New York: Fodor's Travel Guides, 1985)

_____ *1938 in Europe – the Entertaining Travel Annual* (London: Houghton Mifflin Co., 1938)

_____ *Woman's Guide to Europe* (New York: David McKay Co., Inc., n.d.)

Freeman, Roydon, *Sea Travel – The Serious Side and the Humorous Side* (London: St Catherine Press, 1930)

Grattidge, Captain Harry and Richard Collier, *Captain of the Queens* (London: Oldbourne Press, 1956)

Graves, Robert and Alan Hodge, *The Long Week-End: A Social History of Great Britain, 1918-1939* (New York: W.W. Norton, 1994)

Ibsen, Henrik, *A Doll's House* (New York: The Modern Library, n.d.)

Jessop, Violet, *Titanic Survivor*, John Maxtone-Graham ed. (Dobbs Ferry, NY: Sheridan House, 1997)

Jordan, Humphrey, *Mauretania (Landfalls and Departures of Twenty-Five Years)* (Bath, Avon: Patrick Stephens Ltd., printed by the Avon Press, 1988) [first published in 1936]

Joubert, Roger, *Palaces Des Oceans (Journal D'Un Commissaire de Bord)* (Maisonneuve et Larose, n.d.)

Kergus, Yves M., *Normandie – La triomphale traversée* (Paris: Editions de la Plomée, 1999)

Lee, Charles E., *The Blue Riband* (London: Sampson Low, 1930)

MacGinnis, A.J., *Atlantic Ferry* (England: Whittaker & Co., 1893)

Marlowe, Dave, *Coming Sir! The Autobiography of a Waiter* (London: J.B. Lippincott, 1938)

Bibliography

Marler, Regina, ed., *Selected Letters of Vanessa Bell* (Wakefield, Rhode Island: Moyer Bell, 1998)

Marr, Commodore Geoffrey, *The Queens and I* (London: Adlard Coles, 1973)

Mencken, August, *First Class Passenger* (New York: Alfred Knopf, 1938)

Ogilvie, Frederick Wolff, *The Tourist Movement* (London: P.S. King and Son, Ltd, 1933)

Post, Emily, *Etiquette* (New York: Funk & Wagnalls, 1940)

Rimington, Critchell, *The Bon Voyage Book (An Intimate Guide for the Modern Ocean Traveler by "Old Salt")* (New York: The John Day Co., 1931)

Scobie, Dorothy, *A Stewardess Rings a Bell* (Bolton, UK: Stylus Publishers, 1990)

Sowerbutts, Edith, *Memoirs of a British Seaman, No. 1108113* (London: Imperial War Museum, unpublished manuscript)

Spedding, Charles T., *Reminiscences of Transatlantic Travellers* (London: T. Fisher Unwin Ltd, 1926)

Thoreux, Commandant Pierre, *J'ai Commandé "Normandie"* (Paris: Presses de la Cité, 1963)

Twain, Mark, *Innocents Abroad* (Hartford, CT: American Publishing Co., 1869)

Tyler, David, *Steam Conquers the Atlantic* (New York: Appleton Century, 1939)

Vane, Sutton, *Outward Bound* (New York: Boni and Liveright, 1924)

Waugh, Evelyn, *When the Going Was Good* (London: Little, Brown & Co., 1934)

Woon, Basil, *The Frantic Atlantic* (New York: Alfred Knopf, 1927)

Ephemeral Publications

American Architect (1936)
Architects' Journal (1936)
L'Atlantique (1922, 1925, 1927, 1929–30)
CGT Bulletin (1933–37)
The Commodore (1930)
Country Life (1936)
Cunard Business News (1920)
Cunard Line Magazine (1918–27)
The Daily Telegraph (1924, 1934)
The Evening Standard (1931)
Gangplank (1933–39)
Journal du Havre (1938)
Liverpool Echo (1921)
Liverpool Daily Post (1921)
The Nautical Gazette (1935)
Le Petit Havre (1935, 1938)
Revue de Paris (1935)
RIBA Journal (1947)
The Shipbuilder and Marine Engine-Builder (1935–36)
Studio (1936)
The Syren and Shipping (1928)
White Star Magazine (1925–34)

SECONDARY SOURCES

Books

Apollonio, Umbro, ed., *Futurist Manifestos* (London: Thames and Hudson, 1973)

Ardman, Harvey, *Normandie: Her Life and Times* (New York: Franklin Watts, 1985)

Bailey, Chris Howard, *Down the Burma Road: Work and Leisure for the Below-Deck Crew of the Queen Mary, 1947-67* (Southampton, 1990)

Barbance, Marthe, *Histoire de la Compagnie Générale Transatlantique* (Paris: Arts et Metiers Graphiques, 1955)

Barthes, Roland, *The Eiffel Tower and Other Mythologies* (Berkeley: University of California Press, 1977)

Bathe, Basil W., *Seven Centuries of Sea Travel* (New York: Portland House, 1990)

Belcher, Phillip, et al., eds. *Women Seafarers: Global Employment Policies and Practices* (Geneva: International Labour Office, 2003)

Benjamin, Walter (Arendt, Hannah, ed.), *Illuminations* (New York: Schocken Books, 1968)

Bonsor, N.R.P., *North Atlantic Seaway* (Lancashire, England: Stephenson & Sons, Ltd, 1955)

Branca, Patricia, *Women in Europe since 1750* (London: Croom Helm, 1978)

Braynard, Frank O., *Classic Ocean Liners* (England: Patrick Stephens Ltd, 1990)

_____ *The World's Greatest Ship - The Leviathan,* Vol.I (New York: American Merchant Marine Academy, 1983)

Brinin, John Malcolm, *Beau Voyage: Life Aboard the Last Great Ships* (New York: Congdon and Lattès, 1981)

_____ and Kenneth Gaulin, *Grand Luxe: the Transatlantic Style* (New York: Henry Holt & Co., 1988)

_____ *The Sway of the Grand Saloon* (London: Arlington Books, 1971)

Burrow, J.W. *The Crisis of Reason: European Thought 1848-1914* (New Haven: Yale University Press, 2000)

Burton, Valerie, *The Work and Home Life of Seafarers with Special Reference to the Port of Southampton, 1871-1921* (London: University of London, unpublished PhD thesis, 1989)

Calvino, Italo, *T zero* (New York: Harcourt, Brace & Co., 1967)

Clark, Kenneth, *Another Part of the Wood: A Self-Portrait* (New York: Harper & Row, 1974)

Clères, Christian, *Le Havre-New York* (Paris: Editions Hazan, 1997)

Coleman, Terry, *The Liners (A History of the North Atlantic Crossing)* (Middlesex, U.K.: Penguin Books, 1976)

Conquest, Robert, *The Great Terror - A Reassessment* (New York: Oxford University Press, 1990)

Coons, Lorraine, *"Orphans" of the Sweated Trades: Women Homeworkers in the Parisian Garment Industry (1860-1915)* (New York: Garland, 1987)

Creighton, Margaret S. and Lisa Norling, eds., *Iron Men, Wooden Women (Gender and Seafaring in the Atlantic World, 1700-1920)* (Baltimore: The Johns Hopkins University Press, 1996)

Crow, Thomas, *Modern Art in the Common Culture* (New Haven: Yale University Press, 1996)

Drummond, Cherry, *The Remarkable Life of Victoria Drummond - Marine Engineer* (London: the Institute of Marine Engineers, printed by Burgess Science Press, 1994)

Eksteins, Modris, *Rites of Spring: the Great War and the Birth of the Modern Age* (New York: Doubleday, 1989)

Feifer, Maxine, *Tourism in History* (New York: Stein and Day, 1986)

Bibliography

Foucart, Bruno, Charles Offrey, François Robichon, and Claude Villers, *Normandie: L'Epopée Du "Géant Des Mers."* (Paris: Editions Herscher, 1985)

Fussell, Paul, *Abroad* (Oxford, UK: Oxford University Press, 1980)

Gay, Peter, *Weimar Culture: the Outsider as Insider* (New York: Harper & Row, 1968)

Gregory, Alexis, *The Golden Age of Travel – 1880–1939* (London: Cassell, 1998)

Hamon, Philippe, *Expositions: Literature and Architecture in Nineteenth Century France* (Berkeley: University of California Press, 1992)

Higgonet, Margaret Randolph, Jane Jenson, Sonya Michel, and Margaret Collins Weitz, eds., *Behind the Lines: Gender and the Two World Wars* (New Haven, CT: Yale University Press, 1987)

Hillier, Bevis and Stephen Escritt, *Art Deco Style* (New York, Phaidon, 1997)

Hillion, Daniel, *La Mer S'Affiche* (Rennes, Editions Ouest, 1990)

Hinkey, Douglas, Cynthia B. MacMullin and Ronald L. Smith, *The Art of the RMS Queen Mary* (Long Beach, California: Robert Gumbiner Foundation and Hippodrome Galleries of FHP Heathcase, 1994)

Huizinga, Johannes, *The Waning of the Middle Ages* (New York: Doubleday, 1924)

Johnson, Howard, *The Cunard Story* (London: Whitlet Books, Ltd, 1987)

Kinnear, Mary, *Daughters of Time - Women in the Western Tradition* (Ann Arbor: University of Michigan Press, 1982)

Lanier, Edmond, *Compagnie Générale Transatlantique* (Paris: Librairie Plon, 1962)

Larkin, Maurice, *France Since the Popular Front: Government and People, 1936-1996* (Oxford: Clarendon Press, 1997)

Lears, Jackson, *Fables of Abundance: A Cultural History of Advertising in America* (New York: Basic Books, 1994)

Leed, Eric J., *The Mind of the Traveler* (New York: Basic Books, 1991)

Lewis, Jane, *Women in England, 1870–1950: Sexual Divisions and Social Change* (Sussex: Wheatsheaf Books, 1984)

MacMillan, James F., *Housewife or Harlot: The Place of Women in French Society, 1870–1940* (Brighton: The Harvester Press, 1981)

Maddocks, Melvin, *The Great Liners* (Chicago: Time-Life Books, 1978)

Marin, Pierre-Henri, *Les paquebots ambassadeurs des mers* (Paris: Gallimard, 1989)

Maxtone-Graham, John, *The Only Way to Cross* (New York: Collier Books, Macmillan, 1978)

McCart, Neil, *Atlantic Liners of the Cunard Line from 1884 to the Present* (England: Patrick Stephens Ltd, 1990)

Miller, Michael, *The Bon Marché: Bourgeois Culture and the Department Store, 1869–1920* (Princeton: Princeton University Press, 1981)

Miller, William anad David F. Hutchings, *Translatlantic Liners at War: the Story of the Queens* (New York: Arco Publishing, Inc., 1985)

Mohrt, Michel and Guy Feinstein, *Paquebots: Le Temps des Traversées* (France: Editions Maritimes et D'Outre-Mer, 1980)

Mouron, Henri, *A.M. Cassandre* (New York: Rizzoli Books, 1985)

Offen, Karen, Ruth Pierson, and Jane Rendall, eds., *Writing Women's History: International Perspectives* (The International Federation for Research in Women's History. Bloomington: Indiana University Press, 1991)

Offrey, Charles, *Cette grande dame que fut la TRANSAT* (Le Touvet, France: Editions Marcel-Didier Vrac, 1994)

Pedersen, Susan, *Family, Dependence and the Origins of the Welfare State, Britain and France 1914-1945* (Cambridge: Cambridge University Press, 1993)

Potter, Neil and Jack Frost, *The Elizabeth* (London: George G. Harrap & Co., Ltd, 1965)
_____ *The Mary, the Story of No. 534* (England: Shipping Books Press, 1961)

Prior, Rupert, *Ocean Liners – The Golden Years* (London: Tiger Books International, 1993)

Reynolds, Siân, *France Between the Wars – Gender and Politics* (New York: Routledge, 1996)

Saler, Michael T., *The Avant-Garde in Interwar England: Medieval Modernism and the London Underground* (New York: Oxford University Press, 1999)

Scott, Joan W., *Gender and the Politics of History* (New York: Columbia University Press, 1988)

Silverman, Deborah L., *Art Nouveau in Fin-de-Siècle France: Politics, Psychology, and Style* (Berkeley: University of California Press, 1989)

Smith, Bernard, *Modernism's History: A Study in Twentieth Century Art and Ideas* (New Haven: Yale University Press, 1998)

Smith, Bonnie, *Changing Lives, Women in European History Since 1700* (Lexington, MA: D.C. Heath, 1989)

Smith, Ken, *Mauretania: Pride of the Tyne* (Newcastle: Tyneside Ltd., 1997)

Stanford, Don, *The Ile de France* (New York: Appleton-Century-Crofts, Inc., 1960)

Stanley, Jo, ed., *Bold in Her Breeches – Women Pirates Across the Ages* (London: Pandora, 1995)

Steele, James, *Queen Mary* (London: Phaidon Press, 1995)

Stewart, Mary Lynn, *Women, Work & the French State: Labor Protection and Social Patriarchy, 1897-1919* (Montreal: McGill-Queen's University Press, 1989)

The Story of the Seamen: A Short History of the National Union of Seamen (London: Victoria House Printing Co., 1964)

Susman, Warren I., *Culture as History: The Transformation of American Society in the Twentieth Century* (New York: Pantheon, 1984)

Thomas, Gordon and Max Morgan-Witts, *Voyage of the Damned* (Belton, Loughborough, UK: Dalton Watson, 1974)

Troy, Nancy J., *Modernism and the Decorative Arts in France: Art Nouveau to Le Corbusier* (New Haven: Yale University Press, 1991)

Vard, Kenneth, *Liners in Art* (Southampton: Kingfisher Publications, 1990)

Varias, Alexander, *Paris and the Anarchists: Aesthetes and Subversives During the Fin de Siècle.* (New York: St. Martin's Press, 1996)

Vian, Louis-René, *Arts décoratifs à bord des paquebots français, 1880-1960* (Paris: Edition Fonmare, 1991)

Vicinus, Martha, *A Widening Sphere* (Bloomington: Indiana University Press, 1980)

Wall, Robert, *Ocean Liners* (New York: E. P. Dutton, 1977)

_____ *Ocean Liner Postcards in Marine Art, 1900-1945* (Suffolk, England: Antique Collectors' Club, 1998)

Weber, Eugen, *The Hollow Years - France in the 1930s* (New York: W.W. Norton, 1994)

The White Star Triple Screw Atlantic Liners Olympic and Titanic: Ocean Liners of the Past (England: Patrick Stephens Ltd, 1988)

Willett, John, *Art and Politics in the Weimar Period: the New Sobriety, 1917-1933* (New York: Pantheon, 1978)

Williams, Rosalind H., *Dream Worlds: Mass Consumption in Late 19th Century France* (Berkeley: University of California Press, 1982)

Winter, C.W.R., *Queen Mary, Her Early Years Recalled* (England: Patrick Stephens Ltd, 1986)

Zeldin, Theodore, *France 1848–1945: Ambition and Love* (New York: Oxford University Press, 1979)

Articles

Boccioni, Umberto, Carlo Carrà, Luigi Russolo, Giacomo Balla, and Gino Severini. 'Manifesto of the Futurist Painters', in *Futurist Manifestos*, Umbro Apollonio ed. (London: Thames & Hudson, 1973)

Coons, Lorraine. '"Neglected Sisters" of the Women's Movement: The Perception and Experience of Working Mothers in the Parisian Garment Industry, 1860-1915', *Journal of Women's History*, 5, no.2 (Fall 1993)

_____ 'From "Company Widow" to "New Woman": Female Seafarers aboard the "Floating Palaces" of the Interwar Years', *International Journal of Maritime History*, 20, no. 2 (December 2008)

Davin, Anna, 'Imperialism and Motherhood', *History Workshop Journal*, 5 (1978)

Gilbert, Sandra M., 'Soldier's Heart: Literary Men, Literary Women and the Great War', *Signs: Journal of Women in Culture and Society*, 8, no. 3 (1983)

Hillion, Daniel, 'Un peintre de la marine, Sandy-Hook (1879-1960), Le plus mysterieux des peintres de la marine', *Neptunie*, Vol. 54, pp. 216: 72-77 (Paris, 1999)

Koonz, Claudia, 'Mothers in the Fatherland: Women in Nazi Germany', in *Becoming Visible: Women in European History*, Renate Bridenthal and Claudia Koonz, eds. (Boston: Houghton Mifflin, 1977)

Maenpaa, Sari. '"Mothers of the Sea", Gender Patterns of Recruitment on British Passenger liners 1850-1938', unpublished paper, given at Transporting Gender Conference, York, England, October 2000.

Mulhearn, Rachel, 'Room Service: Aspects of Life Aboard the Ocean Liner', unpublished paper, given at Research Day School, 1996.

Panofsky, Erwin, '*Et in Arcadia Ego*: Poussin and the Elegaic Tradition', in *Meaning in the Visual Arts* (New York: Doubleday & Co., 1955)

Reynolds, Siân, 'Women, men and the 1936 strikes in France', in *The French and Spanish Popular Fronts, comparative perspectives*, Martin Alexander and Helen Graham, eds. (Cambridge: Cambridge University Press, 1989)

Sohn, Anne-Marie, 'Between the Wars in France and England', in *A History of Women: Towards a Cultural Identity in the Twentieth Century*, Georges Duby and Michelle Perrot, gen. eds., Françoise Thébaud, ed. (Cambridge, MA: Belknap Press of Harvard University, 1994)

Stanley, Jo, 'The Company of Women', unpublished paper, given at CNRS conference, Calgary, June 1997.

_____. 'Women At Sea: Four Liverpool Stewardesses in the 1930s', article published by author. (Liverpool, 1987)

Thébaud, Françoise. 'The Great War and the Triumph of Sexual Division', in *A History of Women: Towards a Cultural Identity in the Twentieth Century*, Georges Duby and Michelle Perrot, gen. eds., Françoise Thébaud, ed. (Cambridge, MA: Belknap Press of Harvard University, 1994)

Ephemeral Publications

Architectural Review (1956,1960,1967)
See Breezes (1988–89)
Ship to Shore (1985)

Index

Index